THE BIOGRAPHY
OF
EL CHAPO GUZMAN

*The Life and Crimes
of the World's Most Wanted Drug Lord*

Walter Barnes

TABLE OF CONTENTS

INTRODUCTION 1

CHAPTER 1: POPPY FIELDS 5

CHAPTER 2: EMERGENCE 11

CHAPTER 3: THESE BARS AREN'T STRONG ENOUGH 16

CHAPTER 4: THE NET IS CAST 23

CHAPTER 5: FREEDOM, AGAIN 27

CHAPTER 6: LIFE PLUS THIRTY 34

Introduction

The drug trade in Mexico is an expansive and lucrative industry that employs over 450,000 people and generates up to $39 billion per year in revenue that is disseminated through poor and rural areas, funding hospitals, infrastructural projects, schools, natural disaster relief, and other vastly diverse arenas of life for modern-day Mexicans. Drug trafficking and the laundering of proceeds related to drug trafficking has infiltrated the local and regional economies of every state in the nation, and the increasingly violent struggle to control its ebb and flow has muddied the water between authority figures and sheriff and criminals and bandits.

In a nation that draws in millions of people every year—people from all across the globe seeking to experience Mexico as it is portrayed on postcards—the rash of violence that has been swallowing up its government and military has drawn the ire of the developed world. In today's political climate, the United States has an increasingly cold relationship with its former ally, and the Mexican president's inability to put a cap on the northbound flow of drugs, or to bring any of the syndicates' leaders to meaningful justice has meant that the cartels who truly run the country are growing more powerful by the day.

No figure embodies this burgeoning power more than Joaquin Guzman Loera, a short and squat man, whose physical features are nothing to turn your head for, a man who's diminutive stature has given rise to a nickname that has, in the past and present, spread fear throughout the hearts of people up and down the American continent.

That name: El Chapo.

Beginning his career in the violent and uncontrollable world of Mexican drug cartels in the early 1980s, El Chapo has been considered the most wanted man in the world, and the United State's government, as well as his Mexican government, has declared him wanted dead or alive.

The extreme levels of violence he uses to control his Sinaloan cartel and eliminate his competitors is both prodigious and alarming, and, furthermore, represents a new era in Mexican drug cartel aggression against those who were traditionally considered noncombatants. He is a man who uses violence as a sort of alternative language, displaying not only his cruelty, but his power and influence through the use of violence to send messages to terrorize those who would oppose him. He does this to keep both his enemies in the drug world and those backed by federal task forces at bay.

In his career as a ringleader of the cartels in Northwest Mexico, El Chapo has murdered hundreds of individuals, and the impunity with which he carries out his crimes is a product of the immense power and wealth he commands. He is so rich, in fact, that in 2009, Forbes magazine named him one of the world's billionaires, and even after removing him from their magazine, still asserted "that as the leader of the Sinaloan cartel, he was one of the most powerful men in the world.

His power comes from the wellspring of corruption that is rife within the Mexican government at all levels of its administration. Police and military corruption provide for the transportation routes that cartels use to traffic their wares—which have, in recent years, expanded their inventory to include humans as well as marijuana, heroin, methamphetamines, cocaine, crack-cocaine, and heavy-duty firepower—and also to attain information regarding moles and anti-drug operations. So many of the political leaders in Mexico have been brought up on corruption charges that it is no small wonder why the average Mexican citizen harbors an innate distrust of police officials and often welcomes cartels into their communities for the protection they can provide.

The corruption arises from the sense of impunity with which Mexican criminals are allowed to act. Throughout the nation, there are two different legal systems, if not in code, then at least in practice. The first legal system is the one of the laws on paper, and jails whose cells actually hold people, and police officers who actually monitor the activities of suspected offenders. This is the legal system established by the constitution of Mexico.

The second legal system is the one that applies to people like El Chapo, the immensely wealthy and powerful elite classes of society. This is the legal system that allows for the bribing of guards who let their prisons basically walk out through the main gate, the justice system that has men like Guzman Loera existing in the twenty-first century as if it was still the nineteenth, wantonly committing or commissioning murders, robberies, extortions—all of the activities that accompany running a multinational organized crime outfit.

It is the existence of the double standard in Mexican legal protocols that has created such a violent situation, but at the same time, the violence and gang activity in Mexico can be described as a snake eating itself. Behind-the-scenes corruption and widespread police inactivity allow men like El Chapo to walk out of prison three times in his storied career, just as men like El Chapo and his forebears have generated such enormously weighty power structures that they have managed to dismantle the Mexican legal system. Currently, many sections of the country are deemed extremely dangerous for travelers to stray through, and the long-standing traditions of corruption have weighed so heavily on the nation of Mexico that a situation of unsustainable volatility has arisen, destabilizing entire regions as drug cartels engage in the wholesale murder of civilians, of politicians, of each other.

The country has been deemed a war zone because of the intense drug trafficking and the violence that ensues. The many competing cartels are constantly at each other's throats over the profits margins that are at stake, and, for many years at least, the man who reigned over the largest chunk of the illegal enterprises was a short and portly middle-aged man who could be mistaken for anyone's *tio*, if it were not for the murderous aspect in his eyes, Joaquin Guzman Loera.

Also known as, El Chapo.

Chapter 1
Poppy Fields

Life offered very little to a young Guzman. Long before he became involved with any sort of organized crime, violence had already seeped into his life and represented to him a way of communicating with people, a basic and intrinsic aspect of how people lived, how people got by, and most importantly, how people got what they wanted. He was born in the forties in a rural town in Mexico, where he received virtually no education at all. The nearest school to his mountain hamlet in the Sierras was over sixty miles away. The village had no running water, no electricity, no sewage, no public representation in the greater state government. This town was—and remains to this day—the epitome of what Americans describe as a "forgotten backwater." The only difference between an American backwater and the environs that Chapo first called home, were that American backwaters actually had water.

He spent his childhood under the watchful eyes of an abusive father who made his life hell, and who eventually threw him out of the house. Settling with his grandfather in the same area, he worked in fields, he acquired what little wages he could, and he bided his time until the day would come for him to escape Sinaloa forever. Eventually, though the circumstances are unclear, he was able to realize that dream, after so many others like him failed to do so.

He landed his first job as a low-level lackey for a local drug lord, where he proved his truly malicious spirit through his very public displays of brutality and intelligence. From the start, it would appear that El Chapo had found a career for himself, and one that would take him to heights that he would never have been able to conceive of in his father's house in the one of the poorest and harshest corners of Mexico.

It was an interesting time to be a youngster in the Sierra mountains in the northern hinterlands of Mexico. By the end of World War II, American soldiers began to funnel home, and they brought their morphine habits with them. This proved lucrative for a region that was predominantly given over to the ranching and herding of sickly, emaciated cattle whose ribs stuck out from their flanks. As a high, mountainous region with an arid climate and dry soil, Northwest Mexico is surprisingly good for the cultivation of the flower *popiver somniferum*, which is used to produce opium and heroin.

Though it would be an overstatement to call the fledgling opium trade a booming economy, or a gold rush, it is fair to say that the tired and beleaguered farming communities that were nestled into the nooks and crannies of the Sierra Madres welcomed the ability to foster some economic solvency, regardless of the origins of the money.

Guzman made a name for himself in this industry and worked with his family—despite their frequent feuds—to produce opium that would be processed, packaged, and transported north, for sale in southwest America. As the far-flung region of Mexico began to develop in the 1950s and '60s, train lines came to town, Mexico City was suddenly not so distant, and the upwelling of passersby through the region increased the demand for opium as well as means for its transportation.

When El Chapo began his life of modest family-oriented crime in Sinaloa, it was a rural and rather destitute area of the country, but by the time he was in his early twenties, things had changed for the better. Economic opportunity existed, and the thriving opium industry provided for an influx of capital that led to technological and agricultural developments in the region. Even with the increased profit margins made available through the drug trade and Columbian cartels' use of Mexico as an alternative route for transporting cocaine to America, life was simple for El Chapo and his kin.

The dawn of the Reagan era of American politics changed everything. When the "War on Drugs" was proclaimed by the American president and border agents began roving in force in ensuring that the flow of drugs northward remained at an acceptable minimum, the prices of the drugs that Mexican families such as the ones that worked with El Chapo began to skyrocket. And along with the prices, risks also soared. By 1974, the American and Mexicans governments were working in tandem to prevent the distribution of opium across the border, and before 1975 came around, over 22,000 acres of poppy fields had been destroyed in raids enacted by the joint venture. A clear disaster for the opium industry in Sinaloa that El Chapo and his family relied upon for sustenance, the situation began to grow desperate as the American government donated helicopters and began training Mexican forces.

Ironically, this created a long-lasting problem that neither of the two governments could have possibly foreseen. Faced with utter economic devastation, many decided to simply pack up and leave the state or migrate toward cities where they would find greater chances of landing lucrative employment. But the reality of the situation was not so. As with any great migration of individuals, the stress borne by their various destinations engendered even great poverty, crime, and desperation than had previously existed in their old villages. Some figures cite as many as 2,000 villages "abandoned or destroyed" during the opening volleys of the War on Drugs.

As the situation facing Sinaloans deteriorated, the violence began to percolate.

Although Sinaloa has a long and storied history of endemic violence in her communities, the War on Drugs increased the use of violence as a means to settle disputes between rivals. Army patrols marched through the streets of Sinaloa's cities and villages, rounding up the guilty and the innocent alike, until the crisis took on humanitarian proportions, and, under much scrutiny for the overall failure in curbing the flow of drugs through Mexico, the DEA and the Mexican government put an end to their relationship.

In the wake of the DEA pull out, cartel figures such as El Padrino (The Godfather) rose to power, and it was from these violent and dangerous men that El Chapo would learn how to run an international drug-smuggling ring. El Padrino, born as Felix Gallardo in 1946, was a man with many connections. His predecessors had ins with the Cali and Medellin cartels, and throughout the '80s, he built for himself an impressive empire that spanned the northern half of his native country. By the time El Chapo became involved, the Sinaloan cartel had a virtual monopoly on the Mexican drug trade.

This became an increasingly lucrative monopoly to control as the American government intensified its efforts to keep drugs from entering Florida through the Caribbean. Traditionally, this was a safer route for cartels. The lack of strong centralized governments and the widespread poverty in the island region facilitated the search for customs officials willing to add a monthly stipend to their meager incomes, and business ran smoothly until violence in Miami reached such a peak that the Florida pipeline was shut down. South American drugs, from the mid-eighties on, was trafficked almost exclusively through Mexico, making Gallardo his associated rich and powerful men.

Guzman's first real job in the drug smuggling industry had him responsible for the packaging and transportation of large quantities of drugs over the border. He used trucks and busses and planes, anything that would carry a big enough load, and despite the immense risks involved in such an endeavor, he frequently wanted to up the ante. He was methodical, brutal, and exacting in his work. When shipments were late, he personally executed those responsible for them. When a road washed out in heavy seasonal rains, drivers who didn't make their pickups on time were handled in a similar fashion.

Over time his role began to expand. By the mid-eighties, he was overseeing plane conscriptions, trucking routes—the entire vast network required by an organization the bribed officials of numerous countries, contacted numerous buyers across America, and dealt brute force to those who wouldn't fall in line. The Sinaloan cartel expanded their influence greatly because of his efforts, and it wasn't long before he was brought into Gallardo's inner sanctum.

Throughout this time, El Chapo retained a low profile. He lived on a ranch outside the capitol of his state and rarely ventured into the city limits, where flashy and soft gangsters flaunted their wealth. He had a family and three children and lived his life the way normal businessmen of today's era do. He went to work, he came home, he ate with his family. Ostensibly, nothing connected him to the ever-growing empire of murder and violence that jumped to life at his beck and call. Even DEA personnel were not immune to the wrath of the Sinaloan cartel. Corruption was so rampant in Mexico that when on the southern side of the borders, nothing but firepower and military training ensured their survival. Sometimes, it didn't go as planned. Their power had grown to such levels that even after the corpse of a DEA man was uncovered in Guadalajara, Gallardo and his men still enjoyed the political protection of a corrupt government.

This heyday of drug trafficking activity and lawlessness commanded by the Gallardo regime lasted throughout the 1980s and did not cease after the ringleader was arrested by federal agents on April 8th, 1989. Leading up to the arrest, Gallardo had been vesting more and more trust in his men—El Chapo included—in an attempt to distance himself from the drug empire that he built. Still, he had the connections. On the day of his arrest, he was in Guadalajara to visit a powerfully corrupted police official of the city, when federal agents surrounded him and brought into custody.

While it may have seemed to Gallardo's underlings that the time had come for them to go to ground, to cease or at least curtail their operations, for El Chapo, who had made a reputation for himself as an ambitious businessman, the fun was only getting started.

Chapter 2

Emergence

The fallout of El Padrino's arrest created a tremor that rose to a state of serious unrest within the Sinaloan cartel. With their leader in prison, the men who had previously worked cohesively under him began to squabble over control of the routes and the products, the connections and the political influence. With so much money on the table, sides were chosen. Officially, the reigns were passed to four brothers—the Arellano Felix brothers. They were based out of Tijuana and controlled the Baja peninsula and the surrounding regions—areas that shared borders with El Chapo's native Sinaloa.

The problem with Gallardo's arrest is that he functioned as the glue that held so many disparate gangs and cartels together under one flag. Under his rule—bloody though it may have been—the cartels worked together at their joint endeavors and everyone made piles of money on the drug trade that became more and more risky as the U.S.'s War on Drugs continued to rage on both side of the border. So, when Gallardo was pulled off the map, when he sat in a cell in a maximum security prison with a hefty sentence for his complicit role in the murder of a DEA agent, the delicate balancing act was thrown off kilter.

Before long, tensions rose between the Sinaloan and Tijuana cartels, and these tensions exploded into an all-out war in the streets of Mexico by the end of 1989. To describe this conflict as a gang war is an understatement. With heavy firepower and an uncaring or inefficient federal government, the blood shed by Mexican cartels during this period would make the criminal exploits of famous America mobsters seem like a schoolyard argument.

When El Chapo and his second in command, his most trusted lieutenant—Luis Hector Palma Salazar—defected from the Gallardo organization, they faced immediate reprisals from the more powerful brothers to their north. Palma, nicknamed El Guero, received the bulk of the brothers' wrath. At the start of the long and brutal cartel war, El Guero's wife and children were kidnapped by operatives working for the Arellano-Felix brothers. His wife was extorted for upwards of $7 million dollars. After she withdrew the funds she was shot to death by the hitman, who then kidnapped El Guero's two children, brought them to Venezuela, and threw them over the side of a bridge.

The fighting continued, with both sides putting hits out on the other, and gang murders accumulating in the piles of unsolved mysteries that abounded in Mexico during this time. Throughout the fighting, the government remained relatively inert and did very little to prevent the violence from spreading. The rampant corruption of high ranking officials may have contributed to this situation, but the heat was turned up on members of both the Sinaloan cartel and their rivals in Tijuana after a tragic case of mistaken identity brought the scourge of drug violence in Mexico to the attention of worldwide audiences.

In November of 1992, El Chapo escalated his war against the Tijuana cartels through a daring, commando-style raid at a disco in the city of Puerta Villarta. On the Pacific Ocean, at the meeting points between the greater ocean and the lesser Sea of Cortez that separates the Baja Peninsula from the Mexican mainland, a busy tourism season was underway, with many vacationers enjoying music, drinks, and entertainment at a popular disco and dance hall. Receiving information that the Arellano Felix brothers were enjoying themselves at this bar, Guzman ordered 40 of his best soldiers to storm the building and kill his rival. They allegedly severed the phone lines and locked the doors, preventing escape or outside assistance. Then, armed with automatic rifles and submachine guns, they entered the bar and began to open fire on the crowd, massacring the patrons. Death tolls vary, but it is believed that somewhere between six and nine people were slayin that night.

Unfortunately for Guzman, the Arellano Felix brothers were in the bathroom at the time of the attack, and all of them escaped unharmed out of a window. His assassins' inability to locate and kill their target would have long-reaching effects on the solvency of the Sinaloan cartels and would lead to drastic and costly reprisals. What could have ended the war in Guzman's favor ended up being a botched hit, and the force with which the brothers struck back would send tremors through the international community, and indirectly lead to Guzman's incarceration in the following couple years.

After four long years of internal conflict tore up the infrastructure and command chains of both cartels, The Arellano-Felix brothers finally bought some useful information that they would use to end the war immediately: El Chapo was on the move and would be boarding a flight out of Guadalajara.

On May 24th, 1993, Guzman's car pulled into the parking lot of the airport at Guadalajara, with gunmen waiting for him in ambush. He exited his vehicle, grabbed his bags, made for the entrance.

And his assailants waited.

Fortunately for Guzman, another man had recently pulled into the same parking lot, with a similar car. He was a short and portly man, and though he wore a priest's frock and habit, and should have been easy to demarcate from the true target, the assailants—on the payroll of the Arellano-Felix organization—walked up to the Cardinal Juan Jesus Posadas Ocampo, stuck an automatic weapon into his chest at point black range, and shot the man dead with a rapid burst of 45 bullets. His driver was also killed in the shooting, as were three passersby on their way to catch their flights.

None of the three individuals were El Chapo.

In the wake of the murder of Cardinal Ocampo, widespread derision of Mexico's inactivity on the drug front ushered in a new era of enforcement throughout the country. Massive bounties of $5 million dollars were offered for information that would lead to the arrest of not only the Arellano-Felix brothers but also on Palma and Guzman. For a country that had witnessed an enormously devasting wave of violence as the two factions fought for control of the lucrative drug markets, this proved the final straw. Despite their suffering, the murder of important politicians, civilians, children and women, the death of the Cardinal was a tipping point in the war against the Mexican drug cartels.

Spurred into action by the massive outcry against the violence that held the nation in thrall, the Mexican government began arresting traffickers, disrupting the flow of drugs, and seizing money. After a long manhunt, Guzman was arrested in Guatemala, where he went into hiding after the failed assassination attempt. He was sentenced to over 20 years in prison for various guns charges and trafficking charge and was eventually convicted and sentenced to spend a long time in a heavily fortified prison. Despite his political connections and his role as a potential victim of the gunmen at the Guadalajara airport, neither his money nor his might was sufficient enough to get him out of trouble.

His new home in the federal penitentiary—The Federal Center for Social Rehabilitation No. 2, lovingly referred to by its occupants as "La Puente Grande," or, the Big Bridge—did not prevent him from administering to his expansive criminal empire, however. While he was on the inside, Guzman bestowed the power of authority and control of the entire operation to his brother. He would spend many years in prison—almost a decade—but before long, the immense power of drug money in Mexico proved its worth once more, and before his sentence was even close to being served, El Chapo found himself back on the outside and enjoying life as one of the most powerful men in the world.

Chapter 3

THESE BARS AREN'T STRONG ENOUGH

Though he was locked up, Guzman's power did not diminish, and despite the efforts of the Mexican government to decapitate his organization, the Sinaloan cartel remained one of the most powerful criminal organizations in North America through the nineties and into the new millennium. With his empire under siege on numerous fronts, Guzman heard waves of terrible news while he stewed in prison. The government succeeded in arresting dozens of associates and family members after his own downfall and even seized nine properties that belong to him or his associates while he was in prison. At the same time, rival cartel members murdered his son and his brother, and his colleagues in prison after they had been arrested.

These were not easy times for El Chapo, and with his empire on the brink of destruction, he began to cook up plans for an escape. With vast and incalculable sums of money still at his disposal and a growing network of connections to help him both inside and outside of prison, El Chapo found himself in a position to leave behind the penitentiary—hopefully for good.

He enjoyed a luxurious life in prison thanks to his bountiful drug money and the endless corruption of prison guards and officials. He is reported to have enjoyed the company of high-end escorts as well as catered food, and, with the general state of lawlessness in Mexico, the money continued to flow in, allowing Guzman to build for himself not only a kingly existence within the confines of his incarceration but also a reputation as a folk hero. In a land that is enamored by a culture of banditry and rebellion, stories such as those featuring El Chapo were warmly received by the populace, and his named represented to many Mexicans the success of a man who made his own way, who lived by his own rules. But even while he sat safely in lock up, his empire was feeling the effects of his absence, and he could not allow this to continue. According to a former mistress, his childhood of extreme poverty engendered a fear of returning to such a state of financial destitution, and perhaps the increasingly violent news that reached his cell fomented his angst and accelerated his designs to bust out.

Regarding El Chapo's first escape from prison, two stories exist. In the first version of the account, El Chapo found himself stuffed into a laundry cart with the help of prison guards who were on the take. He was buried in dirty laundry, wheeled through the corridors of the facility, and taken right out of the main gate of the prison. The guards allegedly dismantled the security cameras that monitored the hallways, allowing the ruse to go off successfully. After he was pushed through the gates, he jumped up out of the pile of smelly laundry, brushed off his clothes and walked away from this prison a free man. The official government line that sponsored the investigation into this daring and brazen prison break led to the arrests of 71 prison employees for their role in aiding the drug lord's escape.

Many in Mexico do not buy this story, however.

Alternate accounts circulate—whether based around his subsequent reputation as an impossible-to-catch bandit with the mystique of a Robin Hood figure or on actual fact is hard to say—and the effect of these stories has been to entrench El Chapo in the milieu of Mexican folklore for the rest of his career as a cartel patriarch. One such account has two very high-level prison officials walking up to his cell, turning the key in the lock, and telling him that he was free to leave. El Chapo is purported to have literally walked out of the prison through the main gates.

No matter which story is true, the fact remains that in 2001, Chapo Guzman cut his lengthy sentence in half and became a free man once more.

Though it is still an unsolved mystery, the story of his escape pales in comparison to the story of what he did with his freedom. Immediately after breaking free from the prison, El Chapo went to work rebuilding the crumbling façade of his empire. A large and lengthy manhunt turned up no usable evidence as to his whereabouts despite the fact that he was frequently sighted in public during these years. His openness and his involvement with the drug trade during the years of his supposed "manhunt" have contributed to his legacy as a bandit of old-time bravado, and many corridos and Mexican ballads were composed in his honor.

This was a reputation that Guzman put to good use. Stories about him paying for the meals of an entire restaurant, about him giving money to the poor and disadvantaged, and his philanthropy projects—they all served a greater purpose for Guzman in his endless quest to evade recapture by the Mexican government officials.

Whether the stories are true or not is unimportant. What does matter is the legacy of those stories. Suddenly, rather than being portrayed as a violent mass murderer who would stop at nothing to achieve his own aims—no matter what the body count may be—he is seen by the populace as a "man of the people, of God". Throughout the nineties, and until his later capture at the hands of the Mexican government, he would use this reputation to receive aid from people who had no love for their government authority figures and saw him as an important part of their culture, a man who helped his fellows.

His fine reputation was not the only thing that helped him evade capture by his foes. While on the lam from prison, he waged a rather successful gang war against the cartels that had moved in on his territory during his incarceration. During this time, the collapse of the Columbian cartels at the hands of the American government was a powerful boon to the Mexican drug industry, and the organizations involved in the smuggling networks were more powerful than ever before. A cartel out of Juarez had succeeded in gaining control of the northeastern section of the Mexican-America border, and their leader, Rodolpho Carrillo Fuentes, oversaw his operation in much the same way as Guzman administered his during the eighties. Many of his underlings were dissatisfied with life living under the don of Juarez, and after a long time on the run, El Chapo made his move.

Meeting with top officials of the Carrillo Fuentes syndicate, El Chapo put a plan on the table to assassinate their leader and absorb the business, to divide it among the underlings and usher in a new era of prosperity for the Mexican cartels under his own leadership. In Monterrey, El Chapo met with fellow cartel criminals to create a new pact that would put them—former members of the Carrillo Fuentes cartel—in power with Guzman after they helped him topple the reign of their leader and his alliance with Los Zetos cartel out of Southern Mexico. Though the operation went smoothly, it would engender a decade long spree of violence that would bathe Mexico in blood for years to come.

Originally, El Chapo hoped for a truce. He sent one of his ambassadors to meet with the stalwart leader of the Juarez area cartels. This man, Ismael Zambada Garcia, was not able to succeed in brokering a peaceful negotiation of territories and supply routes. Rather than accept the offer, Carrillo Fuentes reportedly refused to shake Guzman's hand, earning him El Chapo's ire.

In 2006, after exiting a movie theater with a police escort and his wife, assassins paid for by Guzman gunned down the rival cartel leader in Culiacan. His wife was also murdered in the attack, and the fallout of the assassination would perpetuate the long war between the northern and southern cartels.

Though this assassination helped El Chapo regain and consolidate his power, the glory of its success was not shared by all of the conspirators, and within a few years of this key moment in the history of Mexico's modern drug wars, most of the men who worked with El Chapo to overthrow Carrillo Fuentes were also dead as a result of their involvement with the seemingly unstoppable drug lord.

The Beltran-Levya brothers, who had worked under El Chapo for many years, began to earn his distrust over their flashy lifestyles and their poor decision making skills. For an older gentleman who earned his living in the drug trade while maintaining an air of silence and respectability—a man who lived in seclusion and did not flaunt his wealth in public to the degree that so many others did—these were serious offenses. As the pressure to act on the issue of Mexican drug violence continued to increase through the late nineties and into the 2000s, El Chapo began to pass information to governmental agencies and American law enforcement that would aid in the defeat of those who posed the biggest threat to his own operation. As the new century wore on, that increasingly meant the Beltran-Levya's. Over time, he gave information that would lead to the arrests of their most notable hitmen, of their leadership and eventually, of themselves. After some time, control of the Beltran-Levya organization, which by now had splintered away from the larger and more powerful Sinaloan cartel, was passed on to one of the younger brothers, Arturo. He did not do well in keeping out of trouble, nor did he patch things up with his former boss.

In retaliation for El Chapo's work with governmental agencies—whether Guzman's storytelling actually happened or not—the Beltran brothers began to fire back. El Chapo's eldest son was murdered, and the cycle continued. Furious at the death of his son, Guzman released a wave of violence that spread throughout the country and claimed the lives of some two hundred individuals that summer of 2008.

In 2009, Arturo Beltran-Levya was gunned down by commando marines acting on information allegedly passed on by Guzman himself. They shot the man so many times that the bullets nearly severed his head, and his body was left in the streets outside of his home with dozens of bullets in it.

These stories indicate how brutal El Chapo was in exacting vengeance against those who spurned him or those who disobeyed his orders. Through all of this killing, with Los Zetas attacking his people and him returning fire in the streets of Mexico, in her deserts, and along her coveted drug corridors that rake in millions of dollars per year for those who control them, El Chapo was supposedly still a wanted man. The inefficient regime of Vicente Fox did little to stop his killing and his reign of terror, but before long, the tide of Mexico's government began to turn, and in 2006, a new president was elected who promised to bring the war back to the cartels and pledged military support for those combating the drug forces that had plagued Mexico for so many years. Felipe Calderon took office and declared El Chapo a top priority of his regime. Though the "fugitive" drug lord had been operating with impunity for so many years, his reign would soon come to end, and the military backing that police organizations received made a huge dent in the Sinaloan cartel's operations.

Before long, after so many murders and so many kidnappings, after a storied prison escape and a well-documented time as a fugitive, El Chapo once more became the center of a widespread criminal investigation spearheaded by the Mexican military. As numerous close associates fell to the government, stories began to circulate that the notorious bandit and folk hero of the Mexican deserts was increasing his range of motion. In the early 2010s, information related to his hideouts and his patterns in the Sierra Madres surfaced, leading to a massive effort aimed at bringing him to justice.

Chapter 4
THE NET IS CAST

Throughout his fugitive years, Guzman oversaw his operation from the relative safety of the sharp and unforgiving mountains that he had called home for most of his life. The landscape and the cultural climate of the area facilitated his constant evasion of capture, but as the investigations into his whereabouts began to uncover some useful information, members of his cartel began thinking about their options.

In November of 2013, the first of many raids against members of Guzman's cartel brought in a notable arrest. The son of his long-time friend and associate, Ismael Zambada—the same man who helped him win the drug war against the Juarez cartel and the Beltran-Levya's—was arrested by federal authorities at an illegal border crossing tunnel that connected the city of Nogales, Arizona to the Mexican deserts to the south. This arrest spelled disaster for Guzman and his crew, and before long, the seemingly endless well of corruption that kept Guzman and his people safe from federal intervention apparently ran dry. Following the arrest of Zambada's son, lieutenants were killed while evading Mexican police, assassins were arrested by international police efforts in Amsterdam, henchmen were being rounded up by the dozens. The men targeted by this operation were no small fish, either. The man who was killed by Mexican police—who gunned him down form a helicopter on the coastal highway that runs along the Pacific coast—was considered to be a go-to assassin, and the man who was brought down in Amsterdam had El Chapo's first job. He was the chief of logistics and operations. This meant he had an intimate knowledge of everything that the Sinaloan cartel did, every road they used, where they kept their weapons and the drug caches, and who worked for them. His arrest was a crushing blow to the cartel, and even El Chapo could not escape the dragnet that ensued following this raid in the Netherlands. All across Sinaloa, police were bringing in massive quantities of drugs and firearms and information related to the now multicontinental operation that had for its epicenter the humble region of the Sierra Madres in the heart of Sinaloa.

The immunity that the Sinaloan cartel enjoyed while all of their competitors were being toppled by the newly elected government of President Enrique Nieto, and his predecessor Calderon, had come crashing down, and El Chapo found himself with fewer and fewer friends on the outside.

Product shipments were affected as well. In the early months of 2014, their leading assassin was arrested on the road, as was a man who was transporting 4,000 hollowed-out cucumbers stuffed full of cocaine. As members of the cartel turned to avoid life sentences for their crimes committed at Guzman's behest, government authorities were gaining ground on the fugitive drug lord who still lived like a king in his mountain hideouts. The final front of this legal war against the cartels came when the security personnel that had been rounded up in the recent raids began to give over information regarding El Chapo's most recent movements.

Growing tired of a squirrelly—if not luxurious—life in the mountains of Western Mexico, Guzman began traveling secret byways through the mountain passes to enjoy the cultural scene along the Pacific coast and in the Sinaloan capitol city of Culiacan. Perhaps he merely getting old and wanted to enjoy some leisure time after decades of hiding from both the law and his drug trafficking enemies. Perhaps it was poor planning or a leak in his crew that fed the information to the government. If anything is incontestable, it is the fact that El Chapo Guzman made a dire miscalculation of venturing out of the mountain range he called home, where people loved and respected him, where he knew every crag and valley and hiding spot the terrain offered.

The information gained through the many informants, wiretaps and state's witnesses who decided they didn't want to serve a life sentence for the betterment of their billionaire boss led to El Chapo's second arrest. Eventually, after a tireless investigation into the kingpin's movements, the authorities found themselves at the door of Guzman's ex-wife, where they knew he was holing up in the coastal resort city of Culiacan.

Raiding with force of numbers and firepower on their side, the governmental forces were stymied after numerous attempts to barge through the steel reinforced door. In the time it took them to gain entrance to the villa, Guzman had succeeded in slipping away through a series of tunnels that he had established, using the sewer system to connect six different locations throughout the city. Once again, Guzman was a wanted fugitive with the police in hot pursuit. Though he escaped the city, the police—aided by the American DEA—traced his movements in a southerly direction and set up shop in the nearby coastal resort city of Mazatlan.

It was there that Guzman was brought in for a third time, ending his run of 13 years as a fugitive from the law after his first jailbreak scheme at the infamous Puente Grande. After a short investigation, they traced him to a luxury condo with a view of the Pacific, where they arrested in the predawn hours of a Saturday morning in February of 2014. Within four months of the arrest that sparked his downfall, El Chapo himself was brought in after being dragged—with no resistance and no shots fired—from a seedy condo that had sparse furniture and no food save for a dozen eggs inside. It seems that after his life of luxurious riches and his many villas and properties, Guzman was arrested in a living situation not dissimilar from his humble, childhood abode in the Sinaloan desert.

He was brought before the press, looking nothing at all like a bandit hailing from the rich and storied lore of the Mexican deserts. Rather, he was middle aged, growing fat, had deep creases in his face, and said nothing to the cameras before being shoved into a Blackhawk.

By the spring of 2014, El Chapo was again incarcerated, and his empire dismantled, but he was still not out of the fight. Before long, he would regain the international spotlight, and rejuvenate both his reputation and his empire for the second time. Mexico had not seen the last of its fabled and sometimes beloved narcos.

Chapter 5

Freedom, Again

Chapo's second stint in a Mexican federal prison did not allow him the luxurious lifestyle he had enjoyed a decade prior. Though he was still able to corrupt prison officials and guards, he did not receive visitation rights from prostitutes, or catered food, and his life was spent in a tiny, L-shaped cell that had a camera in the corner to monitor his activity. He shared his new quarters with many of the men whom he had put in prison and many of his old associates. His family was permitted to see him, and he is reported to have had an allowance of under $50 per month for personal hygiene products and spent 23 hours of every day in solitary confinement in his cell. While he was incarcerated, trouble was heaped on top of trouble, and a joint effort from law enforcement agencies on both sides of the border succeeded in indicting the cartel ringleader on charges of attempting to assassinated government officials, former business associates and rivals, and witnesses. The list of charges continued to grow as he awaited trial, just as his list of allies continued to shrink. These conditions were nothing like his first cell, but he remained undaunted.

Despite the fact that he was a maximum security facility and his power was beginning the decline, the tiny jail cell would not prove strong enough to hold such a slippery convict. This time, rather than a laundry cart, El Chapo slipped through the prison bars with a much dastardlier and bandit-like style that was fitting with his reputation and the place he commanded in local folklore.

Not even eighteen full months after his arrest, the sun rose on El Chapo's prison, but guards did not find him anywhere. Rather, when they searched his cell, they found a hole in the floor in the section not visible from the corridor. The hole went 32 feet down into the foundations of the prison via ladder, where it connected with a tunnel system that stretched for over one entire kilometer and came out on the outskirts of the nearby town. According to the National Security Commission in Mexico, he was "last seen entering the shower area" a little before 9 p.m. and disappeared into the very walls of the prison to renew his life of crime.

To make matters worse for the federal government in Mexico, an investigation of the tunnel quickly led to the discovery of mechanized equipment for carting away soil and rock, as well as infrastructure built into the tunnel to allow for lighting and the flow of breathable air through the tight space. The exactitudes with which it was engineered implied not only help from within the prison but also help from outside. Within a short while of the escape, as many as eighteen guards were being interrogated by specialists in organized crime investigation, and the prison that was supposedly secure enough to hold El Chapo was on lockdown. The scandal damaged Nieto's domestic and international reputation, as he had campaigned on promises to battle the drug cartels until the day was won and mocked his predecessors for their own inability to handle the wayward drug lord. Despite the president's faith that the law enforcement agencies under his control would see that El Chapo was caught for the third time and that he would never again be given the opportunities to escape through the corruption of his captors, many people—including the head of the DEA—believed that he would never be seen again if he made it to the Sierra Madres.

The situation was worsened by the refusal of Mexican authorities to extradite the criminal. He was, after all, still wanted in the United State for money laundering and drug trafficking and other crimes, and given the long-standing tradition of Mexican prison corruption, could have easily been held captive in America, serving the rest of his life in a prison that he would actually be contained in. But the government saw this as an affront to their sovereignty and their national pride and refused the request.

To have lost track of the wealthiest and most notorious drug lord in the world after such a refusal, according to Rolling Stone reporters following the story, turned the Nieto administration into something of a "global pariah."

In response to the international outrage sparked by the fugitive's second escape from prison—aided by corrupt guards—a massive, multinational manhunt was issued for the short, stocky, and aging drug lord. His face was well known by Interpol agents and security personnel at all the major international airports, fleets of helicopters scoured the hills surrounding the prison, widening their field of search as the days pressed on, and agencies on both sides of the border collaborated with one another to ensure that he would not reach the safety of his mountainous home.

But they were thwarted.

They searched for days, for months even—the search did not let up for his entire ephemeral moment of freedom, and they found him only through aid of one of his careless followers, and this, not before American actor Sean Penn, along with a Mexican actress Kate Del Castillo, were able to secure an interview with the notorious and highly pursued fugitive.

Indeed, El Chapo made it back to his refuge, his safety. From his homeland—the state of Sinaloa—he invited the actor and actress to meet with him at an undisclosed location after he had contacted them through a series of anonymous emails, burner cell phones, and lawyer meetings. Though it seems like a surrealistic daydream in a saga that is otherwise populated by the all-too-real corpses left in the wake of his meteoric rise to power, El Chapo Guzman reached out to the pair and invited them for an interview, so that he would be able to tell his story to the world as he wanted it told. He wanted to solidify his legacy. Perhaps he was conscious of the noose closing around his neck and he sought the opportunity to speak his last words to the world.

In any case, the interview went off, with both del Castillo and Penn receiving scrutiny for what the general public considered complicity in the plans of a fleeing escape artist wanted on too many charges to list. It was published in Rolling Stone magazine in America on January 10, 2016.

Strangely enough, the day after the pair left Guzman's Sinaloan hideout, he found himself under siege from the Mexican government forces. They, along with the DEA agents working with them, had succeeded in tracking one of the cell phones carried by a man in El Chapo's retinue. They had pinpointed his location after a long manhunt and wasted no time in descending upon the ranch property he was stopping at. Penn and del Castillo left El Chapo's presence on October 2, 2015, and the raid began the next day.

Reports from locals in Sinaloa tell tales of helicopters being shot down, communities being raided, ranches being seized and occupied by government forces. In the end, El Chapo and his capture proved to be of such import to the Mexican government that they turned the state of Sinaloa into a battlefield, using all of the firepower they could muster to root out cartel members who had gone to ground, turning the gangsters into insurgents in the process. Though accounts of the raid—the extent of the damage and the scope of the military action—are conflicted, the military action is believed to have lasted almost a week. Reporters covering the story frequently asserted that El Chapo was targeted in a precise and militaristic manner, that the roundup was small and featured only those who were working closely with the fugitive drug lord.

Others insist—included Guzman himself—that he was merely wounded, and that the *federales* needed to bring in everything they had to throw at him, and still, it proved to be only just enough.

Following the conflict, El Chapo once more went underground, traveling from place to place in lands that revered him for his bravery and affrontery to a mostly corrupted government. After many nights in the jungle, Guzman ended up in the city of Los Mochis. Resting on the Pacific coast in Guzman's home state, the small city was likely teeming with men and women who would be eager to support his escape and continued freedom. As a hotbed of cartel activity, though, it had a very active police force. This active police force—along with the federal agents from both America and Mexico—tracked one of Guzman's close associates to Los Mochis, one of the men who helped him engineer the tunnel that proved so vital in his most recent escape from prison. This man was responsible for digging tunnels that would serve to facilitate Guzman's escape from the house he planned on staying in while he rested in the coastal city. When monitoring police officials became aware that an important target was imminently using the house to lay away, they had no idea who would be staying there.

But they waited.

And, in the end, the waiting paid off.

At 4:30 in the morning on January 8th, 2016, Mexican marines stormed the house and were met with a hail of gunfire from the men guarding their leader. With an elaborate series of escape tunnels dug into the very building—there was a hatch beneath the refrigerator, as well as numerous entrances concealed behind pieces of furniture—El Chapo attempted to escape. As his men shot it out with the police authorities in the upper levels of the seemingly normal home, Guzman crawled through muddy and narrow passages, exhausting himself to the point of collapse, before finally coming out clean with one of his closest lieutenants on the other side.

He crawled to the surface and came out of a manhole—stinking of filth and suffering from hypoxia—right in front of a Walmart store on the edge of town. He stole a Volkswagen, but it broke down a few blocks away. He hijacked a Volvo and attempted to flee the neighborhood before the Marines were able to circle it and cut off his escape route.

And he almost succeeded.

His lieutenant and himself—in the commandeered Volvo—made it the state highway, there own road to freedom. Had they been slightly faster, the story of El Chapo Guzman might have ended with him escaping into the night, retaining his mystique as a master evader of the law and a hero of his people.

This time, however, he was not so fast.

The Mexican military personnel that had been pursuing him finally caught up, and he was arrested on the side of the highway leaving town. After a bloody gun battle at the house in the middle of the city, he went silently from the stolen car, and into police custody.

Chapter 6

Life Plus Thirty

Immediately after Joaquin Guzman Loera's arrest, the Mexican government began the complicated legal process of extraditing him to the United States. He was still wanted on numerous charges of racketeering, money laundering, murder, drug trafficking...the list goes on for quite some time. Though it took almost an entire calendar year, Guzman was eventually sent to the United States to face nineteen charges spread over six indictments.

His trial began on November 5th, 2018, in Brooklyn, New York. Throughout the trial, the prosecution called 56 witnesses to describe in brutal detail the entirety of his story. Before the jury of twelve individuals, his story was told in its completion. After three months of testimony, the jury had heard a myriad of tales relating to El Chapo's exploits as the leading drug man in Mexico. On top of the well known and frequently recounted stories, they heard about the time he tortured two captives for hours with a stick before blowing their head off and throwing their corpses into a bonfire to destroy their remains down to the skeleton. Witnesses told of El Chapo forcing his victims to dig their owns graves, burning people with clothing irons, and letting people waste away of starvation until his employees complained about the stench emanating from their still-living bodies.

Stories were endless, detailing his brutality and the sadistic nature of his personality that would allow him to suffer no slight, no insult. It is alleged that he offered bribes upwards of $100 million dollars to officials in the Mexican government as high up as the president himself. Certainly, Nieto denies such allegations, and they are likely untrue. But the trial increased the man's mythological, folkloric stature as much as it dragged his reputation through the mud. These stories that were told at his arraignment and during his trial, they have already become the stuff of legend.

Perhaps this is the most telling aspect of his legacy.

Regardless of how hard any government tries to tear down the reputation of a person that his held in high regard by his own people, the stories of that person's heroism and decency will still proliferate. Accounts to the contrary will always be a skewed narrative. The jury listening to these stories, however, was not as moved by the latent heroism of the dispossessed drug lord. After 56 witnesses testified to his guilt, the jury agreed decided that Joaquin Guzman Loera was guilty on ten charges, and in that same month, the judge sentenced him to life in prison. Aside from life in prison plus an extra thirty years for good measure, the courts also underwent an extraordinarily precise and calculated appraisal of Guzman's net worth and ordered him to forfeit every penny that he had earned through illegal narcotics and human trafficking operations. All told, after the sentencing hearing in February of this past year, Guzman is into the federal government of America for over twelve billion dollars.

Certainly, Forbes was correct to put him on the list of the world's richest and most powerful men. Throughout his career, he exercised near total immunity as he ran his businesses with cruelty and calculation. The hundreds of bodies that he put in the ground (or left in the streets) are a testament to his power, and the multimillion-dollar endeavors of digging elaborate tunnel systems both in his safe houses and under the US-Mexico border are a testament to his prodigious wealth. In the world of drug trafficking, he is a legend, and as the corridos continue to be written, his reputation as a renowned bandit and anti-establishment hero of the Sinaloan people will only grow. The innovations that he made revolutionized the drug trade, and his cunning business practices have become standard for the cartels that have risen to fill the gap in his wake.

For all this, however, he has nothing to show.

After the federal government seized his assets, froze his bank accounts, and tore down his empire, he was left with nothing and has returned to a state of poverty not dissimilar from the one in which he was born. He had a life of adventure, and the shadow that he cast on US-Mexican relations stands in stark contrast to the nickname that he is alleged to have hated.

El Chapo's career may have ended in a spectacular gun battle, but his life is likely to end in anonymity after years sitting in a cell. He is currently being held at a supermax prison in Colorado, where he is under constant surveillance. This facility has been dubbed "The Alcatraz of the Rockies," and is home to both domestic and international terrorists, high level organized crime figures, and other nefarious personas that warrant such stringent oversight. Cells are soundproof, and inmates spend 23 hours a day in solitary confinement. They are constructed of poured concrete to eliminate the possibility of suicide and offers virtually nothing useful to the wily criminal seeking a way out. His network of corruption is out of reach, and he has none of the allies in America that he enjoyed in Mexico. Though it seems that he is securely confined in a prison that will prevent his third escape, the ways of the criminal are constantly evolving, and only time will tell if the facilities of America are any more fool-proof that those of Mexico.

If anything at all can be discerned from El Chapo's life of crime, it is that, in the end, everything comes full circle, and that drug trafficking ends in the same way for multimillionaires as it does for street level pushers. You are either killed by rivals, killed by government agents, or spend your life in a cell, waiting for the day a heart attack claims your life.

But in the case of El Chapo, we can only wonder if words he spoke to American actor Sean Penn still ring true. On the day before the Mexican government zeroed in on the fugitive, he was asked if he would change anything in his life, given the chance.

His answer?

For me, the way things are, I'm happy.

Perhaps this is still true, despite how everything turned out. After all, he is still a legend among his people, and he has reached a level of folkloric heroism that few can claim. Despite his reign of terror and the thousands of bodies left in his wake, he is still considered a modern day Robin Hood, and people still sing songs about his most daring exploits.

Printed in Germany
by Amazon Distribution
GmbH, Leipzig

Trusting the Actor

Brian Astbury

Copyright 2011 by Brian Astbury

All rights reserved.

No part of this publication can be reproduced or transmitted in any form or by any means, electronic or mechanical, without permission in writing from Brian Astbury.

Cover photograph of Yvonne Bryceland
in The Space production of
Trevor Griffiths' *Occupations*
by Brian Astbury

brianastbury@ymail.com

Quotes

An idiosyncratic, challenging and practical guide to the craft of acting, crammed with anecdotes and humorous insights
Richard E. Grant Actor/director/writer
(*Withnail and I, The Player, Wah-Wah* and many others)

...a unique figure in British theatre. Provocative, controversial, doggedly inspiring and fearless in his pursuit of the truth, he empowers and questions with equal passion. Immune to the distractions of pretence, he has been the pivotal teacher, enabler and mentor for me and countless others.
Rufus Norris Director
(*Festen, Cabaret, Market Boy, Tintin, Vernon God Little, Blood Wedding*)

If you think this book is just going to be about 'acting' you would be very wrong. Brian Astbury could easily have titled this excellent book 'Everything you will ever need to know about Acting' and even then not have come close to describing its worth. part memoir, part practical workbook - Astbury takes us on a journey of his understanding of how actors work, illustrating his insights with funny, affecting stories of his thirty plus years as a drama teacher.. I cannot recommend it highly enough...
Stephen Moyer Actor
(*True Blood, NY-LON, Prince Valiant*, the RSC)

Trusting the Actor is a conversational (almost chatty) love story, a tale of a theatre company's struggle against Apartheid, an irreverent look at life in an educational system which paradoxically helps breed some of society's cultural reformers while being opposed to reform itself.
If the key to understanding the arts or the sciences lies in our understanding of the patterns life throws up, then reading these pages may help some of us unlock a few more. David Mitchell says, 'Knowledge exists only when it is given'. Brian Astbury is a giver.
Alexander Siddig Actor/director
(*Deep Space Nine, Syriana, Un Homme Perdu, 24, Primeval, Hannibal*)

Brian Astbury was, without a doubt, the biggest influence on me while I trained at LAMDA.
20 odd years and 70 movies later, I have realized that everyone develops their own hybrid of all the methods they have learnt.
Brian's teachings are still what I go to in trouble, and more importantly, way back in a church hall in Earls Court, he taught me to be proud of whatever talent I had, and confident.
Without confidence no actor can risk, fail, brush themselves down and try again.
It's in the taking of risks, and being brave, that we can really excel.

Jason Flemyng Actor
(*Lock, Stock and Two Smoking Barrels*, *Snatch*, *The League of Extraordinary Gentlemen*, *The Quatermass Experiment*, *Drum*, the RSC)

...a truly inspirational teacher.
He taught me that you can have a social conscience and be an actor;
that you can affect change through your work.

Julie Hesmondhalgh Actor
(Hayley, *Coronation Street*)

CONTENTS

Debts and gratitude   1

Introduction   4

Prologue   8

Logue   9

Orestes   16

LAMDA   22

Left-Brain Dominance   23

The Sound of the Gods Laughing At You   25

Even My Dog....   31

The Broken Chair - a belated apology   33

Breaking Down Walls   38

Mountview   45
    A Word about Degrees... .45

The Road to Damascus   55
    A Word to Budding Directors... 55

The Bicycle and the Mud   64
    A Note about Thinking...67
    A Note about Repetition..69
    A digression - on types of actor...71
    A further digression - this time on the subject of plays and society....74

The Problem of Acting   79
    A Word about the Brain....................................... 82
    A Word about Stanislavski...5

Image Streaming	90
On Emotion	99
A Word about Vanity	105
'Why does everything have to have a message?!'	110
The Final Stretch	127
The Exercises	129
Under-reading	129
Mind-Mapping	134
The Basics of Image Streaming	140
The Anger Run	145
The Basic Exercises	149
Things to watch out for... and why...	155
A Word about Tetany	155
Rebirthing	159
Defences	164
A Question of Control	170
A Word about the Imagination	176
Exercises for disabling the Left Brain	180
A word about auditions	184
...and a final word	185
Epilogue	186
Feedback from Workshops	196
Bibliography	201
Index	203
About the Author	206

Debts and gratitude

To all those students at LAMDA, where I spent eight very happy years; to those at Arts Threshold, who demanded that I put my money where my mouth was and start putting all the ragbag of techniques I had been developing with them into a workshop format; to the extraordinary groups of Mountview students who then took on the further development of these workshops, and willingly - and with awesome trust - allowed me to try out ever more extreme exercises and techniques, giving invaluable feedback which allowed us to junk those that didn't work and develop and refine those that did; to other students at Guildhall; Manchester (when it was a Poly); back at LAMDA; and in Boston - who were open to trying out these methods in productions; and finally to the students at E 15 who were so supportive, especially when the exercises came under attack from those who refused to give up time to see them in action - Thank you - you all know who you are - you have the scars...

To the John Hodgson Theatre Research Trust for their generous grant which enabled me finally to write this down.

To the readers who ploughed through my endless digressions and helped me make some sense of the narrative (I hope), especially to Andrew Weale, Dan Horrigan, Kezia Cole, Maisie Tomlinson, Milja Fenger, Maria Rabl.

Finally, three women need to be mentioned without whose help this book would not exist. Jessica Beck - one of those students you dream about, who never lets you relax, asks difficult questions and, like a particularly vicious little terrier, won't let go until you answer. As a director, she has taken on board and developed even further many of the exercises. At a time when I really wanted nothing more than to sink into my rocking chair and gaze into the distance, she finally goaded me into writing this book. And, on several occasions, she bolstered my flagging faith.

Emma Brown found me at Mountview and played a large part in developing the techniques. Her clarity and calm faith, and her extraordinary teaching abilities, kept me inspired and on track.

Yvonne Bryceland - my late wife. For 30 years I lived in the warmth of her giant shadow, watching in awe her ability to transform herself into characters seemingly way beyond the reach of her 5'3' frame; how she could connect to their terrible pain, and then communicate this to an audience night after night - changing lives and healing. This is not idle - I still meet people who, years after her passing on to the next phase, will tell me how a particular play affected them, inspired them, gave them hope and succour. Her work is the touchstone of courage, honour, honesty and total commitment against which I have judged all my own work, and that of others. Impossible to equal. But imperative to attempt to match.

Introduction

Emotion is at the heart of this book. All theatre - you could say all human life - revolves around it.

This emotion is tied to the force on which our entire Universe is founded: Energy. Throughout this book you will find references to energy and emotion. There is a whole section exploring emotion as it relates to acting, and living.

However, I first need to place my journey in context.

For nearly 100 years most actor-training has been rooted in the system devised in the early 20th century by Konstantin Stanislavski - unquestionably one of the great founding figures in this field.

Much of this training ignores Stanislavski's own later reservations on his system and his moving on to a different one - the Method of Physical Actions.

It is undeniable that he would have moved on even further in the light of subsequent events and discoveries. The Second World War, the Atom Bomb, the Holocaust, Vietnam and all the other wars, Freud, Jung, Gestalt, Reich, Lowen, Laing, film and television, the Internet, high-speed travel, the exploration of Space etc., etc., etc. - all these would have excited him enormously. He was always researching and exploring in the new fields of the mind - mesmerism, psychology, psychiatry.

But there is one field that I think would have excited him above all others - the findings of research into the function and limitless possibilities of the brain that have mushroomed so dramatically and exponentially in the last few decades.

Why? Well, let's listen to the man himself speaking through his alter egos in An Actor Prepares.

In order to express the most delicate and largely subconscious life it is necessary to have control of an unusually responsive, excellently prepared vocal and physical apparatus.

Who would disagree with that?

... the very best that can happen is to have the actor completely carried away by the play. Then, regardless of his own will he lives the part, not noticing how he feels, not thinking about what he does, and it all moves of its own accord, subconsciously and intuitively ... (I'm sure he was addressing Olga Knipper and his other female actors as well)

But then he goes on:
Unfortunately this is not within our control. Our subconscious is inaccessible to our consciousness. We cannot enter into that realm. If for any reason we do penetrate into it, then the subconscious becomes conscious and dies. The result is a predicament; we are supposed to create under inspiration; only our subconscious gives us inspiration; yet we apparently can use this subconscious only through our consciousness, which kills it. Fortunately there is a way out ...

The control of which he is speaking is conscious control, and our understanding of this has changed dramatically in the past decade. Now we know that all our decisions are made subconsciously and we only become consciously aware of them a second or so later. And our attempts to control the subconscious can be disastrous - especially for actors.

Stanislavski's *'Fortunately there is a way out'* is followed by:
To raise our subconscious to creative work there is a special technique. We must leave all that is in the fullest sense subconscious to nature, and address ourselves to what is within our reach. When the subconscious, when intuition enters into our work we must know how not to interfere.

So far, so good. But then:
One cannot always create unconsciously and with inspiration. No such genius exists in the world. Therefore our heart teaches us first

of all to create consciously and rightly because that will best prepare the way for the blossoming of the subconscious which is inspiration. The more you have of conscious creative moments in your role the more chance you will have of a flow of inspiration.

Creating *'consciously and rightly'* is precisely the problem. If we could do this without getting in the way of our inspirational flow there would be no problem. Any attempt at using conscious 'creative' control leads us inexorably out of that area of mystery and is in every sense an act of interference. I am not talking here of the preliminary, preparatory work, which is essential, and which must always be done 'consciously and rightly'. This work must be done by the actor before entering the rehearsal room.

Once there, a different process awaits.

The answer to this paradox does not lie in our consciousness as it follows belatedly behind our subconscious. It lies in that phrase: *'... when intuition enters into our work we must know how not to interfere.'*

There is also an implicit assumption that somehow the subconscious is some alien entity and not us. That we are controlled by this 'being' with the further assumption - it seems to me - that this 'being' cannot be trusted.

The methods I have evolved over the past two decades all have their roots in the practical struggle, with many young actors, to find ways to utilise the power of the subconscious without paralysing it with conscious thought; to free intuition to do its proper work; to shift emotional and physical blockages – the defences - which stand in the way of performance; to learn to trust this 'being' which is, after all, an essential part of ourselves, the part that for every moment of our lives keeps us alive and functioning properly. Stanislavski's : *'We must leave all that is in the fullest sense subconscious to nature'*... seems to me to send us down the wrong road. It is not *'nature'* to which we must leave it. We need to learn to understand the processes of this subconscious so that we can find ways to liberate it from the blockages that our defences put in its way - and let it to do what it does best.

Over the years I have come to understand that the best way in to clear these blockages and open the pathway is through the use of energy techniques. I can best outline these techniques by telling the story of their evolution.

I have been told that one should not apologise when writing a 'serious' book. I should do so here. I have a disease which afflicts my writing. It is probably terminal. Its medical name is Unrepentant Facetiousness. But it has served me well over several decades of trying to keep young acting students awake. Some have indeed found me quite funny. Others have just groaned. So, in the spirit of the preceding words of this paragraph: I make no apology.

Prologue

This book comes in two sections. The first is anecdotal, telling in stories which sometimes overlap or skip backwards or forwards in time, how I came, with the aid of umpteen eager, brave and foolhardy young acting and directing students, to evolve this set of exercises. The actual exercises are described in more detail in the second section, together with further illustrative, anecdotal stories - and a major, important section on defences.

All of the exercises arose from the needs of the actors and students with whom I was working. They were road-tested on the originals and then retested and refined on many subsequent students and professional actors - approximately 800 at the last count.

I need to make my debt to these willing 'victims' clear. I was a director/teacher trying to find solutions to problems of acting and directing Without their courage and blind trust nothing would have happened. Actors can at-one-and-the-same-time be infuriating, self-centred, pig-headed and amongst the most courageous people on earth. 98% of them are in the profession because of what I call the Mommy!-Mommy!-Look-at-Me!-Syndrome. They are there for the validation of applause, the 'rewards' of fame and money. I have been very fortunate in working with a disproportionate number of the 2%. Actors who were there for more mysterious reasons. Reasons which are difficult to fathom. Reasons which turned their craft into a vocation - which, practised properly, can raise them to the status of healers, helping those who watch them from the darkness to realise that they are not alone. To grant them understanding and new perspectives. Practised at this level theatre is a noble art. If you feel that it is nothing more than an entertainment, that it can have no place in the process of change, then this book is not for you.

Logue

An actor stands alone on a stage. Facing into a darkness of the soul that is terrifying to those of us watching from the safety of the stalls. With a courage that is beyond awe s/he plunges into realms of pain and rage that seem beyond the capability of the human soul to survive.

This act has a strange effect on its watchers. The Greeks called it Katharsis. It doesn't happen often, but when it does, you know. After a particularly extraordinary production of O'Neill's *Long Day's Journey into Night* - which left its small audience sitting in silence for many minutes afterwards - I found myself trying to describe what effect the play had had on me. 'It was like being scrubbed clean with acid', I said. Despite being taken on a journey into the darker hinterlands of the human spirit, I felt cleansed. Great theatre does that.

So, forgive me if I go back now to place my own personal journey in context.

I was born a country boy in a beautiful small town called Paarl in the Cape Province of South Africa. Raised in the 50s, as Apartheid was formulated and developed.

For those who are, fortunately, too young to know what this was: Racial discrimination exists all around the planet. It is only in the last 50 years that humanity has begun to get to grips with this disease and attempt to eradicate it. In the period I am talking about here the great heroes of this battle - Martin Luther King, Nelson Mandela, among many others - were only just beginning to emerge, following in the hallowed footsteps of Mohandas K. Gandhi. In America there was segregation in schools and on buses; in Australia you could find park benches with Whites Only emblazoned shamelessly; in India the caste system was only just beginning to be acknowledged. Most of this was de facto, the way it had always been. South Africa took this a stage further and, when there was a major change of government in 1948, began to enshrine these practices in law. So, we had the Immorality Act which forbade inter-racial marriage, or even any form of sexual contact between Whites and other races. The Pass Laws forced the Black members of society to carry a pass-book and restricted where they could live and work. There were many other laws which proscribed all areas of life for all sections of the population, culminating in an attempt to segregate the Black population in so-called Bantustans, far away from the affluent and privileged Whites (while, of course, ensuring that enough of the former had passes which would enable them to keep the wheels of industry, the gold and silver mines, etc., going. Also to work as servants for the latter). It was a cruel and iniquitous system which, hallelujah!, came to an end in the 1990's.

This impinged little on what was a very happy childhood. I was a privileged White. Our parents were not well-off, but we wanted for little. Theatre did not play a large part in my early years. Films and books were my main influences. But there were major formative influences in this field. At the age of five I was taken with my sister to see Tommy Trinder in a pantomime in the magical darkness of the old Alhambra Theatre, Cape Town, with its fairy-tale columns and stars twinkling artificially overhead.

One memory remains. Someone, probably Tommy, singing 'Me and my Shadow', while behind him on the set his own shadow is projected large. Magic to a five-year-old. Two years later and we're back. This time the wonderful red curtains pull open to reveal - wonder of all wonders - a huge field of corn. It was *Oklahoma* that stole my heart. I fell head over heels in love with the magic of theatre. Coincidentally it also started a process in which I fall helplessly in love with every leading lady in almost every play I see. But that's another story.

For the rest, there was a truly boring rendering apart of *Hamlet* by the University-of-the-Big-City-Nearby Drama Department. This featured a Laertes who manfully put his leg on a plinth to deliver a speech and could not understand the hilarity of the small-town cretins. Always wondered when he found out that he had a large hole in his black tights. The peak of pure comic heaven for us rugger-buggers, however, came with a messenger rushing on to the stage to tell of something or other. He screeched to a halt without taking into account the pride of the local Nationalist Party. wives in the floor of this political party hall and its high-gloss shine. The crash as he cannoned into the offstage left wall like a drunken ice-skater is still one of my all-time prized theatre memories.

Moira Lister came and introduced me to the joys of Dorothy Parker. But, there was nothing else, apart from a paralysingly boring play-reading, staged by the apprentice-dentist who had spent an entire mid-year holiday instilling a lifelong fear of dentists in me by drilling his way – with one of those old-fashioned slow grinders - through about 10 of my teeth. It was a toss-up as to whether his dentistry or his acting abilities induced the most pain.

I left Paarl for a new adventure in the Big City - Cape Town - where I was to fail miserably at playing University. On the way to being censured, and finally dismissed from my librarianship studies because, and of this I was left in no doubt, librarians didn't read the books – I majored in film at the other 'universities' of Coliseum, Metro, Broadway, Van Riebeeck, the Odeon and, of course, the Alhambra – magical emporiums where I imbibed Cinema. Up to five times a week, I could be found slumped in my comfy front row chair before the big screen. Here, I was introduced to one of my major influences: Ingmar Bergman. *The Magician* was the first film to bring me out in goosebumps.

While still at the other University doing the BA section on my BA Lib Dip, I was put off Jane Austen for far too long by a tutor unwilling to take the time to explain to a country boy why he should love this great writer. It took a further 33 years to remedy this lack. It was an example of teaching at its worst. I would have sunk without a bubble but for two inspired teachers. One was my cousin, Cynthia - a schoolteacher - who, in two hours one night, opened up the Tragedy of *Dr Faustus*, showing me what the other idiot had so singularly failed to do. It takes so little to light an unquenchable flame in a young student.

The other provided lessons for me in several different areas, not all to do with university studies. His name was Mr Van der Westhuizen. He taught Anglo-Saxon. This was not too much of a problem for me, as it is very close to Afrikaans. English Literature was the problem. I went to him in despair. You have to understand how much despair. Mr Van der Westhuizen was a Cape Coloured, a Non-White, a Non-European. At that stage Apartheid had not progressed far enough and some people of colour were allowed to attend, and even to teach. I had grown up surrounded by sincere and well-meaning people who believed, as an article of faith, that Black and Coloured people were not as advanced as us Whites. At most they could rise to be teachers, of their own kind, of course. But there was a ceiling. So, going off to one of these for help should tell you what pit of despair I was in.

He didn't have to see me. I was asking for help that other tutors should have given. Over three or four extramural unpaid hours, he gently opened my eyes to many new vistas, when he could have been home with his family. Most of all, he opened my eyes to the huge lie that I had grown up with. Mr Van der Westhuizen had no ceiling that I could see. He was far more intelligent than the vast majority of Whites that I knew at that time.

In 1998 - 37 years later - I had the unutterable joy of recognizing him in the cafe at the Baxter Theatre in Cape Town. Still the same modest and kindly man. I think he was rather taken aback at my fulsome, blurted thanks for his inspiration, but he accepted them with his usual grace. Great teachers come in the most unusual guises. I hope I am 1/10 of the teacher that he was.

The following year any doubts I might have harboured about Black intellectual capacities were well and truly eviscerated when I joined Dr Jordan's Xhosa class. He was - in retrospect - not happy to be constrained to teach his own language to us smug and lazy young members of the privileged class. He was so intellectual that he frightened me. His daughter was in my class. Why she had to learn Xhosa I never understood. But she was also scarily intelligent, hugely confident. I had been put firmly in my place by destiny and happenstance.

Theatre? Well, one matinee afternoon in 1960 I found myself in the Hofmeyr Theatre, sitting in the 'love' seats (they were joined in twos without an arm-rest in between, and I'll leave the rest to your imagination - they were right up at the back and very cheap). Alone, I hasten to add, I had not yet met the love of my life.

On the stage, a young actor was delivering a speech which, for the first time in my theatre life, induced in me that tunnel vision in which everything vanished but the person speaking and the visions he was creating in my head. Now I know this is the kind of semi-trance state that good actors are in when they perform, and into which they draw the audience. Then it was quite disturbing. Disturbing but exhilarating. My first exposure to the drug of theatre. The speech came from a character who had been lobotomised. The play - Harold Pinter's *The Caretaker* - the first play to show me the power of theatre. The actor - a talented and promising young man called Nigel Hawthorne. Born in Coventry, he grew up in South Africa, where he was educated at Christian Brothers College in Cape Town. I followed him faithfully through several more years and some wonderful productions - his *Yes Minister* character receiving its first airing there in *Beyond the Fringe* - before he left to return to Britain. Sadly I never got to tell him what a huge influence he was on my life.

At the end of that year a meteor crashed through my murky atmosphere and changed my life forever. I took a holiday job in the Cape Times newspaper library and met my future wife. At that stage, a divorcee struggling to bring up three daughters, combining her library work with ghosting a column for Drum Magazine, appearing in radio plays, and attempting to keep working at her passion - theatre. There was little professional theatre in Cape Town, and it couldn't support a single mother and her children.

Despite her reputation as one of South Africa's top radio actresses, Yvonne Bryceland was struggling. I'd love to tell you the story of our courtship and marriage, because it's quite interesting and very funny at times, but that's not what this book is about.

In 1964, at the age of 39, Yvonne was finally able to turn professional and began to practice her craft with the local Arts Board - a government- sponsored theatre organisation with the money to engage a full-time company. I had, in the meantime, morphed into journalism, via a glorious career as a trainee Mail Order Executive. It lasted two weeks - one to work, and one to work out my notice. I had actually applied to a newspaper to be a photographer - a craft I had discovered almost by accident. They turned me down, inviting me back the following year to train as a journalist. I kept a thriving part-time career as a photographer going. Through Yvonne I became a specialist in theatre photography.

And so, in case you were wondering what the relevance of all this is, I found myself crouching in corners in rehearsal rooms, in the stalls in theatres, watching with fascination as actors and directors and dancers and singers and designers and stage management - good and bad - practised their craft. My photographic bent trained me to be a good observer. Following productions from rehearsal to performance was more than intriguing. I was learning.

Another meteorite crashed into our combined atmospheres. Playwright/director/actor Athol Fugard came to town. Yvonne had known him briefly some years previously, when he had been working for the South African Broadcasting Corporation; in his private time staging 'very weird' plays with his wife, Sheila, a poet and novelist.

One of my first times of actually taking Yvonne out on 'a date' came while I was still at university was in 1962. *The Blood Knot* was the play. It was a stinking hot summer evening in Cape Town. The play was being presented in the hall of a synagogue. Apartheid was taking hold and the usual theatres were not available for the mixed race cast. The curtain was delayed for some time. Then the company manager/producer, David Bloomberg, stepped through the curtains. There were problems with the lights. The play would be staged in one lighting state with no fades - only black-outs were possible. By this time the full house had progressed beyond glowing gently to sweating profusely.

Just short of three hours later Yvonne and I staggered into the humid night - our lives changed forever. For me it was like discovering, for the first time, your own language. Up to then all my cultural references came from overseas. British radio, American film, plays, novels – everything was imported. Here was a man speaking to us in our own language. Even though the story line - two brothers, sons of Black and Coloured parents; one able to pass for White - was not in my experience, I heard, for the first time, the sound of a playwright's dialogue with the society in which he, and I, lived.

And the acting! Zakes Mokae and Athol himself. We had seen nothing like it.

Four years later - after huge battles with the authorities, who took umbrage at Blood Knot's success overseas, Athol's forthright views on Apartheid, and his hand in setting up the Playwright's Boycott - Athol reappeared in Cape Town. This time in *Hello and Goodbye*, with Molly Seftel, directed by Barney Simon. Once again we were bowled over. Yvonne was, by this time, a seasoned professional, had won two Best Actress awards, but was still writing an entertainment column. She interviewed Athol. As with John Kani and Winston Ntshona later, this proved a marriage made in theatrical heaven. Yvonne began to make plans to leave the safety of her government-sponsored job and join Athol and Barney to work on plays that had meaning for us.

When she went to hand in her resignation the Arts Board asked to see the play she was going to do with Athol - *People are living there*. It was not one of his 'political' plays. Athol and Barney were hoping to earn some money through this production to fund further, more direct work through Phoenix Players in Johannesburg.

The Arts Board offered a fully-funded co-production with all their facilities. Yvonne would not have to leave her job. Athol's precarious financial position would be alleviated. They could take the play to Johannesburg.

The play's scheduled three-week run was sold out within one day of its opening - something new for Cape Town. Athol's next play, as yet unwritten, had been commissioned by Professor Guy Butler of Rhodes University for the Grahamstown Festival. The Arts Board, flushed with the success of *People*, climbed on the bandwagon and offered a five-week run in Cape Town. They were rather startled to find themselves presenting *Boesman and Lena* - a play about two Coloured down-and-outs who scrape a living by digging for mud-prawns to sell for bait - whose tin shanties are constantly being bulldozed by the White authorities, forcing them to move on to another nowhere. A dying Black man comes to their fireside.

The crit in the morning Nationalist Party newspaper - Die Burger (The Citizen) - was written by the doyen of South African Afrikaner critics, Professor W. E. G. Louw. It began (and this is from memory - and in translation): *'This play says that in this country we bulldoze people's homes and move them on without providing alternative accommodation. I do not believe this.'* My heart sank. He went on: *'But, in the first years of the Second World War, I was a student in Germany, living a few miles from a large concentration camp - and I did not know of its existence.'*

This was my first real experience of the power of theatre to be a part of the process of change in a society. A very important doubt had been cast in a very important mind. He went on to praise the play, the performers, and the director (Athol both directed and played Boesman) in the highest terms.

The Arts Board relaxed. The audiences poured in. Intoxicated with this success the Arts Board now made Athol an offer he couldn't refuse. 'Choose your own actors - the whole company if need be - write a play for them, direct it.'

Athol chose three actors - Yvonne, Val Donald and Wilson Dunster - and vanished into a rehearsal room above the Labia Theatre for nine weeks. I shared several of these sessions, watching and photographing, in awe as this extraordinary man - at that time certainly the greatest director I have seen before or since - challenged and bullied, provoked and inspired his small team.

The result was *Orestes*.

Orestes

Now I know I keep talking of life-changing events - but this is, after all, a quick tour through the highlights of my life.

Of all milestones, however, *Orestes* was the biggest. 65 minutes of physical and a visual metaphor (only 200 words, telling no story), its extraordinary intensity - I'm not sure I could have coped with many more minutes - changed my life irrevocably and forever. Not all at once, and in ways I only realised much later. Two of the most important: I became a vegetarian. I founded a theatre. The theatre grew out of many late- night discussions after openings and parties, with the exhilarating mix of actors, directors, writers, designers, poets, painters, dancers who formed Cape Town's small artistic community at that time. Time after time I would hear an actor or director moan: 'If only we had a space in which to work'. If only. *Orestes* wrecked my ability to echo this sentiment. If you know something needs to be done then you must do it. Don't wait for someone else. I can't tell you that that was the 'message' of Orestes. But it was part of the challenge it threw down for its audience. Work of this calibre had to continue. The Arts Board was terrified by the connection Athol made between the Greek myth and the more modern story of John Harris, South Africa's station bomber. He had placed a suitcase on Johannesburg railway station and succeeded in blowing up and killing an old lady and badly wounding a young girl. He was hanged for his troubles.

On one level *Orestes* was saying 'How can a caring, intelligent person remain sane in a society like this?' Helped by liberal doses of Sophocles and R.D. Laing, the four collaborators produced a piece of theatre which gave you, the audience, a stark choice: Do something - or become part of the problem. I'd love to say it was all this clear to me back then but I'm no intellectual and it took several years to understand just exactly what a seismic effect *Orestes* had had on me, and what consequences had resulted.

I had gone on to found - with the help of countless rather wonderful, unselfish and generous Capetonians - The Space.   It was set up as a venue in which Athol, Yvonne and many others could work, free from commercial pressures. They would have to work for a pittance but no-one would interfere with the statements they wished to communicate. Almost by accident The Space became South Africa's first Apartheid-era professional, non-racial theatre. We had never expected to be allowed to play to mixed audiences, setting up a legal club to cope with this. But from the start we never turned anyone away - waiting for the Government and its police to take action, which, in turn, we would make sure was highly visible. While there were some hiccups, in hindsight it seems clear that we were deliberately left alone, possibly as a small experiment by a government whose business backers were already telling it that change was inevitable.

We opened with *Statements after an arrest under the Immorality Act*, which firmly nailed our colours to the colourful frontage of our theatre in Buiten Street. I have never thought of this before but Buiten means Outside - and that's what we were.

Our first invited company was Athol's Port Elizabeth group of amateur Black actors - Serpent Players. One exciting Easter Sunday night they presented their explosive version of Camus' *The Just* - retitled *The Terrorists* - there was no pussy-footing around with them. This introduced John Kani, Winston Ntshona and the fearsome Nomhle Nkonyeni to us. John and Winston were so turned on by the experience - their first in a professional theatre - that they decided to attempt a full-time professional life. Athol approached us, we gave them a date - a Sunday in September - and contact was made with Ian Bernhardt's Phoenix Players in Johannesburg, M. A. D. S. in Durban, Rob Amato's Window Theatre in East London, to see whether, between us, we could guarantee a livelihood for them.

On September 10, 1972, *Sizwe Banzi is dead* opened to a full-house audience at first stunned, then overjoyed and exhilarated.

We immediately arranged, with the help of Helen Suzman's Progressive Party, for it to return for a late-night run of three weeks. All the proceeds from these performances went to the two actors. One of our stage managers - Bee Berman - wore her fingers to tiny stumps typing up the transcripts of five or six performances which we had recorded. The play was devised anew each night in those early runs. Athol was finally able to put a script together.

Our club - still functioning, but now as more of a supporters club under the chair of Moyra Fine - commissioned another play, and the following July, devised and rehearsed in free time from their tours to other venues, *Die Hodoshe Span* opened. Now known as *The Island* (a title we couldn't give it as any mention of, or reference to, Robben Island - the prison where Nelson Mandela and the leaders of the struggle were held - was forbidden by law) this play, plus the other two went on to form *The South African Season* at the Royal Court in London in 1974. British playwright/director, Donald Howarth, had been working with us when *Sizwe Banzi* opened. He wrote to Oscar Lewenstein urging him to import the play to London.

Pardon my dwelling on these details. It has been extremely frustrating for those of us originally involved to see inaccurate accounts appearing in supposedly well-researched books and journals. I have only once been approached by such writers to confirm details about that period. This one exception is Dennis Walder, whose series of *Collected Plays by Athol Fugard* is the best source of information of that exciting period.

Getting back to our story: the next development came when I inadvertently became a director. This was not an intentional career move. I had never had any desire to direct. I had no training. I sat in on rehearsals with really good directors like Athol and others. The quality of directors in Cape Town at that time was high. I only realised this when I came to London where, for the first time in my life, I fell asleep in the theatre. I was helped to recover from the shock, shame and guilt by Athol and Yvonne, who had already seen the production with its famous playwright, director, starry actors, at one of the leading companies. 'You fell asleep because it was boring. Wasn't your fault.' They were laughing at this innocent losing his theatrical virginity.

So, in our second year, when we sat at The Space with an upcoming opening date looming like a train in a tunnel, we were in trouble. We now knew quite clearly the consequence of a dark theatre. No Subsidy + No Box Office = Death. Every single director we knew, every single wannabe director, was busy. Yvonne and I were due to go to London on a working holiday. Leaving the theatre dark would result in a return to no theatre at all.

Attempting to calm my state of extreme panic Yvonne said: 'Why don't you direct a play?', and shut my protestations up with: 'You laugh easily - direct a comedy'. The night before she had turfed me out of bed because I was laughing so much at Joe Orton's *What the Butler Saw*.

With trepidation I discussed this with our small group of regular actors - Bill Flynn, Jacqui Singer, Chris Prophet, Maralin Vanrenen. They had little desire to see their theatre close, probably thought they could direct the play themselves behind my back (probably did). So, with the addition of two older actors, I found myself sitting in a rehearsal room - with Joe Orton's lively ghost - falling about laughing at the group of genuinely funny actors for 3 1/2 weeks. I knew nothing of blocking, motivation, etc., just let them go their own way as long as it made me laugh. We cobbled together the worst set ever seen at The Space, and opened the night before Yvonne and I left. Houselights down, stage lights up (no curtain - we played in the thrust), actors on - and the audience started laughing almost as much as I had. I still remember my sister, Brenda, with whom I share a sense of humour, laughing at the few ideas I had personally contributed. 'This is so easy', I thought - and left for London. The production became our top earner. I glowed with pride. The fact that the lead was played by Bill Flynn (anyone who knows anything about South African performance in the years from 1972 to 2007, when he sadly died, will know that Bill was a very special actor, capable of the serious depths of Johnny in *Hello and Goodbye*, and certainly one of the three or four funniest actors I have come across in my life); also that Jacqui Singer (who told me at the start that comedy wasn't her metier but that she would take it on for the good of the theatre) won the Best Actress award for her wonderfully funny, po-faced interpretation - had much more to do with its success than I did.

I went on to find other intelligent comedies by writers like Hugh Leonard, Woody Allen, Murray Schisgal, Feydeaux and, helped by casts of talented and funny actors, was able to develop some sort of craft and be of more assistance to them. These productions enabled our more serious work.

I did suffer guilt pangs, however. 'I know nothing about directing', I said to the long-suffering Yvonne. 'How do I find out?' She sighed. 'Well, if you want to, you need to read books on the subject.' 'Where do I start?' 'Stanislavski is supposed to be the basis of all actor training.' Yvonne had no formal training as an actor. She had had to learn and develop on her own, through work in amateur theatre. She suggested I start with *My Life in Art*, but I added *An Actor Prepares* and started studying.

It was like reading a foreign language. *My Life in Art* was better, but still little help. Back to Yvonne. 'To tell the truth,' she said, 'I did try to use Stanislavski but he was no help to me at all.' At that stage this was no help to me either. Subsequently I have discovered that, despite the widespread use of Stanislavski in drama schools, very few actors ever actually use the system in their working lives. More about this later.

I bumbled through several more books - Michael Chekhov, Uta Hagen, Viola Spolin, among others. None of them seemed to have anything to help me with the problem I was already facing. Even with comedies. Very early on I started to identify the moment when an actor is confronted by an emotion - and the consequences of this problem: tightened jaws, shallow breathing, losing lines, bodily tensions.

I began to look for exercises to help actors push past these blockages. Books on acting - or at least the ones I had access to - didn't even seem to acknowledge the existence of the problem. I started looking at books on psychology. *Games People Play*, *The Primal Scream*, Alexander Lowen's *Bioenergetics*, Kermani's *Autogenic Training*, Gestalt Therapy - you name it, I read it. Many of these taught me a lot about the human condition and the reasons why people were driven to take certain actions - all good grist for the motivational mill - but few helped in any concrete way.

After a few years I decided to try my hand at more serious theatre. The problems multiplied. Mostly I had to rely on actors finding their own way through the maze.

In 1979, after eight exhilarating but brutal years of running The Space, and in a state of near terminal depression at the condition of South Africa and the seeming impossibility of change ever coming - except through the barrel of a gun, something neither Yvonne or I could be a part of – we gave up and came to settle in London.

Yvonne had by this time established a name for herself in London and was asked by playwright, Edward Bond, to play the title role in his play *The Woman* at the National Theatre. A new era had begun for her.

I spent five years becoming naturalised, working in my old profession of photojournalist; attempting to start a film company; being a house-husband.

Then, in 1985, Yvonne was asked by Roger Croucher - one-time director of the Royal Court's Theatre Upstairs, then Principal of LAMDA, one of the top drama schools in the UK - to come and talk to his students about acting.

Yvonne was a shy, modest person and occasions like these took their toll on her. But she believed in ploughing back her experience, especially to young actors. She always stipulated that it had to be a question-and-answer session. There would be no speech or lecture from her. There was one further stipulation: no political questions. If you wanted to know about her politics you had to watch her stage performances. As a concession she started taking me along. I was not shy about speaking on South African politics. So at the end of 75 minutes of lively questioning, Roger said: 'We have 15 minutes left in which you can ask Brian about politics and South Africa.' This part of the session expanded to 45 minutes and had to be stopped so that they could have something of a lunch-break.

On the way home Yvonne said: 'You really enjoyed that, didn't you?' Quietly spoken though it was, it was the understatement of the year. Faced with 26 lively young minds asking difficult and sharp questions I had had a ball! 'Why don't you ask Roger if you can direct at LAMDA?'

In reply to my letter Roger invited me to meet him. He didn't feel ready to take me on as a director, but what about teaching a class? I had never taught in a formal setting. What would I do? 'You've worked closely with Athol and at The Space. Talk to the students about his plays.'

LAMDA

So, one really cold day in January, 1986, I found myself squashed into LAMDA's minuscule staffroom with six young people. (Oh! the joys of teaching small groups - now sadly gone for most of us). I had not the vaguest idea what I was going to do, how to teach. I took the register. The third name: Olivier, Julie-Kate. I looked up into the intense, dark eyes of the young woman huddled suspiciously in a coat four feet away from me. A chill crept up from my toes. I would be 'teaching' Olivier's daughter. Suppressing an intense desire to run, screaming: 'I confess - I'm a fraud!', I commenced the lesson.

It was one of the most wonderful mornings of my life. An epiphany. Some time later, describing it to my wife, I said: 'I had the feeling of a square peg slipping into a square hole.' I had come home.

Not everyone is granted the luxury of finding their obsession. It had taken 45 years for mine to find me. I was, and am, a teacher.

Whether those early students of mine remember me with the affection with which I recall them I don't know. I do know that everything else in my life slipped into a poor second place. Talk about *The Joy of Sex! - The Joy of Teaching!* turned me into the most boring obsessive/compulsive. I went to sleep dreaming about it; woke up thinking about it. At parties I was even more boring than usual. The process taught me all I needed to know about obsession.

In the next term I was asked to take scenes from Fugard plays and work on them. I came crashing up against something I had only had an inkling of in South Africa: Left-Brain Dominance.

Left-Brain Dominance

I know the brain is more complex than a simple left/right divide - nowadays I tend to think of it as a conscious/pre-conscious divide - but it's a handy terminology and one I will use, without further apology, throughout this book.

Specifically, I would add, English left-brain dominance. English as opposed to Welsh/Irish/Scottish. The English character with its clichéd stiff upper lip and belief that the display of emotion in public places is rude, throws up huge barriers to the actor. Having to overcome years of repression and the habits that grow from this is difficult.

I'm not saying that other nations find this easy, but, for the most part, there is a permission that many English people don't have. Foreigners are allowed to show emotion.

I quickly became aware of all the defences that the mind and body erect to make sure that feelings will not cause any disruption to the orderly process of life.

As the young actors battled with the intense emotions of Fugard's characters I began to see, with an increasing clarity, the physical defences. Shallow breathing, tense jaws and shoulders, strangulated voices, swallowing - the symptoms are many and varied. So my quest began. It had only been dimly understood before. Now, day after day, it came sharply into focus.

Over the next eight years I went on to teach as a freelance at LAMDA. My first 2nd Year play was Brecht's *Caucasian Chalk Circle.* My first 3rd Year full production in the flexible challenge of the MacOwan Theatre was David Edgar's *Entertaining Strangers* - an enormous promenade using all 27 members of the final year (frightening - the biggest cast I had ever worked with). I also taught classes in everything from audition technique to Greek Tragedy.

I have much for which to thank Roger Croucher. A strange, idiosyncratic man, he operated occasionally on the rather peculiar basis of finding out what you didn't want to do and knew little about, and then making you teach that. I only realised what he was doing much later. One mid-year 'holiday' period was spent sweating blood as I researched Greek Tragedy in order to teach a 2nd-year class. I swore and cursed as I slogged through the extraordinary amount of verbiage written about Greek theatre. Very late I realised that these walls full of books by renowned professors were based on very little but the sketchiest evidence. It was mostly speculation. Roger's method ensured the teacher arrived in the class in a ferment of new knowledge and ideas, and that this excitement would communicate itself to the class.

At the beginning of that term I sat in his office one morning. What, I asked, did he want me to do with them? He smiled, enigmatically. 'Inspire them' he said.

With Yvonne, Mr Van der Westhuizen and Athol (in a more indirect way), Roger became the fourth great mentor of my life, teaching me the centre of learning. Inspire them; light a flame under them; make them want to learn, to find out. I'm not sure he cared what you did in the class as long as, when they emerged, they were better actors.

My battle with the Left Brain intensified.

The Sound of the Gods Laughing At You

My first really big battle came with a young actor playing the title role in a second year production of *Uncle Vanya*. Andrew was an Oxbridge MA graduate and had been driving every director who worked with him insane with his pointy fingers. No matter what he did he would emphasise the words with stabbing points of his fingers. I was told about this in my briefing. One director had made him play an entire part with his hands in his pockets, which led to an outbreak of two-puppies-fighting-in-a-sack-syndrome. I had personally seen him in a Shakespeare in which the director had shrouded him in an all-encompassing, floor-length black cloak. I will leave the result to your imagination. He also had a very powerful voice which he fell back on whenever he was insecure. I battled with him over the rehearsal period. He was sharing the role with another actor, who was playing the first half Vanya. As I was working then in a very linear fashion I only got to his big scenes in the third week (apart, of course from the sketchiest of mappings-out in the first week). The enormity of the problem almost bowled me over. He had no control over the famous hands, no connection to the deep emotions felt by Vanya.

It peaked one afternoon as we rehearsed the scene in which Vanya realises how much his brother-in-law, Professor Serebryakov, has been taking advantage of himself and Sonya. He confronts the professor in a big speech filled with rage and pain and the realisation that they have all devoted their lives to a man of straw. Andrew's rage was splendid; his powerful baritone voice filled the room to overflowing. Several of the actors winced at the volume. It all signified, to quote some other playwright, nothing. I tried everything I knew to get him to connect to the real feeling. The battle stretched over two afternoons. In despair I said: 'Think of it as Vanya at the end of his tether. Chekhov's comedy is not drawing-room comedy. It's the sound of the gods laughing at you. So, laugh at him - as though you find what he's done a great cosmic joke - nothing left to do but laugh.' 'I can't do that,' he said, 'I'm not very good at laughing on stage.' Resisting a sincere desire to strangle him I pushed him towards doing the action. 'What's my motivation to laugh?' 'I don't care, just laugh.' This went on until it reached the heights of ludicrosity with me, the entire cast plus stage-management clustered around him, falling about laughing with varying degrees of success. It was so ridiculous it became very funny. In the centre Andrew Weale sat, mournful. Not a chuckle.

I went home that night thinking it had not been one of my better days. 'Some ideas are better than others.' I told Yvonne. She had no idea how to help.

When I arrived at rehearsal the following afternoon Andrew looked at me with ill-concealed hatred. He hadn't slept all night, he said, bitterly. We went straight into the scene. I had resolved to cut my losses and move on.

Andrew began his rant with a small attempt at a chuckle. This immediately morphed into an intense, softly-spoken speech filled with real anger, and even more real pain. It brought tears to the eyes of several members of the cast - and mine. We moved straight on into the next scenes. The emotional connection he had made leaked from one scene to the next. A very talented group of young actors picked this up and fed off it.

The following week we performed the play twice for an audience of friends, fellow students and staff. At the end of the first performance the entire front row of hardened tutors was in tears as a wonderful young actor, Karen Cass, delivered that final speech of Sonya's in a way I had not heard it done before, and have not since. She had found this more-or-less by herself, but aided by Andrew's bemused open wound of a performance. He had stumbled through the last days of rehearsal in a daze, as previously locked-in emotions tumbled from him without his seeming to do anything. 'How did you get him to stop with the fingers?' two members of the staff asked. I had not the faintest idea.

I discussed the process with Andrew. He said that he had gone home from the 'laughing' rehearsal in a rage, had been unable to sleep, arrived the following day in a state of complete exhaustion, haunted by the possibility that he could not, in fact, act. He was expecting some discussion of the previous afternoon and possibly some other exercise, and had been taken by surprise when just asked to play the scene.

Beyond that he could remember nothing. He had no idea how he played the scene, or what happened. Neither did he remember going on to the next scene.

This was the first step for me in the realisation of a particular process. It surfaced at first when I discovered over many years and performances, both of my own casts and watching many performances my wife gave, that actors are the worst possible judges of their own performance. This developed into one of the maxims, rules, commandments that I bore my students with. It goes like this: If an actor comes off after a performance and says: *'That was the best I/we have ever done the play!'*, you have a strong 90% chance that it was truly dreadful. When they come off moaning and whinging and saying: *'That was the worst it's ever been! Couldn't concentrate, everything went wrong. Props had a mind of their own!'* then you have about a 60% chance that it was really rather good*. The third response comes when the actors come off looking a little bemused and say: *'Can't remember a blind bloody thing about that performance....'* In this case you can be 95% sure that it was the best it's ever been. Here I am being statistically unkind. (*These percentages are approximate guesses, based on personal observation and haven't been researched by an accredited research agency)

A small addendum: Immediately after *Uncle Vanya* I was asked to direct Moliere's *Misanthrope* with many of the same group. Andrew was once again with me but this time in the small role of Clitandre - a fop. I arrived at the first rehearsal in a state of complete funk and abject guilt. I had not yet managed to finish reading the play, falling asleep after about 10 pages each time. I was not looking forward to the experience. But life teaches us many things. Terrified that I would fall asleep again as we read the play I busked and asked them to do the reading on their feet. 'Just make up the moves as you go along.' I airily told them, hoping in this way to be kept awake. One of those wonderful theatrical miracles occurred that have been the joy of my life. As the first actor - a young man called Richard Wigfield - launched into the opening scene, Moliere reached down through the ages, grabbed me by the throat and said: 'My plays are not meant to be read - they are meant to be ACTED!'

The text began to sing. I hadn't realised quite how funny and how moving it was. My previous two experiences of viewing Moliere had both been dire professional productions.

We were rehearsing in the gloomy old Avatar beneath the Russian Church in Kensington - a place of many ghosts. Andrew vanished out of the main door into the room, to prepare for his first entrance. Afterwards he told me: 'I was standing out there without the faintest idea what to do with the part. Then I heard my cue and opened the door.'

From our side Andrew marched in and played the scene in a way that left most of us helpless with laughter. It couldn't have been more correct. Nobody was more amazed than Andrew at the laughter. 'It just came out that way.' he said. I had watched through two productions as an actor learnt how to be 'in-the-moment'. That production is still one of my treasured memories. Discovering, with that talented young cast, the greatness of Moliere, his incredible depth and understanding of the pain and foibles of humanity, his deep knowledge of what will and won't work onstage, was a joyous experience.

Really good acting, in my opinion, is a kind of light 'trance-state'. A story about this. My wife was playing at the Royal Court Theatre Upstairs on her first appearance in London in Athol's *Boesman and Lena*. One night I arrived on my hired motor-scooter (the only way to get around London) to fetch her after a performance. As I entered the empty theatre one of the stage-managers greeted me with: 'We had quite a night tonight.' Apparently a slightly disturbed member of the public who harboured an unspecified grudge against the Royal Court, especially when he had too much to drink, had come up the stairs during the second act. The box office staff had gone and he was able to walk into the theatre where he proceeded to deliver his own speech of recrimination, being particularly harsh apparently on Oscar Lewenstein - at that stage Chairman of the Royal Court.

Two stage managers had wrestled him outside and sent him on his way. The other S-M now joined in: 'What's really funny is that afterwards, when I congratulated Y' - many people called her this - 'about how well she handled the interruption - she just went straight on as though he wasn't there, afterwards two members of the audience asked if it was part of the show - she said 'What man?'.' The two roared with laughter. 'She didn't even notice him.' Yvonne herself, was a bit fazed that she hadn't become aware of the interruption. I took it as an indication of the fierce concentration with which she played each role.

Three years later she told me of another incident which illuminated this concentration, and explained something which I had long wondered about. *Statements after an arrest under the Immorality Act* - the opening play of The Space - was also invited to play at the

Royal Court. Athol had played the original Errol Philander. He now cast Ben Kingsley in that role with the South African actor, Wilson Dunster - one of the original cast of *Orestes* - playing the policeman.

The play was invited to tour Europe, finally ending up in what was then Yugoslavia at the BITEC Festival in Belgrade. This festival gathered productions from all over the world. It had, however, a 'special relationship' with Moscow. This was pre-Berlin Wall. One year Moscow would send an officially approved theatre company. The following year the Yugoslavians were allowed to choose. This was the rebel year and they had chosen Moliere's *Don Juan* as performed, I think, by Yuri Lyubimov's Taganka Theatre - then one of the most radical companies in the USSR.

Athol and his cast were invited to an official reception for all the companies shortly after their first performance. Standing feeling a little isolated they found themselves being approached by a phalanx of men, dressed in grey flannel suits of old-fashioned cut. Most looked friendly, though there were some more inscrutable faces. They brought with them a translator who introduced them as the Taganka company. Yvonne did a very funny impersonation of Athol's bemused switching between shaking hands and bowing. They had seen *Statements* the night before, were very complimentary and wanted to invite the company to see *Don Juan*. They had done their research. *Statements* was a short play, ending before their interval. They would arrange for a car to pick up the *Statements* crew and race them across Belgrade to their theatre in time to see the second half. They left with much bowing and shaking of hands.

'You know who those other men are?' - one of the BITEC officials whispered to them. 'Those are their KGB minders. They hold their passports and they all have to travel everywhere in a group in case anyone tries to defect.'

The following night they rushed to change and got to the other theatre just in time. Standing at the back - the performance was crammed - Yvonne was approached by a member of the audience. She had seen *Statements*. On hearing that they would be standing, she invited Yvonne to share her seat. Perched on the edge of the shared seat in the front row, just feet from the stage, Yvonne was entranced. 'I've never seen acting like that,' she told me. The leading man especially. 'He looked so totally relaxed and at ease. And he was wildly funny. Even though it was in Russian I could follow everything. He had a scene with his sidekick Sganarelle, during which he jumped off the stage and landed right in front of me. From 18 inches away I could feel a barrier of heat around him. He was so relaxed, yet so concentrated, that his body heat had gone up to the extent that I could feel it from that far away. That's the moment I felt proudest to be an actor in my life.'

I have attempted to find out who the actor was. I think it must have been Vladimir Vysotsky, though I can only find a reference to the film of *Don Juan* by Lyubimov - also the director of the Taganka Theatre. Vysotsky was a hugely popular cult poet - much banned by the authorities. Apparently he was akin to a rock star in Russia, reading his poetry to huge auditoriums of fans. When he died in 1980 at the age of 42 his funeral was attended by crowds estimated variously as more than 40,000, and in one article, a million people.

The question of his raised temperature answered a question of my own that had intrigued me for years. From the beginning of our relationship, as I picked Yvonne up after a performance, we would walk hand-in-hand. After a while I stopped commenting on how hot her hand was. This was not usual - she had the coldest feet on the planet - but it was always there after performance. She just shrugged her shoulders when I noted it. For years I tormented my casts by going backstage and feeling their foreheads. A cool forehead was received with disapproval. Little did I know it but I was being introduced to the central components of one of the great mysteries of acting - being 'in-the-moment'.

Even My Dog....

My first real encounter with the challenge of being 'in-the moment' came early in my new career as a teacher at LAMDA. After a first-year showing of some scenes the cast were being given 'crits' by a panel of the staff. While I taught at LAMDA (I can't talk about afterwards) we received a constant stream of very talented young actors from Oop North. Especially from Accrington, where an obviously inspirational teacher called Martin Cosgrif worked. One of these, Joe Alessi, was told by two of the tutors: 'The problem, Joe, was that you weren't 'in-the-moment'.'

At the lunch break that followed Joe approached me. 'I'm always being told I'm not 'in-the-moment!' How the hell do I get there?!'

I had no answer.

The question, however, set me off on a search. The answer came in dribs and drabs over the next 10 years as I haphazardly put techniques together in response to particular problems of particular actors in particular classes and productions.

For the moment let's put that aside as I continue my linear way through these discoveries to introduce another question to which I had no answer.

It was a bright, sunny early spring morning in Earls Court Road. I was on my way to a rehearsal. I passed the Church Hall which was one of LAMDA's wonderfully idiosyncratic rehearsal spaces. Sitting on a wall outside was a young actor - Julie Hesmondhalgh – another Accringtonian. She appeared to be crying. I sat down next to her, asked what the matter was. Her face lifted. She was, indeed, crying - but they were tears more of rage than pain. 'I have just been told,' she said through gritted teeth, 'to go home, find an 'affective memory', come back tomorrow - and CRY!'

She was rehearsing a second year production of *Three Sisters* - the part of Masha. Suppressing a sharp desire to go into the Hall and punch the assistant director who had instructed her thus, I tried to talk her down from what, I am sure, was the same impulse.

Again, I wasn't very successful. No answers. She continued: 'I haven't got any affective memories. I had the most marvellous childhood. My mum and dad are still alive; my brother's one of my favourite people on earth; all my grandparents, my aunts and uncles are still around - I've never lost anyone.' She took a deep breath. 'Even my dog hasn't died.' Tenderly funny as this is, I knew I couldn't laugh. A few useless words of encouragement and I was on my way.

Two weeks later Julie was on stage giving a deeply moving interpretation of the tortured Masha. I came out of the performance confused. If she had no 'affective memories' on which to draw, where did this intense feeling come from. She was either telling lies (and Accringtonians don't lie) or something else had fuelled her acting.

Another question to set me on another road.

The next major discovery came via a broken chair.

The Broken Chair - a belated apology

I was asked to do a class on 'Audition Speeches' throughout the term - 3 hours, once a week. I did not take it on with any joy. I would personally never cast anyone from watching an audition speech. It is possible, with sufficient coaching and the right approach, to make the weakest actor look quite good. Their only use is if you have the time to get the actor to throw away their coached certainties, give them some different - and preferably ridiculous - interpretation, and then see how they cope. The ability and courage to cope instantaneously with change is what defines the good actor.

The term was, I was sure, going to contain three hours of sheer boredom each week. I worried myself to a near ulcer trying to work out how to make it bearable. On the first day I sank into the unbelievably comfortable chairs of our rehearsal room - a small theatre, the name of which shall be hidden for reasons that will become clear. LAMDA at that stage had its headquarters in the furthest corner of Kensington - across the busy Cromwell Road it became Earls Court. The large house was not big enough to contain all the necessary studios, so classes and rehearsals were conducted in an eclectic and widespread set of hired rooms. The freezing, stone-floored hall of St Mary's Church next door, where we would all huddle around the 19th-century radiators waiting, generally in vain, for some heat to emerge; the Poetry Society - down at the bottom of Earls Court Road, carpeted, properly heated, and with lovely low winter sun streaming in through ceiling-high windows; a convent in Kensington Church Square; and, my favourite - the wonderfully ghost-ridden Avatar, situated under a Russian Orthodox Chapel in a large house in Kensington.

This was another (nameless, remember...) - by far the best. Fully equipped with stage and those comfy, almost-armchair seats. In which the rest of that first class prepared to go to sleep while I dealt with the first speech.

By the end of the speech they were, in fact, asleep. I was yawning but desperate. This was even worse than I thought it would be. The three-minute speech dribbled to an end and Ethan stood on the stage awaiting guidance, direction, a miracle.

I knew I had about seven minutes with each student. Three of his were gone. Once again I sat in front of an actor with no answers. In what turned out to be one of the more inspired busks of my life (there was another, but that's for later) I said rather limply: 'That sounds as though he's really angry. Why don't you try the speech again, playing only the anger.' 'Why would he do that?' was his what-is-my-motivation response. Having no real answer and limited time I said, confidently: 'Don't worry about that - just be very, very angry.' Fortunately for me Ethan was not an actor to hold back (he was American), and he set off in a splendiferous rage which grew and grew, culminating in his destruction of a chair that was haplessly sharing the stage with him. We hid the pieces behind the curtains in a dark corner, to my shame, and never reported it. The reason for the secrecy now? It may be two decades ago but who knows how long this crime may have festered in the caretaker's mind.

This led to the institution of a set of rules:

- **no handling of any piece of furniture or prop**

- **no touching of another actor**

- **no kicking or punching floors or walls**

The most interesting thing for me was that a) nobody was now asleep in the auditorium; and b) he had spoken many of the lines with appropriate emphases and understanding. Up to then I always spent hours around the table thrashing out text and meaning with the actors. In the two minutes (anger runs obviously speed up the text) it had taken, Ethan had made perfect, if rather loud and overwrought, sense of the speech. I asked him to do the speech one more time without the anger - unless appropriate, of course. I was fascinated to see that, in the areas where the character was indeed angry, there was a distinct residue of this anger, even though Ethan was not attempting to play it.

Thus I discovered what I call *Imprinting*. What's that? Well, if you press your thumb on a jelly you will leave an imprint of your fingerprint. But more meet to our discussion here is the actual printing process - particularly litho-printing. The image is etched photographically onto a large, thin tin sheet (very useful for thunder effects, incidentally). Through a combination of chemical processes beyond my understanding, when the ink is applied it sticks only to the areas where the image is; falling, dissolving, whatever, from the areas where there is no image.

In the same way, the anger Ethan had expressed fell away from the parts of the speech where it had no relevance, but remained imprinted where it did. We experimented further with this throughout our three-hours-a-week term. Instead of being boring it became fascinating for both myself and the other actors. For the most part only the really good actors feel there is any use in watching other actors working, assessing and learning. The rest would rather read or sleep or learn their own lines.

Astbury's 1st Law of Theatre

By and large actors would prefer to be in the pub

However, put some real, raw emotion on the stage and everyone - and this includes the audience - is fascinated.

Along the way we found various other small techniques but they'll come out later in this narrative. What I did find myself developing was a set of exercises that actors can do on their own, in the absence of a director to make quick and basic connections to the characters.

A Word about Directors...

'In the absence of a director' could apply to having to learn an audition speech or lines for tomorrow's telly quickly and without access to a director. It could equally apply to working with one of the many completely useless directors who litter the Earth. This is not my own experience, it comes from many, many of those actors I have trained who have gone out into the real world to fall prey to people who would probably not know an actor if they fell over one, and whose ability to help is usually limited to some Eng Lit work on the text and the application of ill-digested Stanislavski.

Setting up a training course for directors is very difficult. Actors train by learning the various techniques and then putting them into practice in fairly large groups. Directors need such large groups to practise on. As most drama schools are loath to hand over their trainee actors to a trainee director, this becomes a Catch-22. The answer is to engage actors on a professional or semi-professional basis. This is prohibitively expensive. I have been involved in the setting-up of two such courses. It generally involves the directors having to seduce or suborn actors on the other courses to work outside of hours on projects with them. While such said action is a talent that needs to be learnt in itself, the system rather relies on the willingness or un- of actors. For the rest they do a lot of assistant-directing, observing hopefully good directors at work. This really was how I learnt. Sitting in corners watching. Seeing what worked and what didn't, and why. When I set up my first such course I asked several of the best directors I knew how they had learnt. Not one had come from a formal course. Even those who had come the acting route attributed most of their learning to observation. 'You learn most from a bad director' said one.

Sadly the system here in Britain is predicated on the fallacious belief that a literary degree from the appropriate University immediately qualifies you as a director. I have never understood this belief, but it is entrenched and powerful. Two directors with whom I have had close acquaintanceship came via this route. Both are really nice people, they have worked at many of the top theatres both here and internationally. Both have won awards. Both can talk the hind leg of a burro about the play and its background. Ask the actors who work with them and they will tell you how nice they are, how intellectual and intelligent they are. But do they help them as actors? No. The actors, pro's all, manage by themselves. It happened to my wife on more than one occasion. Also to many of my other actor friends.

I have no answer to this problem. Only: Find a director. whose work you really rate and ask to sit in the corner, observe, ask questions, and make the tea. If you're going to read Stanislavski please read the whole canon, paying particular attention to what he was saying at the end of his life - with special reference to the new system he was developing: the Method of Physical Actions. Follow how this was developed further in Russia by his disciples, resulting in new processes like Active Analysis. (Read Bella Merlin's *Beyond Stanislavsky*). See especially where Grotowski took it in his various exercises. (Read Steven Wangh's *Acrobat of the Heart*). As I have said if Stan was still alive he would undoubtedly be following with fascination all the developments in film and media, psychology and the discoveries on how the brain functions. He would have taken into account another World War, Atom bombs, the Holocaust, Vietnam, ethnic cleansing, genocide, information overload, the Web, etc, etc, etc. There is no way his system would have stood still. He was already disowning elements of it in the 30s. Elements that are still religiously taught today.

The only question any system has to answer is: Does it work?

If not, bin it and move on.

Breaking Down Walls

The next major development for me came with the establishment of Arts Threshold in Paddington.

I had been pushing a group of young LAMDA students. Approaching graduation they were sliding into the terror of the unknown that grips drama students. What if they couldn't find an agent? What if nobody wanted them? What if....? Too much Stanislavski in there with his 'Magic if...'.

'You've built up a good ensemble over three years. Some really good plays and productions. Take one or two to Edinburgh.'

The Festival followed hard on the heels of their graduation. It was a challenge. Some of them took it up, went to Edinburgh to find out what to do. Came back disheartened. No theatres available. Too expensive, etc.

They counter-challenged. 'You've got such a big mouth - show us what to do.' This was during their final term of the year at LAMDA. I was faced with a dry summer doing little but play cricket. I took them up on it. 'Find a play', I said. Their ideas were a bit hackneyed. Revivals of famous plays everybody was always reviving. Revivals of unknown plays which were unknown for very good reasons. Plays too recently done.

Finally I brought a play to the table. In 1979 in South Africa at The Space we had premiered David Mowat's *The Guise* . It was a play about a theatre company trying to survive in London in the 1640s, coping with censorship, the closing of the theatres, survival. It was intense, funny and very, very violent. A cast of seven - 4 men, 3 women. They loved it as much as I had back in the 70s. I had not directed it then. It had lasted for three nights before the censors banned it.

We had 16 actors who were interested. Mowat was very keen for it to be done again after an unfortunate experience with the British production which followed ours. I double-cast it - we would play the companies in repertory. 'Where are we going to stage it?' they asked. 'I don't know.' I said, 'Something will come up.' 'How are we going to pay for it?' they asked. 'I don't know.' I said, 'Something will come up.'

Astbury's 2nd Law of Theatre

*If you wait for the money to arrive,
or for a venue to materialise,
you will never open*

Four weeks into rehearsal - LAMDA had allowed us to use their out-of-term facilities - one of the cast's father, impressed by their dedication, gave us £1000. Now we could print posters, flyers, programmes, buy the basics of costume and props.

Somebody had a friend, who had a friend, and designer Katrina Lindsay entered the fray with us, taking on the daunting task of coping with my idiosyncratic ways with designers. I am a minimalist. Not an intellectual minimalist. I've just never worked in any theatre that had any money. My training was to discard.

On the acting side the battles were intense. Actors of little faith were falling by the wayside. Finally we were down to one cast.

On a Saturday afternoon in a large rehearsal room at LAMDA. I worked with the two leading actors on a very difficult and emotional scene. It was the woman's scene and she was pushing the emotion away, big-time. I had tried all my tricks, nothing was working. There were some Alexander head-rests in the studio. Small sponge neck-cushions. I said to the actor: 'As you do the speech, kick the cushion around the studio.' She set off. As the poor cushion rocketed around the room, bouncing off the walls, she followed it grimly, each kick getting more potent. She fought to hold on to the text and keep the action going. Suddenly both connected and a huge flash of rage flooded from her. So huge that I failed to notice the connection. I had never been in the presence of such intense anger. I had no idea where she was, how to help her through, whether she might actually topple over an edge in her psyche and damage herself. I calmed her down. As she panted quietly, fists still balled, I looked around. The other actor was sitting with his head held between his hands, unable to look. A stage manager who was helping us was standing looking ostentatiously out of a window, whistling tunelessly.

We had tea and disbanded for the day.

At home I told Yvonne about the incident, about my fears for the actor's sanity. She was unimpressed.

'You should have pushed harder,' she said, 'Actors are much tougher than you think they are.' This was not the response I expected. I argued lamely but Yvonne was unrepentant.

Later I realised how badly I had failed the actor that afternoon. She was one of the most talented actors I have ever trained. Able to make the telephone directory interesting. What I had done, I realised much later, was stop short of the full connection. When we rehearsed again her defences were so high that I never got beyond them - to her distress and mine. She finally left the company. 'I know what you want from me, and I can't do it. It's driving me mad.' If I'd known then what I know now... Sorry Emma. I hate failing actors.

These developments were what I now took into our new venue at Arts Threshold. The venue had grown from success of *The Guise* in the following progression:

- Nearing the end of our rehearsal period we still had nowhere to stage the production;

- at the last moment a theatre became available in Tufnell Park, 10 days before we were due to open;

- this production was seen by Dee Bidmead of the Etcetera Theatre in Camden;

- he recommended us to a scout for the Richard Demarco Gallery in Edinburgh;

- the scout came to see us at a specially-staged re-run at Pentameters in Hampstead, run by the blessed Leoni Scott-Matthews;

- we were invited to stage the play at the Gallery the following year;

- at the Festival we won a Fringe First award;

- were invited by Ion Karamitru - Romania's greatest actor and a Vice President in the temporary government that overthrew Ceauçescu – to tour to that country;

- Benny Chia of Hong Kong Fringe Festival invited us there;

- an American company in Chicago extended a similar invitation;

- after all the excitement of these tours we set about in earnest searching for a venue;

- a Church Hall in the basement of a block of flats in Paddington was offered to us

- once again many wonderful people poured in to help;

- the actors built their own theatre;

- we opened with a bang - 3 plays: *The Guise, Julius Caesar,* and a new play - *The Fisherman's Ring,* written by one of the actors.

Easy.

The actors, all volunteers, worked like the rest of us, for nothing. Their ambitions did not stop there. There would be workshops each Sunday. 'Good.' I said. Nobody gets me out of bed early on a Sunday. They looked at me. 'What are you going to do?' I had not run a workshop in my life. 'Nothing.' I said, hoping to hold on to my warm Sunday morning bed. 'Why don't you do a workshop about all those techniques you use?'

Some actors are the spawn of the devil. 'I won't start before 11 a.m.' I said. 'That's okay.' they said.

I cast around for a name. The week before I had been directing a play at LAMDA and one of the actors - struggling to make a connection – had said to me: 'It's like there's this wall in front of me, and I can't break through it.' This was not the first time I had heard this. Another actor had gone further. 'I'm in a bloody fog and I can't even find the damn wall!'

So - *Breaking Down the Walls* became the title. One Sunday morning at 11.15 (I had to wait for them to finish their coffee) eight actors and I gathered in the theatre for my first workshop.

I had asked them to bring an emotional speech. To separate out what the dominant emotions were in the speech. We would then play the speech over and over, each time using a different dominant emotion. I was hoping that this would lead to a thorough imprinting of the various underlying emotions. Each actor had religiously mined their speech. Shame, guilt, love, jealousy, envy, disgust, contempt, anger, pain – the lists were long. Each had identified between 6 and 10 emotions.

At the end of the first day we summed up. A big surprise awaited us. Only two emotions worked. Anger and pain. They found it difficult to play any of the others.

One more Sunday of finding the same thing and my mind was working overtime. I came up with a theory. Emotion, I surmised, was something like light. Depending on what theory of light you use, our conception of light is formed by the mixing of three colours - red, blue and green (I know, I know - cyan, magenta, yellow - stick with me - I'm just using it as an example). Mix them together in various ratios and you get all the colours of the rainbow, and many, many more. Mix pure emotions, I thought, and something similar will happen. So, as there are Primary Colours, there must be Primary Emotions. Problem: I only had two - Anger and Pain. The third was revealed to me the following Sunday when one of the actors struggled to their feet after a hectic and emotional set of exercises (many of the exercises are done lying down with closed eyes). '#*$@#!!!', she said, 'isn't there any joy in anything you do?!' Bingo! Anger, Pain - and Joy - my triumvirate was complete! Anger we had lots of; Pain was there in spades; Joy ... well, that doesn't feature much in audition speeches, I rationalised.

It took 18 months more for me to realise that my theory was wrong. It's actually about a journey - a journey which starts with joy - or rather perfect peace - which state is broken by pain and fear which cause anger. More about this later. There were eight Sunday workshops during which I discovered all kinds of new exercises involving muscle tension, breathing, etc. We had a big black cushion that became central to much of the work. I had read of an anger workshop in which participants had been encouraged to beat the living daylights out of a cushion. It worked a treat for us, too. Interestingly, the first time I used it one young actor went into that flash of rage which had so scared me a year earlier. This time - Yvonne's strictures in mind - I was much more prepared. She smashed her fist into the poor cushion with a venom that had the rest of the class aghast. A young director who had asked to observe, later told me she had felt like a voyeur. She was sceptical about the value of the work. 'I didn't want to be a watcher - I wanted either to be doing it - or not to be in the room.' This despite her doubts. Some of the other actors were also disturbed at the level of emotion released. Not for the last time the fear was expressed: 'What if someone is really close to an edge? Won't it topple them over?' I clung to Yvonne's words, though, in those early days before I became used to such levels of emotion, there were occasions of doubt.

This young actor ended in floods of tears. The pain was connected very strongly. Later she told me what had happened. I never encourage people to tell me what is behind their pain. I do not consider that it is my business to delve into their personal lives. However, she wished to tell me so I let her. It was the triggering of a personal memory that she had partially buried. There were two really positive outcomes. The first was that she finally spoke to the person involved - whose face had appeared on the cushion to be punished. It was a good, loving relationship. The anger was the result of a misunderstanding. The relationship prospered. It was very satisfying.

The second came four weeks later. She phoned, excited. 'I have just had my first singing lesson since the workshop. My teacher says my voice has expanded by nearly an octave!' It was not the last time I was to hear this.

A note: It's not usual in these exercises to get such a specific memory. I can only remember about two other occasions where a specific buried memory surfaced. Both of these had positive outcomes as well.

We continued over eight workshops to experiment and develop. Working now with trained actors who were out in the real world I was able to begin articulating to myself what was happening.

Then I got a job.

Mountview

I have been a freelance for most of my life. It's a risky but exciting way of living. It also gives you a degree of freedom of choice. One of these choices is to starve, obviously, but it is your own choice. I applied for a job out of pure financial necessity. It is very difficult to carve out any form of existence on the fees paid to freelance teachers of drama. I held out no hope of even getting an interview. I had no letters behind my name. No degree. The one I had received from the University of Life was of no use.

A Word about Degrees...

In South Africa I had only once had to apply for a job - the mail order fiasco. In Britain I tried on several occasions - and came up against a Great Truth. If you don't have a degree you won't even get an interview. Sorry about that all of you who are trying to convince your parents that you don't need to go to university. Listen to them. They're right. Despite the fact that many degrees are worth much less than the paper they're written on in copperplate. I once interviewed a young wannabe director applying for a place on a director's course. She was bright and chatty, but vague. On her resume I noticed she had spent a term on Theatre of the Absurd. Hoping to get her relaxed and talking about something she knew something about, I asked her who her favourite Absurd playwright was. She looked blank and started to tap-dance around the question. Name any playwrights of the Absurd, asked another member of the panel. The tap-dance grew more frenzied. She couldn't name one. The names of Beckett and Ionesco stirred not a flicker of recognition. We moved on with an easier one. What theatre production was your favourite, and, obviously, why? Here she had an answer though it was shrouded in clouds. It took a bit of time to get the name of the play. '*Lear!*' she said, triumphantly. By this time two of the three panel members (me being one) had given up. The third soldiered doggedly on, finally extracting from her enough information (she'd seen it with her school before going to university - couldn't remember where) for us to realise that she had been to Stratford to see Robert Stephens' much-praised *King Lear*. Stratford rang no bells either. This prized exhibit of our education system had been granted - by a university which shall remain nameless in its shame - the degree of BA Hons. She would have got an interview ahead of me. I'm not bitter...

This time I had got an interview, and, to my utter amazement, found myself offered the post of Head of Courses at Mountview Theatre School. Run by a wily old fox, Peter Coxhead, Mountview was much bigger than I had been used to. The 'Courses' I was 'Head of' turned out to consist of one Acting stream, one Musical Theatre (with a total of nearly 60 students on them in each of two years), plus a One-Year Postgraduate Course, with similar streaming between Acting and Musical Theatre. This varied but could bring in as many as 45 students in a good year. One of my first tasks was to add a director's course.

So, each year I had control of over around 220 students. I soon realised that Peter - to whom I owe an enormous debt of gratitude for seeing beyond my lack of a university degree - was an absentee Principal. He sat in his lair up in Crouch Hill surrounded by the Finance, Publicity and Technical Departments, and left the running of the teaching side in bosky Wood Green to me - except for his weekly visits to auditions.

I would have drowned without a band playing but for a wonderful Administrator, Jude Tisdall; a scheduler of unquestioned genius, Kathy Bowman; and a staff who had been drifting leaderless for nearly 18 months, trying desperately hard to provide coherent courses. Most of them fell on me with relief and generosity and we spent nearly a term reconstructing the courses. Peter, a very wise old fox indeed, had given me the last term of the year to assess where the school was. I sat in on classes, attended rehearsals, learnt the new audition process - and its one drawback. This was at a time when Thatcher's depredations had laid waste to the grant system and many talented young actors applied in vain, with no hope of getting a grant from their Local Education Authority. Peter solved this by the simple technique of taking anyone who had the money and could walk across the audition room.

The academic year ended and it was time for me to 'take over'. One of the first tasks handed to me consisted of a list of 18 names. They were all students going into their third and final year. My task was to write them a letter telling them that, as they had failed to make the requisite progress, they were to be put on Limited Casting in their final year. I had heard of this. When I was offered the job I was still running Arts Threshold. A talented young actor working with us was a Mountview graduate. 'What was it like?' I asked. He looked mournfully angry. 'It was the worst time of my life.' 'Why?' 'In my third year I was placed on Limited Casting.' This meant that the school did not need to cast him in any role if it chose. Mostly he would just cart spears around.

It was an extraordinary year, he said. 'Like being in Purgatory. Other students wouldn't even sit with our little group in the canteen. People I'd thought friends were suddenly avoiding me.' He was a really good young actor. How had this happened? He had no idea. Only theories.

So, on being given the list I said: 'I won't do this.'

'You have to -' I was told, 'it's what happens.'

I clenched my little fists and stamped my little foot, didn't quite say: 'I won't! I won't! I won't!' - but they did realise I was serious. 'So what are you going to do?' I'd known this moment was coming, had given it some thought, and was prepared. 'I'm going to do workshops with them to see for myself what the problem is.' They raised their eyebrows long-sufferingly - 'On-your-head-be-it' looks in their eyes. I still had to write some form of letter. So I penned a missive which stated that in the coming year casting would depend on talent and ability. If people were seen to be improving they would be given better roles. If not.... we reserve the right, etc. The letter was sent to the entire third year and Kathy never quite forgave me. Apart from being the glue which held the schedule together she helped her lovely sister, Liz, who answered the phones. Panicked calls choked the switchboard.

On the Tuesday evening of the first week of term I walked into one of the studios to confront 18 fraught young students.

Thus commenced one of the most exciting periods of my life.

I began by putting them all - one-by one - through a set of the basic exercises that had been developed at LAMDA and in the Arts Threshold workshops. It took two more evenings that week to work my way through the entire group. By then two things were very clear. Two of them should never have been allowed on the course - they couldn't act for toffee.

I don't say this as an insult. I can't act for toffee. Neither can I play the piano in any way that is not painful to the listener. This despite the fact that the greatest pianist who ever lived resides in my head. It's just that his abilities end at my wrists. Tragedy of my life. I have had some experience in hiding people who believed they could act. With effort you can camouflage them. But it's always at the expense of the other actors.

So, two down - a year full of camouflage-casting ahead. That left 16. 16 very blocked but not talentless young actors. Fortunately for me 16 incredibly desperate young actors, willing to try ANYTHING to get themselves cast.

I worked 2-3 nights a week and all day Sundays. Word spread among the non-Limited Casting actors. Several of those blessed actors who are always looking for ways to improve themselves asked if they could join the classes. A large percentage of the others stayed away in case they were tarred with the LC brush.

I won't claim that I turned 16 young actors around and converted them into potential Olivier's or Judi Dench's. It was remedial work. Some of them were lazy and had not done the requisite technical work in voice and movement that was needed to support their acting. Some were so blocked that it took almost the whole year to open them out. But four of them ended up playing leads, and, with two exceptions, nobody just carried a spear.

With the very obvious success of the workshops - they were now 32 students signed up - others started enquiring to join. Something else also started to happen. Something which has been the bane of my life.

As the word spread, controversy grew. It was a controversy that I understood. 'There's this teacher who is pushing people to the edge. They scream and cry and come out with voices a bit rough the next day.' I would also be suspicious. I let it be known that the workshops were open to any staff or visiting tutors/directors that wished to attend. I was still developing the work and desperate for feedback from outside.

A pattern emerged. Those that took up the invitation, came, saw, agreed, disagreed, argued - contributed. Those that didn't, criticised.

I cannot tell you how much I hate people who condemn without evidence. Several, when challenged, were unwilling to give up an evening to observe. 'I work really hard, need some time off.' At that stage I was working 80 hours a week.

Among those who did attend was Emma Brown. Former actor, turned Alexander teacher, Emma was freelancing for the Voice Department. Hearing about the workshops early on, she asked if she could watch. She sat in on several evenings, giving very valuable feedback.

After one she said: 'You never touch them?' All my exercises were done at a distance. 'I don't believe it would help. I don't know what to do. Also it opens the classes up to misinterpretation. Think of the headlines in The Sun - *'Randy Old Teacher Gropes Nubile Young Students!!'.* Emma laughed. She understood my fears - we both knew teachers of acting and Alexander Technique who had abused their positions of trust - but, 'You're missing out on a very valuable additional technique.' I was not convinced. Good Alexander teachers have magic hands which seem to be able to draw emotion from their clients with no apparent pressure. I had seen Emma at work and she had such hands. 'At the next workshop, if you see a moment when you think it will work, feel free to step in and show me.'

The next time I was working with a young man. A lot of my work takes place with the actor on their back on the floor. He was proving very resistant. The speech he had chosen was filled with pain. I was beginning to despair. Emma silently appeared by my side, placed a hand on his stomach at belly-button level, and gently pushed it back and forth, side-to-side. There were only about four or five of these motions before the dam burst and the young man began to sob. Real pain poured out into the room. We let him cry, then Emma returned to her seat and I took him back to the text. An irrevocable connection had been made. As he calmed down he was able to do the speech quietly, with a small smile, but with the emotion radiating from within. No big histrionic tears, no loud emoting. Several of the other workshop members were in tears at the end of his speech. He was a little stunned.

What was she doing, I asked afterwards? Disturbing the pathway that emotion has to take to emerge. The seat of emotion seems to be in the gut. The road up is through the solar plexus, lungs, heart, throat, jaw, and finally out of the mouth, guarded by the huge defensive walls I had been fighting to help actors break down for so long. Disrupting these defences by putting a cross rhythm in place helped the emotions to escape from their prison.

This set me on another journey of discovery as I began to explore working on pressure points in the body. This work - by far the most controversial (understandably) part of what I do - will not be covered in this book. It is too open to abuse and misunderstanding. I only teach it to directors and actors who are willing to take the plunge and go through the whole process themselves - so that they will know what the effect is, understand the depth of emotion that can be released.

Emma brought me an outline for a voice/acting class for which she had been trying to find a home.

We gave her a couple of experimental classes with second year actors. These worked well. In the next academic year I asked her to take a class with the Postgraduate actors. This was a one-year course populated by more mature actors who were either from a university background, or who had a lot of experience in theatre, both amateur and professional. She worked with the entire year in two groups.

We had wondered what to call the classes. What pigeon-hole did they fit? My '*Breaking Down the Walls*' was adjudged too violent. '*Permission Workshops*' was possible as it was evident from the beginning that giving actors permission to vent their feelings loudly and uninhibitedly took them into new and, for some, quite exhilarating territory. We are all taught from very early on to harness, control repress our emotions. It's not polite to scream and rage and cry. Life would be chaos. Unfortunately this teaches most of us to show no emotion whatsoever. This is dangerous for our everyday health, but terminal for actors and performance.

Finally we settled on *Emotional Access* classes. Most of the students rather referred to them as *Emotional Release* classes, but

Emma and I stood firm. She ran the class throughout the term. I sat in on all the classes for one of the groups. After each we would discuss and compare notes. Emma's methods are very different from mine. She is gentler, kinder (I'm a bit of a sadist) and uses a wide range of techniques drawn from Grotowski and other practitioners. However, we did continue to develop what I should probably call the Resistance Techniques – pushing against the wall, punching and in other ways abusing a large, defenceless pillow, etc.

The interest spread, and in the Easter holidays of 1994 we ran a demonstration workshop over two days. This was attended by 25-30 teachers, directors, voice and movement coaches. We used volunteer students from the 2nd year Acting Course who had, as yet, had no experience of the techniques. While we could not obviously show how the process worked itself out over a full rehearsal period, we were able to give a good introduction. The feedback - both from the students taking part and the watchers - was generally favourable. There were tough questions and some reservations. A few of the staff members who came were concerned as to where it should be placed in the curriculum. They felt it might be too advanced and taxing for actors early in their training. It was decided to put it into the final term of the second year. These classes were all run by Emma. I continued with the extramural workshops.

At the end of the first year of classes with the 2nd year students, we had a feedback session. The general opinion from the students was that they would have liked to have done this work earlier in the course, as it was having beneficial knock-on effects in other classes. We moved it to the first term. The same feedback process was repeated the following year. Once again the students felt they would have benefited from the work earlier in the course.

We moved it again into the final term of the first year. We got the same reaction - 'Wish we'd had it earlier'. It seemed to be helping in other areas - voices became more released, physicalities became freer.

There has never not been controversy about this work. Singing teachers were especially chary of it as the occasional student would arrive with a slightly rough voice after a workshop.

Time for a disclaimer. At the time of writing I have personally done this work with coming up to 800 students. Emma must be nearing that number herself. Not once in that entire time has anyone suffered damage to their voices beyond the normal kind of short-term strain that comes whenever a muscle is pushed to its limits. This should happen in every area of skills training. At every drama school at which I have taught there have been days in which half the class have been limping around after a particularly stretching movement or dance class. I never rushed off to berate the tutor for damaging the poor babies. 'Good!' I would think, 'they're really being stretched.' I would watch in satisfaction as they extended their range. As for real damage: on three occasions at one school we had students walking around with their necks in a brace after an exercise in their voice class. Here we did finally have to caution the tutor not to use this exercise.

Time and time again students would comment on the broadening range of their voice.

Another question - frequently unspoken - was answered at the beginning of the second year of Emma's classes.

This was finally articulated after another workshop/demonstration. It arose after further unease had been expressed. My Principal, Peter Coxhead, spoke to me about it. He had, personally, no problems with the work. I had talked to him about it at length.
There had been concerns expressed, he said. He knew how irritable this made me. My workshops were open. Anybody who wanted to exercise this 'concern' could come on any one of the three evenings a week and every Sunday, see, express their concern, speak to the students, initiate a dialogue with me. As I have said, some did. Many ignored the invitation but felt free to continue to express 'concerns'. 'Frankly', I told Peter, 'I have no time for people who are so 'concerned' that they can't afford to take three hours one evening to sit in. This does not seem like concern to me.'

There was also concern that - as I was responsible for most of the casting in the 2nd and 3rd years - I would be biased in favour of those who came to the workshops.

I showed him the result when I put up a notice at the beginning of my third year, advising of the workshops and inviting volunteers to sign up. There were 57 students in the new second year - 39 of them volunteered. I couldn't actually fit them all in. To cope I was scheduling every-other-week workshops. I had approached them all to ask if they were sure that they wanted to take part. Nobody backed out. 'I'm asking for volunteers NOT to do the workshops.' I told him. There were also 3rd year students who wished to continue the sessions. I had nearly 68 students that I was attempting to fit in. This answered the next question as to whether they felt their casting would be affected if they didn't take part.

Nonetheless, he said, he had to address the issue. I agreed with him. To stop them having to give up a precious evening of their time we arranged that Emma would give one of her normal classes - observed by the entire staff and any other interested parties. Their classes would be subbed by other tutors, for which the school would pick up the bill.

To further ensure that all questions were answered, a psychotherapist would be asked to observe the class to monitor the work and answer staff questions. I was not wildly enthusiastic about this. I had no personal experience, but several friends had entered such therapy. Of the eight or nine people that I knew who had undergone the process only one had come out 'healed' - and even he felt that just talking about his problems had had the major therapeutic effect. This approximately 15% success rate, of course, is way above that of psychoanalysis.

But it was going to happen and I didn't want to argue. Emma did her demo class. As we walked away from the rehearsal studio to the staffroom where she would face questions, the therapist asked me: 'Do all your staff have to undergo this scrutiny of their methods?' 'No.' 'I'm really amazed to see work like this happening in a drama school. It's very exciting.' She complimented Emma on her handling of the class.

The 'unspoken' question was finally asked by a staff member. It was the one which had hovered uneasily in the back of my mind for some time. 'What if someone is very near the edge - couldn't this work push them over?' 'And into insanity' was the unspoken.

'No.' came the answer, 'Somebody who is that close to 'the edge' - a breakdown - would do one of two things. They'd either refuse to do the work, or 'act' it for you.' She went on to explain that we have a very good internal health system (which we spend most of our lives ignoring). For people on the verge this would be operating on high alert and would prevent them from engaging in the work.

This has, in fact, been my experience. Among the hundreds of actors I have pushed through the process there have only been three who fitted this bill. One politely declined to do the work - my workshops were always voluntary - I have never forced or blackmailed anyone to take part.

The second would put up a huge smokescreen of emoted over-acting. Those who have sat through one of these workshops will know that it soon becomes very clear if someone is 'faking it'. The room becomes very charged with real emotion, voices have an authentic sound which is difficult to ignore. Nobody is bored. Our 'avoider' lost the attention of the class very early as she wailed and writhed and overplayed the text.

The third had made me nervous from her arrival in the school. When she asked to join a class I had serious doubts. At her first session I started her off at a very low level. She didn't commit to the work. Afterwards she came to me: 'I don't think I want to do this sort of work.' That was fine with me. Towards the end of the year she came back. She'd been watching the results on her fellow students. She could see it worked. She wanted to be a 'serious' actor, and felt it was necessary for her. Could she come back? I was still not convinced, but allowed her back in. Again I only put her through a very light exercise. Once again she didn't commit. And once again she told me she didn't feel happy doing the work. With silent gratitude I let her go.

A year later she manifested fully-developed Bipolar Disorder which resulted in her withdrawing from the school for a year to undergo treatment. The treatment consisted of putting her on lithium and she was allowed back at the school too early, while they were still battling to balance the medication. Frequently she would appear in what one of the tutors unkindly called 'Zombie-mode'

Our psychotherapist answered questions for an hour, gave Emma and the work a clean bill of health, and for the remainder of Peter's time as Principal of the School this controversy was laid to rest.

The Road to Damascus

Earlier - in my first official term at Mountview - I had a rather startling experience. In my first, observational term I had on one day watched two Shakespeare presentations by 2nd year students on the Musical Theatre stream. Coming straight from LAMDA where Shakespeare was a speciality and the standard very high, I had been fairly pleasantly surprised. While not deathless, there was a good energy and, from most, an understanding of the text. I had been expecting much worse.

The following morning I sat in on their feedback session and watched in amazement as their tutor ripped them to pieces. Several left the room in tears. At the end of the session the tutor sat back and said: 'The trouble with Music Theatre people is - they can't act!' He was not a permanent member of staff and he had already been engaged to direct a third year acting production in the following term, so I kept my peace. It seemed to me to be an arrogant generalisation and was certainly not borne out by what I had seen. His production the following term was average and I never used him again. I have a loathing for directors who use their position to exercise and abuse their power.

My first teaching term arrived and, as luck would have it, my first performance project involved directing the new second year Music Theatre students in a Chekhov play.

A Word to Budding Directors...

The initial impulse, when asked to direct in this situation, is to lick your lips and go for the Big Ones. Mistake. When finally asked to do some Shakespeare scenes at LAMDA (with 1st year students. Roger would never have trusted me with any of the more experienced ones – he had too many real experts on the books),

I chose King *John* . Result: as the other tutors, who, with the other 1st year group, would be the audience for the single showing, filed in, I heard two of them say: 'This is interesting - I've never actually seen King *John*.'. The talented young students did a good job and I avoided competing with the ghosts of everyone from Olivier and Gielgud to Brook, Hall and Nunn.

Now, at Mountview, I put the same theory into practice. I started by choosing *Wild Honey*, Michael Frayn's adaptation of a Chekhov play found among his papers after his death. The title page was missing, so it was generally known as *The Play with No Name* - or *Platonov*, after its main character.

As part of my research I decided I had better read the original. It's a mammoth play. To stage it in its entirety would probably take between five and six hours. Not that anyone would want to. The first two acts are a dense thicket of Russian politics and unbelievably complex relationships between the cast of more than 30. The last three acts, however, are something else - fast, funny, emotional - a bit like Tchaikovsky on speed. What got me though was the end, and what Frayn had done to it. He has Platonov rushing out into the night and getting knocked down accidentally by a passing train. Chekhov has him completely unable to find the courage to commit suicide until Sonya, his mistress, shoots him almost by mistake. This is pure Chekhov in grand gods-laughing-at-you farce mode. It's economical, swings from comedy to tragedy in milliseconds, and is not at all ponderous.

So I decided to do the original, trimming it down to the two-hour maximum time we were allowed. We were rehearsing for 14 hours a week - every afternoon except Wednesday.

We spent the first week filleting the play. In an adaptation of the technique taught me by another of my mentors - Caroline Eves - I split the play into its individual scenes and allocated these to five groups of three actors to cut, 'synopsise', decide which characters and scenes were unnecessary. We concentrated on the first two acts, emerging on the third day with all the politics gone and only 14 characters left. The concentration was now totally on Platonov's wildly chequered love life and its consequences. Two more afternoons were taken up in reconstructing the opening two acts to introduce the characters in rather quick travelogue fashion, and send them on a rapid whistle-stop trip towards Act 3, when the real action started.

On the Tuesday afternoon of the second week we arrived at the real text. Platonov has reignited an affair with an old university flame - Sonya, now married to his best friend, Sergei. She wants him to elope with her. He has been thrown out by his wife, is living in his schoolroom, where he teaches the local children, and has taken to drink. Sonya comes to visit him.

Up to this moment we had done very little actual acting work. By the tea break at 4.15 we had completed our work on the script. At 4.30, refreshed by a lovely cup of Annie's tea, we reconvened. The two actors took up their scripts and off we went - me, unknowingly, being led out on to the Road to Damascus in the unlikely location of a rather grotty Wood Green industrial estate.

My Sonya came on and we plunged headfirst, but without the drama, into what I call 'Floaty Chekhov-land'. There seems to be a fairly widespread idea that the way to play Chekhov properly is to take on an air of deep melancholy and drift around looking sad. The scene is only about nine minutes long, but within three of these the rest of the group - who, up to then, had been energised and enthusiastic - were falling asleep. So would I have been but for the horror that was filling my soul.

I stopped the scene halfway through, desperation curling tightly around my throat. The wicked voice on my shoulder chuckled and whispered: *'What if he was right? What if Music Theatre people really can't act?!'* .I tried to shush it but it reminded me that, in the first week, a young actor called Gerald - a broad Northerner with a beautiful singing voice - had been sitting one afternoon with his feet on the table as they cut the script, and said to me 'I dunno about this fookin' acting lark - I jus' wanna sing!'

Drastic measures were called for. Busking, I asked Sonya - Melanie Barker - to start over again, except that this time she was to come on in a complete rage. This was where I discovered one of the real differences between Music Theatre actors and the straight variety. Music Theatre actors are used to being snapped at by Hitlerian singing teachers: 'Get up!! Sing!!!' A 'straight' actor like Ethan had asked for his motivation. Melanie, however, stalked off and stormed back on in a rage of quite splendiferous proportions.

As I stood on that Road the most amazing thing happened - my Pauline, Road to Damascus moment. The scene took off like an aeroplane, lifted, banked, soared. The actor playing Platonov in that scene (the role was shared by three actors) - a young American, Todd Yard with real improvisational skills - responded and the scene stormed to its conclusion.

There was a hush in the rehearsal room. Nobody was asleep. Even Gerald was watching like a rabbit caught in the headlights. Eager to hold on to this impetus I indicated that they should go on. Anna - Sergei's stepmother, a widow who desperately loves Platonov and wishes to have an affair with him, finding to her intense frustration that he thinks of his relationship with her as the one element of untouchable purity in his life - enters.

Within 30 seconds we were back in Floaty Chekhov-land. This time I didn't wait as long for boredom to sit in. Not wanting to overdo the Anger gambit I went for my earliest variant and asked the young actor - Sarah Hope - to come on laughing the lines out. This did not mean laughing at the lines or their meaning or the situation, it did not mean laughing at and then speaking the lines - it meant just what it said on the tin: 'Laugh the lines out.' They have to be spoken on the out-breath wave of a laugh.

Dutifully she obeyed, and once again I watched in stunned amazement as the scene took flight. After it ended I just let it run on. Next up was Gerard. He, with the rest of the cast, had been watching with intense curiosity. Obviously deciding that this was what all this 'fookin' acting lark' must all be about, he plunged in headfirst. His character entered in a huge emotional torrent in any case.

The plane kept flying. We played two more scenes like this, then ran out of time. The cast looked shell-shocked. So was I.

I went home. Took out my diary. Wrote down all the day's events. I still have the diary. There are only three entries for the entire year. I'm really rubbish at keeping a diary. But I knew something important had happened. I didn't know what or why. The afternoon's events broke every rule of rehearsal that I knew. I had watched young students playing Chekhov - in one moment as though they didn't know who he was, or worse - didn't even know where Russia was. And then, in the space of seconds, they were playing him as though he was their favourite uncle. Words were delivered with appropriate meaning and emphasis, surfing on emotional waves that had depth and strength.

I had obviously, I reasoned, been in the presence of a rare theatrical miracle. Unrepeatable. Maybe there had been a conjunction of the stars? I just knew I would never see it again. What I had seen was impossible.

On the Thursday afternoon the cast filed into the rehearsal room. There was an unmistakable aura of fear and gloom. 'What?' I asked. 'What's wrong with you lot?' They looked at me in despair. 'How are we going to do what we did the other day, again?' Now, as anyone who knows me will confirm, I'm not a modest person. I'm a Really Good Teacher. And as any of the other Really Good Teachers (there are a lot of us) out there will confirm, all Really Good Teachers are quite frequently presented by the little bastards they are trying to educate with questions to which they have no answer. My mind sought desperately for an answer. I had already decided that I couldn't go down the anger/laughter run route. Their defences, I thought, would be too well prepared. The desperately-seeking mind could find no answer on its dusty shelves.
The silence in the room seemed to stretch into oppression.

I did what all Really Good Teachers do in this situation: I busked. At least on the outside. I strung together meaningless phrases like: 'Well............' (*note long meaningful pause*) '... that's a very good question........... very intelligent...' (*note transparent use of flattery*) '... and it's something to which I have given a lot of thought...' (*note proper positioning of preposition*) '... we did really well on Tuesday... very well...' (*flattery again, use of long grave pauses*) '...'

While all this was going on my Inner Teacher was on his knees, hands clasped, begging the gods for help, for an instant answer. You have to have the gods on your side. This isn't easy because they're a tricky bunch and don't like being brown-nosed. However, I had stopped to allow a mother with a baby in a buggy to cross the street that morning on my way to work - despite the fact that she should have crossed 20 yards further along at the very obvious zebra crossing!

They were smiling on me today and sent Mercury with a winged busk that turned out to be The Most Inspired Busk that they have ever given me. I am humbly grateful.

Finally running out of meaningless phrases and grave, thoughtful pauses, I opened my mouth again to make a weak joke about not having the faintest idea, when Mercury screeched to a halt next to me and thrust the following words into the useless gaping hole: 'I'll tell you what we're going to do, or at the least I'll tell you what we are not going to do!' Grave pause to make sure there were some more phrases ready to emerge; Mercury coughed impatiently: 'You are not allowed to repeat anything that we did the other day. Change the moves; forget about how you played the lines. The only thing we will hold on to is that initial impulse of energy as you came into the scene. Even if the character isn't angry or tormented by the gods' sense of fun, just come on, find an energy and play it. Then surf the result like you did on Tuesday.'

Poor deluded innocents: they looked at me as though I was the font of all wisdom ('Over 50 - must be wise...'), took my words for gospel and proceeded - the gods bless Music Theatre actors - to do just that. Even though even I wasn't quite sure what it meant.

For the next two weeks and one day I sat and watched in wonder as they plunged with abandon into the maelstrom of this extraordinarily strange piece of work. Early Chekhov - nobody is quite sure whether he wrote it at 17 or about 22 (my bet's on the later date) - it is raw and painful, wildly funny and able to switch in a millisecond from one to the other. Everything is on the surface. His later, much greater plays, only show the scars, almost subliminally. This one shows you the bleeding wound. It is a play that needs the actors to drive it - to make it work. Afternoon after exciting afternoon they happily and unknowingly broke all the rules. That cast is most responsible for the title of this book - *Trusting the Actor.* From depths that I was only to begin to understand some years later, they plumbed real, believable meanings and emotions. I occasionally had to correct an emphasis - normally connected to an actor not knowing the actual meaning of the word. (Actors are notoriously lazy. Despite the free availability of such things as dictionaries, they will frequently attempt to busk what they think the meaning is. You have to threaten the buggers and run occasional spot checks - otherwise they could happily go into a performance not knowing what 'irony' means... well, maybe that was a bad example).

For the rest they changed moves and meanings daily; cheerfully threw themselves into the deep seas of emotion, swam and gaily surfed the waves of what I finally realised was 'in-the-moment'.

It was a blessed, happy rehearsal period.

I wish I could tell you it had a happily-ever-after ending. One thing (he said, plunging into gloom as he spoke) life has taught me is that fairy tales and fantasies are wonderful, can teach you lots, the beginnings of wisdom especially, but: They rarely come true! All those fantasies we have in our heads, the happily-ever-after stories we tell ourselves in the privacy of our mind, probably have a very good purpose, I suppose - no, I believe. But don't make the mistake of believing that they will necessarily come true. If this were so, I would have won that lovely little Alfa Romeo Sports Coupe in 1962 in South Africa; would currently be on my 20th lottery big win, and as for Brigitte Bardot... but we'd better move on.

Fortunately for my sanity the dress rehearsal we did on the Monday night was attended by a small group of friends and lovers (not mine, theirs). The cast did a cracking performance - all was well with my world. Apart, of course, from this breaking:

Astbury's 3rd Law of Theatre

*A bad dress rehearsal means
a good first performance
...and vice versa*

This law is not totally inviolable - it's only 99% true. If I ever have a really good dress I make absolutely sure that we have one more run or read before opening, to shake out the burrs.

The small audience loved it. Aware of this 3rd Law of mine I warned the actors: 'Treat tomorrow like another rehearsal, don't set anything, change moves, don't drop the energy.' They nodded sagely.

The following morning was to be our only performance. I was in the process of changing this. Actors learn most from Acting. Audience response provides them sometimes with salutary feedback. Mountview was not the only school which only allowed one performance. Performance, it was said, encouraged bad habits. Performance, I and many others of my ilk say, is where you can point out the bad habits; identify and correct them. Some actors are wonderful in the rehearsal room and fall to pieces onstage. The good actors get going - like the tough...

Our first two stripped-down and reshaped acts went OK. This cast had done a good basic job of editing. Later casts added muscle to the bones. Then we hit Act 3 and the real acting task. Faced by a phalanx of 150 of their peers, staff and tutors, the first actors on - I shall spare their blushes - it wasn't their fault, I prepared the next year's cast much more diligently - collapsed under the glare of 300 eyes. They went straight to the moves that had worked the night before.

You know those films of toppling dominoes...

I sat watching in horror as scene after scene collapsed into boredom and disinterest, meanings were lost, emotion sank without a bubble. It might have been my last production at Mountview. Being my first, most of the staff were keen to see what I could do. To the gods I give thanks for Scott Fleming. He was playing one of the three Platonovs. One of our adaptations was to introduce a Narrator/Platonov who introduced the play and its characters (including the other actors playing himself) to the audience. He then sat in the centre of a row of chairs behind the playing area with the rest of the cast, watching the happenings on stage and occasionally making explanatory forays into the action as a sort of ghost.

I watched him watching with horror equal to mine as the play collapsed. We reached the last act, when he would take over and play the final Platonov. He had, as always with people in the last act of the play in these shortened rehearsal periods, been under-rehearsed. The previous night's dress had been only the second time he had been able to play the role with all the stops out.

Today he gathered his horror and his talent and stormed into the final phase of the play with all guns blazing. It was as we had been working in the rehearsals - and it had the same effect. The play finally, and almost too late, lifted off the runway. The audience began to respond. The play tosses you back and forth from wild farce to ridiculous tragedy, especially in those last three acts. He managed to recapture most of these moments and the rest of the cast followed him out of the trenches.

'Liked the last act...' said several members of the staff in various ways afterwards.

I mentally withdrew my letter of resignation.

The cast and I had a thorough debrief session. One of the two culprits who had led the collapse admitted to her guilt. 'I walked on and saw all those faces and heard myself saying the first lines in exactly the same way as I had the night before. I realised I'd even walked on stage in the same way. Then it was like I was on rails, I had no control. I was just taken from one place to another. No matter how hard I tried I couldn't break free, even though I knew the play was dying.'

The Bicycle and the Mud

This 'confession' taught me another invaluable lesson. From then I introduced all my casts to *The Story of the Bicycle and the Mud*. It goes like this: One day you're riding your bike down a pathway. It's been raining and there are patches of mud. You drive through one. It's fun! The next day you are going down the same pathway. The sun's been out and baked the ground hard. You come to the mud patch with its baked-in track. If you make the mistake of trying to follow that track you will fall off. The track will control the bicycle and your balance will be thrown.

Moral: In rehearsals and early performance the first few paces onto the stage, the first words, are crucial. Vary your approach each time. When you've finally found the rhythm of performance and understand how the audience will respond you will find that the moves and inflections settle into set patterns. These will be sustainable. In a long run you might find that these become stuck and you will have to start varying the initial impulses again to keep it fresh. My ideal actors go onstage not having the faintest idea how they are going to play their roles in this particular performance.

As I write this I can already hear the screams of rage and sneers of contempt from those directors who place their casts in the chains of 'blocking'. It's amazing that this system still survives. Most actors I know hate it with a deep passion. It sets up the director as puppet-master. 'Move this way on that line, then sit for these lines, then turn for this line...' Some poor ASM faithfully marks all these moves on the prompt script and heaven help the actor who deviates. It's a system for the left-brain dominant, consciously 'thinking' actor. Many actors who have been crippled by their training and slavishly follow such directions can be completely thrown by the smallest deviation, lose their lines, freeze up. It is antithetical to the improvisation we try to teach them.

The ability to respond to a new offer in the blink of an eye.

The ability to be 'in-the-moment'.

I was getting closer to understanding the answer to Joe Alessi's hard question about getting into the moment six years earlier.

It's not quite accurate to say that the fairy-tale didn't come true. One year later, almost to the day, another cast took on the same challenge. It was Chekhov-time again for the Music Theatre course 2nd year students. The new bunch sat before me on the first day - full of trepids. This time I was prepared. The first thing I said to them was: 'Last year our cast collapsed at the final hurdle despite us having a really good rehearsal period. I'm not blaming them - I didn't prepare them properly because we had discovered something amazing during the rehearsal period and I knew as little as they did about how it works.' I described the process and it's consequences. I had been using it ever since with various 2nd year Acting groups, and was more aware of what to do to make the process work. I ended with a promise:

'If you take on the process, play with it, try it out...

If on the performance day you go onstage with no preconceived ideas in your head...

If you play as though it is just one more rehearsal, one more different way of doing the play...

If you do this - and it fails:

I will take all the blame.

I will personally tell everyone that you all did exactly what I asked of you to the utmost of your abilities.

I will have failed, not you.

If, however, on the performance day you try to recreate the last good performance that you did, it will fail, and when it does I will place most of the blame on you.

I will tell everyone what crap actors you are, unwilling to take risks, pining for a safe haven.'

Though even more trepids appeared on the young faces before me, they sallied forth into a much easier rehearsal period than their compadre's from the year before had had. They now had a text for the first two acts - pre-cut and prepared. We were able to add, hone, tighten and make them more like scenes from a play, less like a travelogue.

We were also able to start with the new process much earlier. I was now doing 'anger runs' as a matter of course. It felt rather simplistic, but it was working, so what the hell.... The same, rather wonderful quick connections with meaning and emotion kept happening. By now I believed it. I had seen it work time and again.

I started to see something else which made me fall even deeper in love with Chekhov than I already was. As we played and replayed the scenes, always taking on different moves and impulses, I watched in wonder as a line which seemed to have this meaning, this sub-text today, had a completely different meaning or tone tomorrow. At first I had tried to hold on to an interpretation which somehow just seemed to hit the spot. Only to watch it die as the actor attempted to reconstruct, 're-create' it. I finally realised I was ignoring the rule I had set up - 'Don't repeat.' So I sat back and watched as endless variations on the text emerged. There appeared to be no end to the list of possibilities of how to deliver a line. More about this later.

I gave the actors almost total freedom in how to play each scene. Each day would be new and amazing and then all its discoveries would be 'thrown' away.

In one of those lovely coincidences in art, I read one day in the middle of this rehearsal period of a group of Buddhist monks who were touring the world, working towards peace. What they would do, apparently (forgive my dicky memory), was to set up next to a river or a body of water. Then, over a period of time - I think it was a week - they would sit around a large wooden board and, with small tubes filled with coloured sand, 'draw' an incredibly intricate mandala. They worked in shifts, as one stepped out the next would take over and continue the drawing. I never found out whether they were drawing a specific mandala, or whether it was 'free-flow' drawing with the overall pattern emerging as they went along. I hope it was the latter. When it was completed they allowed the audience time to view it. Then they ceremonially tipped the mandala into the water, and went on to construct a new one somewhere else. I'm not a very religious person - well not, at least, a follower of 'man-made' religion - but the thought of this wonderful, selfless creation, and dissolution, of a work of art affected me deeply.

Much later I found a saying attributed to Buddha: 'It is in the nature of all things that take form to dissolve again. Strive with your whole being to attain perfection.'

The performance finally arrived. Dress rehearsal was appropriately rocky. I gave them a warning again. This time the fairy-tale did come true. They plunged in without 'thought'.

A Note about Thinking...

I need to explain here that what I mean by 'thought' or 'thinking' in this context is conscious thought. We are thinking all the time. The majority of this thinking is sub- or pre-conscious. That's good thinking and we'll come back to this later on. The kind where we sit and consciously think 'Now I'll do this,' or 'Now I'll do that' is 'conscious thought' and, as I frequently tell my actors: 'Conscious thinking is seriously bad for an actor.'

Back to the performance. As I said, they plunged in. With energy and verve. There was no repetition of the previous night's dress. Everything was fresh and new-minted. The audience began to respond, first with laughter, later with shock at Platonov's outrageous, self-centred justifications, his quite stunning, thoughtless cruelty. I heard something I hadn't heard in years: an audience talking back to play. The cast rampaged on, driving the play relentlessly. Of course it wasn't all roses, it never is, but even the weakest links kept the energy up and the pace going.

At the end - after an exhilarating tour through a wonderful piece of Chekhovian farce/tragedy which has the watchers switching from tears to laughter and back again within three lines - the audience erupted into cheers and shouts. This, of course, is nothing unusual in a drama school - where you have a built-in claque eager to applaud you because they know that next week they'll be onstage and you'll be applauding them. However, there was a genuine spontaneity about the applause and the feedback to the students afterwards confirmed this. Some staff members found it too raw and loud for their tastes, and expected detail in performance way beyond what can be achieved in a short rehearsal period.

It has been a constant source of amazement to me how often this criticism comes up in drama schools in first or second year projects where the large cast has been working over four weeks or so, for an average 12-14 hours a week. These are not trained actors, they are young trainees desperately trying to put a whole range of complex new techniques in acting, voice and movement into practice. To expect the detail that experienced actors might find in such a short period of time is ludicrous.

It also betrays an essential misunderstanding of the process of art. Da Vinci did not begin to paint Mona Lisa's left eye in exquisite detail; Michelangelo didn't start lovingly to carve David's tackle. The former first drew the large outlines, placed layer upon layer, wash upon wash, before finally sketching in the exquisite detail of those eyes and that infuriating smile. The latter first had to hack out from the huge block of marble the statuesque and daunting (to us males) shape, before getting to tinker with a tackle. Detail comes last.

Those two casts taught me huge amounts through their courage and willingness. I continued to experiment.

A Note about Repetition...

Now I'd better address the thought/ criticism/quibble that is probably in several directorial brains. Repetition. Having done this work can actors re-create, repeat, night after performance night?

Depends on what you mean by re-create or repeat.

In the early days (and still occasionally now) when asked to explain the process of rehearsal and performance all I could offer was the following: *'At the beginning of the rehearsal process you're standing at one side of a dense, boulder-strewn, scrub-covered tract of land. In the distance you can see a peak. This is where you need to go. So you set off, through the underbrush. As you're cutting a path for yourself a moment will come when Pain will drop from the branch of a tree above onto your shoulders and give you a right old going-over. You stagger to your feet and continue on. A bit later Anger will pounce from behind a rock and mug you good and proper. Crawling, limping you soldier on. Finally, scarred, weary, triumphant, you reach the peak. You have created your character and laid down its performance trail.*

Performance arrives. You have to do it all again...

So, you set off. As you pass under the tree you cringe, preparing to duck as Pain drops. Nothing. The tree is empty. Later, as you approach the rock, you have your hands covering your tender bits in anticipation. Nothing. The rock is hiding nothing.

So what do you do? Well, it's simple, and tough. Each day you set off and walk the path. Without anticipation. Your tender bits available for mugging. In the early days Pain and Anger (and any of the other emotions) will find you at different stages and in different places - other trees, bushes, rocks, ravines. You have to allow this.' At this stage I generally hold out my clenched fist. *'This isn't acting -'* I say, and open my fingers, palm upwards, *'- this is. As you get more and more experienced the emotional muggings will start to happen same-time, same-place, performance after performance. Ringing like a pure-toned bell, night after night. Trust yourself.'*

In those early days all I could do was to ask the actors to trust me. It would happen, I assured them - though I didn't know why.

I know more of the 'why' now, but it still remains a rather wonderful mystery.

Back in the bad old days of 'blocking', actors were instructed by directors on each move they had to make. As I have said, this was written down by the faithful stage manager. An absolutely marvellous system for exceedingly left-brained actors, used to consciously thinking their way through life and the plays therein in painstaking and, for their audience, extremely dull detail. We shall shortly (I promise) come to an explanation as to why doing things this way CANNOT work.

But first, let me explain what I think re-creation or repetition is, or should be. As always, by way of example. I was with another Music Theatre group at Mountview. A 2nd year Chekhov project, again. This time - *Three Sisters* . At one time not my favourite Chekhov. I'd only seen productions in which the title would more profitably have been *Three Long-Suffering and Boring Heroines* Oh how these poor dears suffered, being cooped up with the cretins. For me a more appropriate title would have been *Three Bitches*. I had always come out with intense sympathy for Natasha, cheering on her destruction of them at the end. Suppressing a desire to vomit as the three stood or sat, always with arms nobly around each other in that last scene, nobly delivering their noble speeches as the band took the grateful army away...

This was on my second *Three Sisters* at Mountview. I started off by telling them of my reservations about the play and my feeling that Natasha might just be the central character. We set off. Anger runs, etc. Played the first Natasha much more sympathetically and the Sisters much more snobbishly.

The interesting thing, however, happened with the final phase of the final act. Vershinin has gone, leaving Masha a wreck; the Baron has left for his suicidal duel; Andrei is wandering mournfully around with cuckold-baby. The three women launched into the first rehearsals of that final scene with grim gusto. We obeyed the rule: no repetition. Throw all discoveries away. Approach it each day without conscious thought or decision.

It became one of my all-time favourite rehearsal periods. I actually became addicted to the scene, almost to the detriment of the rest of the production. Over three days - afternoons - of rehearsals, I sat entranced watching as these three found endless different ways of acting that scene. I have seen the end of *Three Sisters* done in ways you couldn't possibly imagine. The wonderful thing is that, on each repetition the play worked, the words worked. They would say a line in a way that would have my poor brain protesting: 'You can't say the line that way'. Yet it would make perfect sense, in that moment, between those three. I think I was going for a world record in 'The Number of Ways the Final Scene in Chekhov's *Three Sisters* Can Be Played', when the actors from the first four acts reminded me that they were still there.

It was completely exhilarating.

In performance they kept this up. Both showings were subtly different, but made perfect sense.

Later I did four professional productions using these methods and asking the same of the actors: that they never repeat. This might sound like a recipe for anarchy, chaos and disaster to some of you. With bad actors it probably would be. With good actors it is, for me, better than any drug - exhilarating, once again, the only word that adequately describes it.

The actors are truly 'in-the-moment'. In tune with each other, solidly seated in characters which are a wonderful and unique combination of the character on the page, and the actors themselves.

Repetition? If the actors are properly seated in their roles, connected to the emotions, at one with the rest of the cast, then each new night will be a celebration, a surprise - magic.

You can trust good actors.

A digression - on types of actor...

There are, to generalise shamelessly, three different kinds of actors. The first have very strong personas and plaster themselves all over the character - to a certain extent hiding the character from view. You go to each performance knowing exactly what you're going to get. The same as the last. A lot of audiences like this. It is unthreatening, doesn't challenge their imagination. Many critics also love this type. They will frequently refer to them as 'that fine actor'. I first heard that phrase in South Africa in the 60s, where the local well-respected film critic referred to Telly Savalas in that way. Shame, poor bald-headed Telly - throughout his long career he played that one role undeviatingly. He might, indeed, have been a 'fine actor' but, after we all marvelled the first time he played it, some of us got bored and disenchanted. The most recent time I read this description it was in a top London paper and used by an esteemed critic to describe an actor who was part of the company of a large organisation. He was a nice man, so I'll refrain from naming him. Not one of the top echelon, he had been in the company for nearly 25 years. As each play came around you could tell exactly which role he would get. Lazy directors loved him. You could set him off on autopilot and know exactly where he was going to land. I got to know him over about 10 years. Once a firebrand, both theatrically and politically, he was then bored and cynical. I'm sure he would have been a 'fine actor' if he'd been challenged.

I once read an interview with Robert Redford - one of those actors I deeply resent for reasons not connected to his acting abilities. Following *Butch Cassidy and the Sundance Kid*, I was forced to live with a wife and one of her daughters (I'm a step-) who were wildly in love with only one man in the Universe - and it wasn't me.

Redford had just made a movie which he highly valued. In it he played a character far from his normal screen persona. The film flopped at the box office. In the interview Redford mourned the fact that his fans only wanted him to play one role. No wonder he began to look for other outlets for his creativity and created the Sundance Film Festival. Probably why Paul Newman started selling pasta sauces?

Anyhow, that's Type Number 1 - works well for film.

Type Number 2 is characterised by the quote: *'I hide behind my characters.'* This type of actor doesn't submerge themselves in the character, they hide behind a mask of the character. Sometimes they create very successful masks. These often involve physical changes to the face - wigs, a larger nose, plumped out cheeks, etc. What you are seeing is what is written on the page, mostly, sometimes with a change of wallpaper. The character is reduced to a stereotype that can only really be played one way. So much for making a character live for each new modern period and country in which the play is staged.

And so, on to Actors - Type 3. No prizes for guessing which are my favourites. These merge themselves with the role, like boiling water and a teabag - each different blend bringing a unique taste. Done like this there really are hundreds of thousands of utterly unique

Hamlet's, Ophelia's, Nina's, Konstantin's. As each of us has a one-off fingerprint; that totally unique string of DNA, so each actor can allow the character to take them over completely, using whatever the role needs, to create a blend like no other.

Working this way, actors can create magic - and our modern world is sadly lacking in this.

Two more of my endless stock of illustrative (true) stories.

Yvonne and I went with Athol to see *Hello and Goodbye* in London. Athol was interested in Ben Kingsley taking over the role he had played in our *Statements* for the London production. Afterwards he went backstage to talk to him while Yvonne and I waited outside. (She hated going backstage, being very shy.)

Finally he emerged, full of praise for Ben. He was gobsmacked at how 'frisgebou' (South African Afrikaans for 'well-built') Ben was. Onstage he looked every inch the broken, shambling Johnny. Athol kept coming back to it. 'You wouldn't believe how different he looks.' .Finally Yvonne said, gently: 'Yes, Athol - he was acting.' Athol roared with laughter. He, of all people, should not have been surprised at Ben's ability to transform himself, to allow the character to shape him.

10 years later I was sitting in the National Theatre's staff canteen, waiting for my wife's rehearsal to end. I had bought a book of photos on a sale in the NT's bookshop. It featured production shots taken over a decade at the NT. Yvonne's *The Woman* was there. I paged through, looking at all the famous faces and productions. An actor from the cast Yvonne was in joined me. He told me of the plays he had been in, pictured in the book, of those he'd seen. I'd just been looking at a photograph of T*he Elephant Man* in its original stage version. Had he seen that? Yes. He raved about David Schofield in the title role. One of the best acting performances he had ever seen. And the make-up! Extraordinary! I paged back to the picture of Schofield and slid the book over the table to him. He looked at it in amazement. It was a solo shot - Schofield dressed in what looked like a large nappy. No make-up. No prosthetics. 'My god!' he said. 'I remember seeing all the hideous disfigurements.'

Magic.

A further digression - this time on the subject of plays and society...

I said earlier: So much for making a character live for each new modern period and country in which the play is staged. With Actor - Type 2 the play remains calcified in its original state. Now some would say that this is right and proper. You should always remain faithful to the writer's intentions. I'm afraid I don't go with this 'Writer as God' tendency. After a play has been staged for the first time, hopefully as the writer intended (and, if this doesn't happen, a writer can become very badly blocked as s/he doesn't see the full impact of the play on the audience, which is like the final piece being put into a crossword puzzle), it is open to the world as far as I'm concerned. For a play to survive - to achieve universality - it needs to be able to speak to each new generation in a language that generation will understand. If it can't do this it is not a great play.

One of the best, the funniest *Midsummer Night's Dream's* I have ever seen was done by a bunch of Senior School pupils at Cape Town High in the late 1960s. Under the direction of the wonderful Robin Malan, they took the stage on a set which placed the play on Clifton Beach in Cape Town. Dressed - or undressed - in bathing costumes (Clifton was known as Bikini Beach), sporting dreadful, broad South African accents, the joyous young cast brought out most of the play's themes - young love and its silliness, burgeoning sexuality, magic. Out in the stalls this young photographer was having a hard time keeping in focus, so helpless was he with laughter. And the play spoke directly to me and its audience. It was not (hushed, reverential tone) 'Shakespeare'. It belonged to us. Us unsophisticates at the bottom end of Africa. (No pun intended).

Two further stories to illustrate this point.

In the early 70's Yvonne had written to me, while on one of her London stints, of a play she had seen - David Rudkin's *Ashes*. Two of the best actors she had experienced in Britain in a powerful, moving play. She sent me a copy. I was underwhelmed. Stuck in the stranglehold of the South African situation, I found a play about a husband and wife and their struggle to have a child uninvolving. For me the play, while dealing with a very emotional and pressing issue for people in that position, was not important. Two years later I found out how wrong I was.

On June 16, 1976, Soweto exploded in flames. I remember standing in the office/home of a London agent on Cromwell Road - one of the busiest roads on the planet. He was on the phone. I was watching in horror as the images flowed out of South Africa from a television screen in the corner. These, I later found, were not being shown on the censored South African Broadcasting Corporation. Through the high window looking onto the busy road I saw a car pull to a halt in front of the big hotel opposite, smoke rising from its engine. The driver jumped out and opened the bonnet. More smoke. In the middle of the road on the other carriageway a small van stopped. Its flanks advertised some kind of fire extinguishers. I will be kind and grant them anonymity. The driver opened the back, took out a large example of his wares and ran to the car. Whoosh! - a huge cloud of something was directed at the smoke. He stood back. Thank heavens! ...Too soon for thanks... New and bigger flames jumped up from the engine. Back to his van - another type of extinguisher. Another Whoosh! Even bigger flames! I won't string this out.

As he was trying out his fifth product, the ever-growing flames now engulfing the entire car, the Fire Brigade arrived and finally quenched the fires on the burned-out hulk.

The agent and I had, rather insensitively, been going into hysterics at the antics of the fire extinguisher salesman. 'A perfect piece of one-act farce.' he said. On the telly the appalling pictures kept coming - the iconic photograph by Sam Nzima of the 12-year old, dying Hector Pietersen being carried in the arms of Mbuyisa Makhubo, burnt-out schools, police firing tear-gas canisters into rioting crowds. The London scene seemed to provide a metaphor for the South African. Fortunately for us when Nelson Mandela arrived with his fire extinguisher of forgiveness, South Africa did not descend into chaos.

I got back to Cape Town to find people in an odd state of denial. Even the more radically inclined members of our Theatre - White and Black.

Partly this was because of a lack of information. Mostly, however, it was for a reason I only understood some time later.

The riots had spread to Cape Town.

I left The Space one day to go for my normal afternoon tea in Stuttaford's department store Tea Rooms. This allowed me to de-stress and stay sane. I used this time to read plays and think while consuming the best waffles, syrup and cream anywhere, with tea in real silver pots with little green felt holders to protect your fingers from the heat.

As I walked along the Cape Town side street I could see down to the city and beyond. Devil's Peak towered in the frame. Behind it, rising straight into the deep blue sky of a still, early Spring day, was a plume of dark smoke. In another of the great lost photos of my life a large sign in the shape of a revolver hung advertising a gun shop - enjoying a boom in business at that fraught time - the plume of smoke seeming to come out of the point of its barrel. Large in the foreground hanging on a lamppost in front of me was a newspaper banner. It said 'Langa Riots – 4 Killed'. The smoke was coming from the direction of Langa township.

I continued walking to my tea-room. It was only on my second cup that my slow brain put it all together. The closer you are to a large reality the more you disassociate yourself. I had been aghast at how indifferent my associates had seemed to be when I returned from London to The Revolution. Now here I was, suffering from the same condition.

A month or so later, aware that Yvonne's taste and nose for plays was better than mine, I took up *Ashes* again. At its centre I found a long speech I had hardly done more than skim the first time. The husband goes back to his family home in Ireland to attend a funeral. On his return he tells his wife of the experience. I actually started to cry when I read it this time. The speech had one of the most chilling lines I had ever read:

'I: have been part of a muck that only violence can shift.' (Rudkin's punctuation, not mine...)

To a quite significant extent this line marked the beginning of the end in South Africa for me. Neither Yvonne or I believed in violence as an answer. But it was getting very difficult in the situation to ask that Black South Africans - living at the sharp end of those inhuman policies - take a Gandhian view of things. And, for them, friendship with us Whites was increasingly becoming a complicating factor.

We staged the play with our best cast - Yvonne, Bill Flynn and Bill Curry, and a wonderful director, Dimitri Nicolas-Fanourakis. It lasted three days before it was banned.

Second story:

In the middle 80s my wife was cast in the title role of Brecht's *The Mother* - it was for the National Theatre Educational Department. Not *Mother Courage* - his adaptation of Gorki's novel of the same name which is, at heart, a primer in how to mobilise resistance and set up a Communist cell. Under the direction of Di Trevis a superb cast of mainly younger actors set about realising the play. They did a wonderful job and the play toured to schools and community centres, with attached workshops on its various themes, etc.

Throughout, I, and several of the cast, while admiring the production, found the play to be a bit of a museum piece. Time had passed it by. The people were interesting, their situation only historically so. It was given a week's run at the end of the tour in the Cottesloe. At least one of the critics agreed with us. Interesting, but no longer valid.

On the last night I was standing in the small Cottesloe foyer, waiting to go in, when I was delighted to see Julius Mtsaka. He had acted in plays at The Space and went on to become a director. He was in London on a course. South Africa was still in the grip of Apartheid, Mandela still imprisoned. Julius had come to see Yvonne, accompanied by a cultural attaché of the African National Congress. We arranged to meet for a drink in the Green Room afterwards. I went in to take my seat for another one of the most exciting nights of theatre in my life. (I have had far too many boring ones to moan about here, but remember - this is a book of highlights.)

The 'antique' play, the museum piece, suddenly leapt into flaming life as I viewed it through the eyes of two Black South Africans fighting their way out from under an oppressive power structure. It became - as *Ashes* had - a play written yesterday for today.

Afterwards I met up with the two again. They were fizzing with excitement. Julius wanted to do the play immediately back in South Africa.

Given what had happened to us with *Ashes*, I advised him to take the play as a basis, change its title to avoid censors knowing what it was about, rewrite it for their own situation. Sadly, I lost track of Julius and never knew whether this happened.

Three plays written centuries apart, two of them aimed very specifically at a particular audience. All able to transcend boundaries of time and culture and speak to other audiences about the situation in which they were currently trapped.

Well, that was a digression (with internal digression) of Billy Connolly proportions.

Back to our subject.

The Problem of Acting

At this stage I knew that the exercises we had developed worked. However, mostly I didn't know why. I still really had little idea of what being in the moment was, and little idea of how to get the actor into that state.

In 1996 I found a book which began to give me the reasons.

Daniel Goleman's *Emotional Intelligence* is not a book about acting. It's probably more about giving you the knowledge to increase your ability to live as a caring human being . To do this he introduces you to the functions of the brain. As I read the book my head was filled with 'Oh-is-that-whys'.

Goleman owes me a cut of his profits. I personally brought 10-12 copies to give to anyone I thought should or might be interested. One MA degree holder sniffed: 'It's very anecdotal.'

You should read the book for yourself. However, for the purposes of this book, I shall instead take you on a tour through a class I teach preparatory to the first basic application of the exercises. This gives a rough background to the what and why (and makes neuroscientists wince).

I call it The Problem of Acting. (I personally have a problem with prepositions, and never know whether it should be Problem 'of', or 'with', or 'in'. Suggestions, after reading the chapter, on a postcard).

So, imagine yourself for the moment as part of a class of eager young drama students - actors or directors. You're sitting in a circle, with me somewhere on the circumference. I am a sweet old guy, overweight, cracked-up, grey-haired, a neat line in clothes in a style known as Rumpled, my left eye twitches (after a Theatre Injury in the 70s which slightly crushed a vertebra in my neck, trapping a nerve).

Some people think I'm quite huggable - which is nice for me - until they find out what a sweet sadist I really am.

I begin by telling them that I'm going to demonstrate The Problem of (in, with?) Acting. I ask for a volunteer. You are obviously going to have to use your imagination. This is good for you.

When the unhappy-looking volunteer is seated, I tell the rest of the class to get in a group facing Unhappy so that they can see his/her eyes. I stand next to Unhappy. I inform the others strictly that they should under no circumstances look at me - to concentrate on Unhappy's eyes - or they will miss the entire point of the exercise. Unhappy is told just to stare over their heads. When I am sure that all eyes are aimed correctly, I flick the back of my hand at Unhappy's eyes, stopping two or three inches short. Unhappy blinks. Sometimes flinches. Or, at worst, ducks. No, at worst was the time when Unhappy was a woman who actually didn't blink at all! End of demonstration - had to get another unhappy volunteer, who, thank heavens, did blink. I then repeat this action as many times as it takes for Unhappy to stop blinking. This can be as little as two or three flicks - once nearly 20. When I've got Unhappy to accept the flicks without blinking I say, rather smugly: 'The Problem of (with, in..) Acting.

Mostly this is met with complete mystification. (Sons and daughters and lovers of neuroscientists apart, or people who read more books than is good for them).

'What happened?' I ask. 'S/he blinked, then stopped blinking.' 'What does that mean?' I like trying to get people to think things out for themselves. Very few get the answer to this question. 'Did you see my hand coming - and then decide to blink?' 'No', says Unhappy. It was an involuntary action. The brain responded with an avoidance reaction without conscious thought.

Two wonderful little parts of the brain - the amygdala (so-called because they are shaped like almonds - amygdala is Greek for almond, I'm told) are among the first to receive the messages from our sensory system - eyes, ears, nose, tongue, skin - which are gathered by the hypothalamus (I just love the names given to areas of the brain, and these two - with the hippocampus - are my favourites) and distributed to all interested agencies in a jiffy. Together these two qualify as your Early Warning System. If the amygdala senses a dangerous pattern it presses the Emergency Red Button and your entire system is placed in one of three modes -

Fight, Flight or Freeze, the 3 F's of basic survival. You've probably all heard of fight and flight - freeze is not always mentioned, but should be.

The best way to understand this process - its advantages and its dangers - is to read Peter Levine's *Waking the Tiger*.

He deals with the understanding and treatment of Post-Traumatic Stress Disorder. In the book he tells of watching a wildlife documentary - one of those horrible ones which show nature red in tooth-and-claw. A cheetah was pursuing a gazelle. Despite the swerves, kinks, sudden stops and reversals on the part of the gazelle the cheetah finally caught up and was about to sink its fangs into the little thing when the gazelle appeared to drop dead. The cheetah dragged its prey back to the shade of a tree to await the arrival of the rest of the family for their tea. A short while later, and, thankfully before the arrival of husband/wife and kids, an intense shiver ran through the little 'dead' buck, it jumped to its legs and scarpered. I can't remember whether it got away this time. I hope so. I'm really at one with the idea of living inside the cycle of life, the balance of nature - which us human beings don't. I'd just rather not watch it in operation.

The gazelle's survival system, realising the jig was up, put it into freeze, feigning death. When it opined that the danger level was sufficiently low, it brought the buck back to consciousness through that shiver - ready and able to run for it.

The gazelle had gone through two of the F's: Flight and Freeze. Wisely it didn't think Fight would work against the rapacious cheetah.

What has this to do with acting? Well, as actors approach a character and attempt to connect to its thoughts and feelings there comes a moment when the character sends out a flash of emotion, asking the actors to grasp this and make it their own. To understand it and feel what it was like to experience. In high-octane scenes this 'ask' can be very challenging. As the emotion attempts, like a bolt of lightning, to find its way out to the audience through the actor - operating as a sort of lightning conductor - the actor is, especially at an early stage of rehearsals, shocked into one of the three states. Involuntarily. It doesn't require a genius to understand that you can't act while in such a state; while your involuntary system is in control of your survival instincts.

Before going any further -

A Word about the Brain...

This, I warn any neuroscientists who may have strayed unknowingly into this book, is my own highly individual and rather simplistic take on the subject.

Let's first look at the basic structure. Let's get back to the Left Brain/Right Brain divide. It's not quite as simple as that but, for the purposes of this book and because I don't want to further confuse you, we shall retain this old-fashioned view.

The brain is divided into two rather strange and not very pretty, squishy hemispheres. It's an astonishing structure, affording an incredible amount of surface area to cope with the latest developments, but one that won't win any architectural prizes for Aesthetics.

It is, however, without doubt one of the most amazing creations in an extraordinary universe. Consisting of some 200 billion cells (I always tell my classes that some guy in America counted them, but I'm joking, of course), each one of these cells is capable of making a whole set of connections to the other cells (I'm avoiding using terms such as neurons and dendrites and synapses to prevent confusion amongst lay-actors). Now, when I started reading about this in the 90s (Goleman introduced me to the work of Joseph LeDoux, Anthony Damasio, and Michael Gazzaniga), the number of connections was estimated at anywhere between one and 20. Just last week - as I write - another estimate of up to a thousand was quickly followed by an estimate of many thousands. That man in America has been very busy.

This absolutely unimaginably vast network holds something that I can never describe without a sense of real awe. Our whole life. Every moment, every single frame. Each sight, sound, smell, taste, feeling. I look around the classroom and tell them that their faces are now stamped, forever and indelibly, in my brain. 'No matter how hard I try, I'll never be able to get rid of them.'

Part of what this book will attempt to teach is how to access this amazing database of fact and feeling.

Back to the hemispheres. By-and-large (looks furtively over his shoulder for lurking neuroscientists) the Left Brain does its job rather well. I like to think of it, fondly, as the brain's input system. Rather like the keyboard of a computer. Very handy for typing in the facts, but limited. It deals with lists and logic, facts and words, order and pattern. The Right Brain is more about the Big Picture, symbols and feelings, intuitions, emotions, spatial perceptions. It is impetuous and likes to take risks.

There is much more on both sides, of course - find out for yourself - it's fascinating.

Now for that Left Brain limitation. Just as you can only type one key at a time on the computer keyboard, the Left Brain can only hold seven bytes of information in its grasp at any one time. There is some argument as to this number. Some say five, some go as high as nine or 10. I KNOW it's seven. Any neuroscientist who cares to argue can come to one of my rehearsals. I use a system called Under-reading (more later). This involves the actor being fed the lines by other actors or stage management. They do not have scripts. The under-readers have to learn to feed the lines in chunks, trying to keep the meaning. There is one absolute, however. If the under-reader gives up to seven words the actor will be able to repeat them. One more, and the actor will stop and mostly be unable to repeat more than three or four of the words they had been fed.

To drive home this limitation I always then give the following illustration: I ask if any of them can drive, pick one who puts up their hand, take my car keys out of my pocket and say: 'I am going to throw you my car keys. I want you to go down to the nearest cake shop, buy us all a selection of cream-cakes, doughnuts, éclairs...' (I tend to get a bit carried away here), '..come back here and we'll all have tea. BUT,' I add, 'I want you to give conscious instructions to each muscle in your body needed to carry out that set of actions. How long', I ask, 'will it take to carry out that task?' Guesses range from minutes to hours to days. 'The answer is,' I say rather smugly, 'that you won't even catch the keys.'

People tend not to believe this so I then move on to my piece-de-resistance, my all-time favourite demonstration. I'm rather hesitant to tell you this 'secret' in public here, as it were. But, what the hell, it's probably time to release it into the world.

I tell them I am now going to do something so amazing, so-o-o stunning, that they will remember the moment for evermore. Just as we can all remember where we were when we heard of some momentous event. (For us older ones it's usually when we heard of Kennedy's assassination) I am, I say, about to initiate them into this smallish, exclusive club who were present when Brian did this unbelievable thing. By this time you can cut the tension in the room with a scalpel - well, except for the laughing disbelievers. I make them all take three deep breaths to relax and focus them. Ask them to concentrate on me - 'You wouldn't want to miss this...' (Meaningful pause) '... Ready..?' They nod.

Then I lift my right arm and describe a circle in the air before bringing it back to my side. It takes about two seconds. Try it. They look at me expectantly. 'Isn't that amazing?' I ask. They laugh, some mystified, some with that 'oh-he's-just-kidding-us' look. 'You don't think that's amazing!?' I ask, in amazement. Mystification increases. If someone makes the mistake of agreeing that this is indeed 'amazing', I asked them to explain why - which, up till the time of writing, nobody has been able to do.

'I have just taken 18,000 decisions in two seconds. And,' I add, 'if I get up at the same time it multiplies to, probably 30 or 40,000. If I jog and talk at the same time it's up in the hundreds of thousands.' (DISCLAIMER: I got this figure from one of the many books on the brain and I've read - can't remember which one. Sorry. It seems that American man continues to be very, very busy.)

So, we go back to the cream-cake-and-car analogy. 'What would actually happen,' I say to the putative driver, 'is that you would catch the keys, drive to the patisserie, get the scrumptious goodies, and drive back here. Halfway back you might find yourself thinking that you can't remember the last half mile of your journey. But you will not have left a trail of dead grannies and squashed hedgehogs. There will be no flashing blue light in your rear-view mirror.' Even those who walk or ride bicycles will acknowledge these areas of autopilot journeying.

We are now in the territory of the Right Brain, or the pre- or sub-conscious. Your average amazing desktop computer can take 28 million actions in a second. That is mind boggling. Your average human brain can take 58 trillion actions in a second. What's better than mind-boggling? Uncountable numbers of decisions are taken for us every day by this infinitely capable, extraordinarily complex three pounds of mush in our heads.

I end the lecture/demo with: 'Which area would you rather controlled your acting: the Left Brain with its pathetic inability to hold more than seven bytes of information at any one moment? Or the Right Brain, which can take squillions of decisions in the blink of an eye?'

There is, of course, no contest.

Read Malcolm Gladwell's *Blink* to gain a better understanding of this. It reports on the brain research which reveals that we know what we are going to say or do about a second or so before we know what we are going to say or do. In other words our whole life is lived through our sub- or pre-conscious. A perfect explanation for the acting process known as being 'in-the-moment'. To get into that perfect state you cannot be under the control of your survival instincts.

So we move on to the challenge of harnessing the power of both sides of the brain. This is not a Left Brain Bashing exercise. Both areas of the brain need to work in balance with each other. Unfortunately, far too many training systems tend to encourage the use of the conscious left brain and ignore the wonders of the right. The result: dull, restricted, out-of-the-moment acting, able to deliver only one thought process at that time, not the multileveled complexity of the most ordinary of us human beings.

A Word about Stanislavski...

I hate being thought of as a critic of Stan. He was an extraordinary man who left us blessings and curses. There are three problems. Firstly the translations on which all us Westerners have based our interpretations of his work are apparently flawed. Only now are new translations coming out which place some of this work in a different light.

The second is, as I have said before, that the man himself was an incorrigible experimenter. He was up-to-date with all the latest developments in theatre, but also in other fields. He dabbled in Mesmerism, read about the new branch of knowledge - psychology, was interested in humanity and its processes. He unrepentantly junked aspects of his 'method' which proved unworkable (some of which - inexplicably - are still faithfully taught today) and went on to find new ways. If he was still alive today one can only speculate with wonder at where he would have taken his 'System'.

The second problem: Stan first developed his system in response to the need to find and develop new young actors, not petrified in the demonstrative 'acting' tradition which surrounded him in Russia. But he was developing this system for Russians. Without getting too stereotypical - the Russians are a wildly emotional nation. The average Russian can access 25-30 emotional states - elation, depression, excitement, anger, compassion, dismay, disgust, wonder, horror - you name it - in the course of three or four sentences. LISTS?! LOGIC!? 'Ha!!'

Stan had to drag his actors kicking and screaming towards the use of their conscious, list-making, organised, left brain. I saw this process in action when Athol Fugard forced my wife to begin to think, to analyse, to rationalise. She had, up till then, been a wonderfully intuitive, instinctive actor. He enabled her to add the balance of a properly thinking, appropriately functional left brain.

That's fine for that kind of Russian actor. However, in the land of the Stiff Upper Lip, in the Kingdom of Logic and Rational, Considered Thought that is England (once again I don't lump the Scots, the Welsh and the Irish in this equation), this is probably the Worst Possible Technique to teach. Your average English actor is amazing at analysing and understanding a text, can make lists to an Olympic standard, AND can access one emotion each and every single year.

It's a miracle that there are so many fine actors here. They survive despite the chains of Actions and Objectives. Back at Mountview I had the chance to do a fascinating experiment. It confirmed something I had discovered, anecdotally, over the previous 25 years: most trained actors are taught the basics of Stanislavski - very few of them actually use the system.

In South Africa, back at the beginning, I had been the recipient of a stream of young actors from the (very good) local drama school. It was at a time when I was trying to learn how to direct. I didn't just ask Yvonne about Stan - I asked them as well. They were quite willing to pontificate about Stan, but when I asked them how they put it into practice, they all had the same answer - they didn't. In Britain, especially after starting to teach at one of the top drama schools (I have not experienced all the drama schools in this country, so I can't speak authoritatively but I have only heard of two which do not have the Stanislavski System at the basis of their training), I occasionally kept up the querying - always with the same answer. When I moved to Mountview, where I had real control over the content of the course, I started asking more experienced professional actor-friends the same question. 'Do you use The System?' Most said: 'No.' Two said: 'Not consciously.' Nonetheless at Mountview I made sure that the basics of Stan were covered in the first year.

We used to have rather valuable meetings of the acting tutors - staff and freelance - at which people shared their methods. These were fascinating and informative. However, they led to a Stanislavskian backlash. There are more teachers teaching it than actors practising it, I sometimes think. The attacks were strong. How could we ignore the basis of all actor training? Well, we weren't quite ignoring it, and, as for 'the basis of all actor training' - tell that to the Chinese, Japanese, to the Indonesians, etc, etc.

However, I do not luxuriate in the opinion that what I do is right, and all else is wrong. There are, as a vegetarian saying goes, 'many ways to skin an orange.'

So I proposed a test. In the next year - apart from the continuing basic 'Intro to Stanislavski' training in the first year - the 2nd year actors would be given one intensive term's training in the Stanislavskian Method. This would be handled by one of the most passionate of the proponents of The System. She would be given adequate time in classes and projects to teach them how to put it into practice. This would continue through half of the second term, when they would reach their Chekhov project. Then they would be encouraged to use The System - as they worked on the plays written at the time it was developed and first directed by its progenitor.

At the end of the process they would be given a questionnaire to answer. This would be anonymous to allow them to be completely honest. The questionnaire was a fairly simple affair - about 10 questions as I remember, covering each element of The System. Had they used it in preparation, in rehearsal, and how effective it had been for them? All three directors were Stanislavskians to prevent any sabotage. Three groups of 14 actors took on three plays. As always in a drama school the results were mixed. One really good *Three Sisters*, a so-so *Cherry Orchard*, and a curate's egg *Uncle Vanya* (a really good Sonya and Elena, but sadly deficient Vanya/Astrov. This was not the fault of the director - the actors were just not up to it, Stan or no).

Afterwards they dutifully filled in their forms and we collated the results.

Two of them had used The System throughout and thought it helped their performance. 16 had tried to put it into practice throughout, but found it took too much time. They felt ill-prepared when they reached performance. About half of these felt that the process got in the way of performance, as they were so busy thinking of all their actions and objectives, that they sometimes found they weren't listening to the other actors. (Thus breaking one of Stan's cardinal tenets: *'Acting is reacting'*).

That left 24. These ranged from eight of the laziest, who had not even bothered to try (and I must admit that this group was made up almost exclusively of the duffest actors on the course), to 16 who had made various levels of effort to try it, until it got in the way of their process.

A quote I remember was: *'I kept finding that the character's objectives were changing from day to day as the other characters grew and changed. I felt that if I stayed with yesterday's objective I would not be being honest or in-the-moment.'*

Several felt that actioning the play while reading it before the rehearsal process had started helped them to understand the narrative of the play.

Several others came to an even more interesting conclusion. They had all been taught to Mind-Map both character and play in the first year, and this had been reinforced in classes with me in the first term of the second year. One put it succinctly: *'Mind-Mapping is a modern and more effective method of actioning. I'm sure Stanislavski would've been using it if he was still around.'* (More on Mind-Mapping in Part 2)

Overwhelmingly this group felt that, apart from the above, The System was of little use to them.

Disregarding the eight lazy buggers, this left the final score at: Pro-Stan - 2; Indifferent to Stan - 32. I suspect that if the same test was done in any other drama school the results would be roughly the same.

The Stanislavskians protested that judging the efficacy of the work on a 14 hour-a-week-for-five-weeks rehearsal period was unfair. Given the drastically reduced rehearsal periods which have become the norm at all but the biggest, wealthiest companies in the real world, I am not sympathetic.

I became more and more convinced that the methods we were evolving were capable of providing the answer to Joe Alessi's question about not being in-the-moment: *'How the hell do I get there?'*

Image Streaming

One more development while at Mountview took me further down the road of Trusting the Actor.

I was in the old Compendium Bookshop in Camden - then one of the best bookshops in London, now sadly deceased. Looking through the Education section (which is where I originally found out about Mind-Mapping) I saw a spine proclaiming *The Einstein Factor!* (not sure about that !, but the whole cover screamed Exclamation Mark!). Written by one Win Wenger, it detailed various learning methods to turn ordinary old you into a genius. I opened it on to a page called Image Streaming and read about the technique. Halfway through, one of the stages rang a bell. 'That's what actors do,' I thought. (It might appear from this book that I spend a lot of time with my brow creased in thought, but actually I spend much more time vegging out in front of the telly).

I bought the book and read up the technique. It is a way of speeding up learning, has been tested on large groups of up to 2000 students in America, where it apparently upped the average mark by nearly 20%. Recently I read with joy that Scottish Universities are starting to teach it. It can be used for anything from biology to maths, literature to playing the piano.

It operates like this in its 'pure' form.

Let's say that we have a pianist who is studying a piece by Chopin. First make sure that s/he has an outside focus - another person taking notes, or a tape recorder. It is, Wenger says, not as effective without the outside focus; something my own work with the technique has borne out. The 'streamer' closes his/her eyes and concentrates on the piece, an aspect or image, and then begins to describe every image that enters their mind in as much detail as

to describe every image that enters their mind in as much possible, paying attention to the sensory as well as a visual. They must under no circumstances question or judge the images - just describe them. I tell my students that if a Boeing flies through their stream, piloted by a dinosaur in a polka dot nappy, they are to describe it.

In the pure system they go with the images up to a point and then bring Chopin himself into the scene. He watches them stream about his piece. The interesting bit comes next. It's called 'Putting on the Head'. What the pianist does is BECOME Chopin. That's what got me interested. The actor becomes the character.

A week or so after reading the book I found myself with a 2nd year Acting class. 14 students for three hours. We were to work on Chekhov scenes using the techniques described in Part 2. On the first morning I started with two women on the late night scene between Sonya and Yelena in *Uncle Vanya*. Neither knew the play. I gave them the briefest intro. Sonya is the horrible Prof. Serebryakov's daughter. Her mother has died and he has remarried one of his students, Yelena. She is much younger than he is and has obviously not married him for love. She has been sitting up with him. He suffers from gout and makes sure that she suffers with him. (He is probably one of the only one of his characters that Chekhov, a supreme humanist, hates.) Sonya, on the other hand, doesn't care for her stepmother, but does want a friend. She is in love with Dr Astrov. Astrov actually delivered her, loved her mother, and is smitten with Yelena. Sonya has just tried to find out whether he could love her, with no success. He thinks of her as a little girl...

That's all they were told. We worked for about 30 minutes with the basic exercises and then it was time to move on to the next couple and their new scene. While I think that actors should be fascinated by watching other actors working, learning from mistakes and adding the knowledge gained by the successes, many waste this chance. But I was dying to try out Image Streaming. Even though I didn't think it could possibly work this early in the process. They just didn't have sufficient knowledge. They hadn't even read or seen the play. In the pure version two people can do it together. I think this was evolved to help people who don't easily find the images in their head. Most people, when asked to close their eyes and visualise, get only blackness. I'm one of these. However, ask an actor to close their eyes and visualise and from most of them you get *War and Peace*.

I suggested that they sit opposite each other, close their eyes, and start by saying: 'She looks like...' and then follow whatever comes. I gave them my watch which had a timer. I set this for 10 minutes and said that when they heard the beep they should change to: 'I'. So: 'I am wearing...' etc. They should go for about another 10 minutes and then come back and tell me what had happened. Off they went.

At the tea break 50 minutes later they had not returned. I found them sitting in deep discussion in another rehearsal room. 'What happened?' I asked. They looked at me with big eyes. The word that has come to mark the use of this technique was applied for the first time. 'That was really WEIRD.' they both said. What was weird, I asked? Well, said the actor who had just been introduced to Yelena, 'I found myself in a rather odd coach, bumping along a country track. It didn't seem to have any springs. We drove up to this strange, small house.' She described it in some detail. 'I got out and walked up the steps and went in through the door. I could smell this other woman's house - and I hated the smell!' (My italics) The 'hated' was said with some passion. Every director's instinct in my body was rushing around yelling Huzzah's. An actor had made a connection which I couldn't imagine would have come from any amount of hours sitting around a table talking about character. 'The smell of another woman's house...'

Sonya had several similar sensory moments, not quite as dramatic.

The following day I took in a book and showed 'Yelena' a photograph. 'That's just like the house I saw.' she said. It was a photograph of Chekhov's dacha in the country-side outside Moscow. Dachas can share the same design, rather like bungalows, but this had come into the mind of someone who had no conscious memory of seeing any such pictures.

We started using it with each new scene. I was teaching the technique to three different groups. Sometimes, as one group filed out, the next group would file in. They had little chance to compare notes. Two different Olga's, working on the scene between the three sisters after the night of the fire in their town in Act 3, had visions of walking through burning buildings in intense heat. One said: 'My coat kept bursting into flames and I had to beat them out with my hands.' One Konstantin in *The Seagull*, streaming after working on the scene where his mother, Arkadina, re-bandages the head-wound from his attempted suicide, recalled: 'I was in this strange room. I've never seen one like it. Everything was made of wood - bed, cupboards, everything. The bed had a patchwork quilt covering it. I was lying on it with my ear pressed up against the wall.. I could hear my mother making love to Trigorin.' (Trigorin, Arkadina's long-term lover and an established writer, much envied and detested by Konstantin). Gooseflesh time again.

He was particularly worried by the room. 'I've never seen a room like it.' 'Yes you have.' I said. 'One day you were paging through a magazine and there was a picture of a room like that. You didn't even register it. Or you saw a film, documentary, or travelogue and the camera travelled through a room like that. You didn't even notice it. But it was trapped in the web of your brain, left its trace in those 200 million neurons. The character was rummaging around in your brain and found it. 'My room!!' he said.'

One more story from these classes. Early on I suggested that the three sisters image stream together. I listened in for a while. Olga and Irina were going great guns - Masha sat shtum - quiet - not a word. Afterwards I spoke to her. 'This technique doesn't seem to do much for you.' 'Absolutely not!' she said, 'She just wouldn't say anything in front of her sisters.' I gave her another listener and Masha unbundled all her secrets.

We quickly found that two people doing it at the same time was not working. Actors didn't need breathing time, as I said - *War and Peace* just flowed. So we adapted the technique. The actor streaming would give their notebook to the note taker - the outside focus. We found that this person, as with Masha, should not be a closely related character to the one doing the streaming. Lovers, enemies should be kept apart. There are occasions when related characters can stream with each other but, for the most part, this should be avoided.

I began to use image streaming in productions. It had the most extraordinary effect, and, of all the techniques I teach to actors, this remains the one that most continue to use. Early on I would worry about the intricate detail in which actors - especially the women - would describe the 'set'. Surely this would get in the way when they finally arrived on a real set which bore no resemblance to the one the character had drawn from their imagination? 'Not at all', said one actor after the other. 'It doesn't matter what is onstage - the set is in my head - I just use whatever's physically there.'

Odd things began to happen. While working on the scenes, or devising, or running a class teaching the technique I could have as many as six or seven people image streaming at the same time in the same room. The first time this particular thing happened was quite early on. We were devising a play. I was still using the method of two people streaming together at the same time. One couple - two women - were 'debriefing' after a session. 'You know,' said one to the other, 'when you were describing that scene?' - she said what it was - 'I was looking at it! I didn't start looking at it because you were describing it. I was looking at it and then you started describing it!' This continued to happen to them as they developed their scenes.

It, however, also happens rather strangely (I'm trying to avoid the use of the word 'weird') in rooms with several people streaming. Someone working on one side of the room will say to someone who was working in another corner exactly what I've quoted above. What this means I do not know.

For me the Everest of Weird came during rehearsals for a play - *Matchstalk Man* - which I was directing for a run at the Actor's Centre, London.

We were rehearsing in a room above a pub in Camden where two of our actors were employed as bar staff. The play features a psychotic drug dealer and his ditsy girlfriend, plus another young man who spends a lot of his time tied up in a chair being harangued by the psychotic. They are holed-up in a deserted warehouse for reasons that don't much matter here. Halfway through the play another woman appears. It all ends happily with everybody apparently dying in an explosion accidentally set off by the psychotic in the final action of the play.

The play was written by a student of mine at Mountview under the pseudonym of Billy Woods. It had first been staged with great success at the Edinburgh Festival. The offer to do it at the Actors Centre found only the actor playing the psychotic lead available. I was brought in to direct him and an entirely new cast. The man-in-the-chair and the new woman turn out in the end to be brother and sister. You get this information within five lines of the end of the play. Originally the two characters were set in the North of England somewhere, but, as both of the new cast members came from Scotland, we decided, with the approval (well, actually, he didn't give damn) of the playwright, to relocate them there.

From very early on they had problems. Who were they? What was their background? What were the 'why's' of their lives that had lead them to this place and time? At the end of one afternoon's rehearsal this reached crisis point. I phoned 'Billy'. 'Mark,' (his real name) I said, 'who are they?' Etc., etc. 'I don't know,' was his helpful response. 'You must!' I said, 'You wrote the bloody thing!' 'Sorry,' he said - not sounding the smallest bit apologetic. 'No idea.' Did I tell you about the murderous impulses I have stifled over my career towards writers? I badgered him. All he could come up with was: 'They're half-brother and sister.... I think.' After 20 minutes happily spent plotting his mysterious disappearance and death I was left with two frustrated actors drowning in the deep end.

OK, I said, tomorrow we image stream to see what we can find. I arranged for Victoria to come in at 9.30. I would be her outside focus/note-taker. She had a shift in the pub starting at 11. Ian would come in then and I would take notes on his stream till approximately 12.30. Ian went off to his evening shift in the pub; Victoria's boyfriend picked her up, and I went home to find the number for the Mafia hitman I had noted down somewhere. 'What's one writer less in the world?' - to crudely borrow a quote from the doctor in *Three Sisters*.

The following morning I started off with Victoria, blearily, at 9.15. She plunged into the stream and, by 10.45, an entire, fascinating story had emerged.

To her surprise she began to stream the story of a 14-year-old Glasgow prostitute. Mother died, father remarried. She hated new stepmother and left the family home and a younger brother - a seven-year-old - to go onto the streets. She was taken up by a pimp and went to live in his house in a posh area of Glasgow, where he kept her, an older prostitute of 30 or so, and another younger girl of 16. Every evening they would be sent out into the centre to troll for business. There wasn't much detail about the how and where of this.

She was aware that her brother was being mistreated by the stepmother and, as soon as she was settled into her new 'home', she determined to rescue him. Here the stream shifted into what seemed like real-time.

'I go back to my home. It's night. I know my dad and stepmother will be out at the pub. I still have my key. I go into the house. It's dark and gloomy and quiet. I go upstairs and open the door to the bedroom I shared with my brother. He is lying on the bed crying. He has wet the bed again and knows that she will beat him when she comes home. I clean him up and dress him. I pack his clothes and take him down the stairs and out into the streets before they get back.'

She then described the journey from this harsh, poorer part of Glasgow, down onto a pathway along the river Clyde, and up into the posh suburb. Back at the house she had to argue her pimp into taking the boy in, but he did and things settled down. The pimp and her brother would spend the evening watching telly. Coming back from her stint with the others one night she sensed something was wrong. A week later she once again felt that something was happening. She grilled her brother. He finally admitted that the pimp had hit him. While the pimp was away one day she packed herself and her brother and left.

The stream ended here.

It was a rather florid story but better than the nothing we had. 'Where did that all come from?' Victoria asked. None of this cast had been at Mountview when I started experimenting with image streaming. 'Haven't the vaguest idea,' I said. We discussed it a bit further. I felt the idea of a teenage prostitute was a bit hackneyed. She wasn't wild about it either 'but that was what she was in the stream.' We left it at that.

Ian arrived; they said 'Hi' in passing. I didn't want them to listen into each other, or even talk about it until after they had both done at. Ian jumped straight in. He was five and lying in his bed in the dark. It was evening and his father and stepmother were out at the pub. He knew that she would hit him when they came back as he had wet his bed. She hated it when he wet his bed, which happened two or three times a week. He tried to stop but he couldn't. His father didn't protect him, just told him he was a baby. He was crying. The door opened. He was terrified. It was his sister, who had abandoned him when she left after a huge screaming row with her father. She cleaned him up, dressed him, packed some clothes, took his hand and led him from the house, watching out for their parents. She led him down to the pathway along the river. (I have asked various Scottish students over the years, and apparently this riverside walk, linking a poorer and a richer part of Glasgow, exists). They went up some stairs.

As though my disbelieving gooseflesh were not aroused enough, he continued: 'We're walking up the road to this big house. Light is streaming out of its windows. It looks sooo warm. My sister knocks on the door it opens and...' (I can still remember the pause and the look of wonder on his face) 'there's a family! There's a dad and a mom, and there's a daughter. She's about 16. They welcome us in. It's sooo lovely. I have my own room and a lovely bed, and, every evening the mom and the girls go out and I sit and watch telly with the dad. He's a very nice.' There was another pause. This time his face clouded over. 'One evening I say something wrong and he hits me. He's very sorry and he makes me promise not to tell my sister. A week later he does it again - twice. My sister knows something's wrong, even though I haven't told her. She forces me to tell her, and I do. She packs us up and we leave the house.'

The stream ended. I gave myself time for the hair standing on end to subside, then said: 'So when did you and Vicky get together to make that up?' It always takes a bit of time for people to surface after a good image stream. They feel rather 'space-y' for a while. 'What do you mean?' he asked. 'Did you meet her last night, or phone her?' 'I was working here in the bar till 11.30. Then I went straight home. I haven't spoken to her.' 'Pull the other one,' I said. 'You must have worked it out together.' Ian had a rather short temper. 'Look, all that bloody stuff just came out now, as I was doing this weird thing?' 'OK', I said, 'let's go downstairs and tell Vicki.'

We found her sitting in the pub. 'Tell her.' I said. He started off describing his stream. I had to fill in some detail as it is fairly common that people don't remember saying some of the things. Vicki - who is very excitable - started to scream around the time of wetting the bed. By the time we reached the house, everyone in the pub was looking at us.

I was still suspicious. Actors love wind-ups. However, it became more and more clear that they were equally shaken by the coincidences. The only differing detail was his age. Five or seven? They had quite an argument about that until the realisation dawned for them that they were talking about different areas of time and Ian had to move his age up - to seven. I finally capitulated and believed them. What mostly helped me do this was a different perception of the house, the look of wonder on Ian's face as his character found 'a family'.

I have done many image streams since and the number of these odd 'coincidences' steadily increases. The same colours appear, rooms and locations share similarities. One of the oddest came at the end of rehearsal period on *The Seagull*, working with first-year students at Guildhall.

We had had a lot of time to rehearse the play through an entire term. On one of the last afternoons of rehearsal, with not enough time to do another run of the play, I suggested we do one more image stream. This one to focus on the moments after the final line: 'Konstantin has shot himself.' Don't know why I did this. Just interested to find out really. It worked very well for the actor playing Konstantin. His stream was short and to the point, but did help him with his final feelings of complete despair and hopelessness.

The odd part came with two other streams. Masha, who has always loved Konstantin, had an equally short stream. She walked out of the house, avoided seeing the body, which everyone else had rushed to do. Went straight down to the lake, waded in, and drowned. At the end of this the actor was in floods of tears.

Strangely her mother had no room for her daughter in her stream, concentrating, as always, on her lover, the doctor, Dorn.

The rehearsal room was fairly small and the group had split into two for these streams. Arkadina was in the other room. When we reassembled and shared the happenings she stunned us all. She had gone to her son's body, but then she said: 'Something is worrying me. Where's Masha? I leave the body of my son. I know where she's gone. I run down to the lake. I hope I'm not too late. I stand on the shore. In the moonlight I can see this dark lump drifting on the water. I wade in. I'm crying. I pick her up and hold her. I don't want her to die. It is too late.'

'How did you know?' asked the actor playing Masha. 'I don't know. I just knew. It was the first thought that came into my mind as I was holding Konstantin's dead body.'

This was a real surprise for both of the actors. 'I didn't even know she knew I existed,' said Masha. 'Rather oddly,' said Arkadina, 'I realised I'd always wanted a daughter. I knew she was Dr Dorn's daughter, and I'd always envied her mother - Polina - because he loved her.'

For those of you who know the play this opened a very large and fertile can of worms.

Image Streaming is a very powerful tool for giving a character access to the actor's imagination.

On Emotion

As I said at the beginning - emotion is at the heart of this book. All theatre - you could possibly say all human life - revolves around it.

Just what exactly is emotion? It seems such an easy question. We're always 'indulging' in it. We fall in love, get angry, depressed, sad, laugh, marvel at a sunset, feel safe and warm in our morning bed, irritated to leave it, glad when we meet a friend, p'd off at a motorist cutting us up ... the list goes on and on and on. Feelings, moods, passions, sensibilities - all, arguably, come under the heading of emotions.

While writing this book I thought I'd better do a little swotting on the subject. The literature is vast. Everywhere civilisation leaves a record there seems to be someone jotting down thoughts. For us Westerners the Greeks seem to have made the first real stabs at definition. The Stoics, Plato, Aristotle, et al. Then the Romans got in the act with Quintilian's system of gestures and poses - to avoid upsetting the bodily humours.

Later, a partial list would include the likes of Darwin, Francois Delsarte, Descartes, Aaron Hill, David Hume. In the late 19th and early 20th century the floodgates opened. In 1884 William James and Carl Lange independently formulated the James-Lange theory - much misunderstood - which led to various other double-barrelled theories such as the Cannon-Bard, which argued the opposite to the James-Lange.

Freud and Jung opened up the mind and theories came tumbling out. There are Cognitive Theories and Perceptual Theories, the Affective Events Theory and the Two-factor Theory, not to mention the Component Process Model and Dimensional Appraisal Theory. There are even Hybrid Theories which mix and match between the others. Psychiatry examined it, psychology examined it; everything from anthropology, criminology, economics, ethology, linguistics, philosophy, sociology examined it. There are those who base their studies on emotions and their relation to facial expression - Paul Ekman, Nico Fridja. There's even a concept of Emotional Labour, and, more scarily, Affective Computing.

The neuroscientists joined in. The ones who enabled me to understand the function of the brain. Joseph LeDoux, Anthony Damasio, Michael Gazzaniga.

At the moment - and this will change - there's a bit of a barney going on between Neuroscientists and Emotion Theorists.

I did try to understand all these - promise - but it all seemed to me to be a fight about definitions and physical manifestations, with nothing beginning to describe, explain, what my own experience of emotion is.

So, instead of a learned treatise, all I can offer is my highly personal 'understanding' of the subject. As always this is told by way of chronicle and anecdote.

To begin at the beginning. When I first began to wonder about the feelings that gripped me - instead of just allowing them to take me over – I was not the sort of person that spent much time analysing anything, really.

I did notice things. I had always had access to the various basics. Anger at my parents for not allowing me enough pocket money to buy that extra ice-cream. Pleasure at my various (small) sporting triumphs. An inexplicable feeling when the girls in my road suddenly began to develop in ways different to me.

There was, however, a distinct lack. My parents would take my sister and I out for Sunday drives. My father had an unerring ability to find bumpy, dusty, gravel roads to out-of-the-way places. One of my major childhood memories revolves around the smell of roast chicken and gravel dust in combination. My mother would put a foil-wrapped chicken in a slow oven overnight, and it would fall obligingly into tender pieces for us to devour the following day - as we sat overlooking a mountain, a valley, a sea.

At some stage there would be a view or a sunset, and everyone would sigh: 'Isn't that beautiful!' Everyone except me. I would sit there, looking at the vista, and think: 'What are they on about? That's just another mountain with late-afternoon pink highlighting it from one side.' Or 'Another sea with sun streaming through clouds. The gold colour is quite nice ...'

I noticed this so many times that I was beginning to worry. Why could I not see this beauty that seemed so obvious to everyone else? So worried that I even discussed the problem with my three best friends. Fortunately for me, Carl, Tivver, and Jumbo all agreed with me.

It was a mystery.

The mystery plagued me until late one night in January or February, 1962 (forgive my imprecision - there are times I regret my inability to diarise), when the most extraordinary, the most wonderful thing happened to me. A woman's lips touched mine. My virginal, untouched lips.

This is a memory I will die with.

I had been, quite unknowingly, teetering on the edge of a cliff, hovering on the brink of a state known as 'falling in love'. This soft, butterfly kiss toppled me over. The feeling as I fell defies any description. Later, at 3am, my Vespa scooter and I floated back to my digs. I was in love.

Suddenly the mystery was no mystery any more. Or perhaps an even deeper one. Around me colours I had never noticed clamoured now in crisp sharpness for my attention. The Mountain (Table Mountain - I'm a Capetonian) revealed its full grandeur, its spectacular beauty. The sea around me - blue, green, white-capped - glittered with diamonds as the sun sparkled and bounced off it...

I could go on and on with this purple prose. I hope you've been there. You will know. If you haven't, don't worry - the most amazing experience of your life awaits you. I'm quite envious.

Major league emotions now entered my life. Not all of them pleasant. Loss is one of the worst. Jealousy - oh dear, that was a painfully uncontrollable battle. Fortunately, at about 27, another change took place. I'm not quite sure why - maybe I just learnt to trust - but that destructive emotion was unable to torment me any more.

The Goddess bearing all these gifts took up residence in my life, and I in hers, and my real training began.

The ordinary, common-or-garden, daily human emotions continued to function in me. However, I was now in a relationship with an actor, and the world of theatre opened itself to me.

Right from the beginning it was blindingly obvious that emotion played a central role. Theatre is designed to change you, to alter your perspectives, to open up new horizons. It does this through the strange process whereby we are drawn into a story. I call it the 'Once-Upon-A-Time' syndrome.

Just as Nigel Hawthorne had sucked me into Pinter's *The Caretaker* earlier, I now found myself - on a very regular basis - being seduced and beguiled by theatre.

I still wasn't much involved in analysis. I laughed, I cried (I'm a wonderful audience), I felt, occasionally, what later I came to know as Catharsis.

If you had asked me - and no one did - I would have opined that, as far as the theatre experience of emotion went, you would listen to the words, pick up cues from their meaning, tone, the actor's body language and, as a result, feel.

Even after I began to direct, this remained my understanding of the process. As far as I can determine, there are many theorists and neuroscientists who would still, today, broadly agree with this view (in a much more intellectual and structured way).

However, there was a complication. It came in that moment I spoke of at the beginning of this book - the moment when an actor stands alone (even when other actors share the stage), and something happens. Some mysterious process which leaves me, the audience, in tears, involved, deeply moved.

I've seen this happen too many times to question it. Have you ever stood behind an audience when an actor enters such a moment? Watched as all the heads tip towards the side? It's a very strange communal phenomenon. Think of yourself in a moment of empathy; observe yourself next time. You will find your head inclining to left or right and, probably, your hand on your chest.

Emotion happens in real life, but it can also be recreated on stage. By the actor.

Brecht fought hard against this moment, which he thought caused the audience to lose their critical faculties. I don't agree and, ultimately, neither - in my opinion - did Brecht. His great later plays, especially Mother *Courage* and The *Caucasian Chalk Circle,* shamelessly exploit this power.

Just think of those moments in *Mother Courage* when she has to deny that the dead bodies being presented to her are her children? From this came the misunderstood concept of The Silent Scream. I have seen three productions of this play. In one of these the moments were acted out in a way which looked rather like the famous, posed photograph of Helene Weigel. As an exercise in face-pulling disconnection it left me not only un-moved, but also angry.

The other two - Judi Dench at the Barbican, my wife at The Market in Johannesburg - left the audience reeling. There was no questioning the all-encompassing pain of a mother who has not only lost her child, but even worse, caused that loss.

If those moments don't work, the play becomes a rather dull tract. In both the actor just turned her face away from the scene and towards the audience. No 'Silent Scream'. Actually neither seemed to have any expression on their face at all. But pain streamed out inexorably – pervading the audience - helping us to understand, viscerally, how that mother - how all mothers - felt.

I went on unquestioning, right into the 80s, my unexamined theories undisturbed.

Then, one day in about July, 1985 (mislaid my diary ...) I had the strangest experience. My first Pauline Moment.

It was a Sunday. I had been playing cricket, had taken three wickets AND a sharpish slip catch (than which there are few better feelings in life). It was a balmy summer's eve as I arrived home. I was looking forward to a lovely evening meal (my wife's acting talent was almost matched by her ability as a cook).

I felt at peace with the world. As I arrived outside our flat I saw one of my neighbours and his son standing outside their home opposite. The parents had divorced - quite amicably it had seemed from the outside - and the father would collect his son for the weekends. They looked as though they had had a good day.

I pulled around the corner, found a parking spot. As I walked back up the road, I met the father leaving. We had a brief chat. He was very upbeat. I went on to my front door.

As I stretched out my hand to put the key in the lock I heard two words spoken quite plainly and, at the same time, an absolute cloud of pain swamped me from behind. I turned. The young boy was still standing alone at his door. His father was long gone. All he had said was: 'Bye, dad.' He disappeared inside.

As I tried to insert the key my hand was shaking uncontrollably. Finally, using two hands, I managed to open the door.

Three flights up my wife looked at me with immediate concern. 'What happened?' I told her. She made me some tea.

What I couldn't understand, I said, was that a) I had had no inkling that there was any problem - the father was cheerful, I hadn't even seen the boy standing in his doorway; and b) I had my back to the 'happening', and the boy's voice was about as close to emotionless as you could get.

Where had this cloud of pain come from?

For the first time in my life I began to attempt to analyse what had happened. I still have no rational answer. But now, when I first talked to young actors about emotion and its transmission, I tell them a 'bowdlerised' version of that story, and then state my anecdotal, unprovable theory:

Emotion is a physical force - an energy field - which is communicated, transmitted through the air.

And, just in case they think that these are the ramblings of a senile old man, I take out my mobile phone. 'When I switch this on' (mobile phones should always be switched off in classes and in the theatre) 'it might just ring, and I will be able to speak to someone many miles away. How does this voice reach me? Invisibly through the air. If you have a dusting of iron filings on a sheet of paper and hold a magnet some way away beneath them, you can make them reshape themselves into various patterns.'

The world is full of energy - transmitted in ways we can't see. Radio, TV, radioactivity, X-rays - mass hysteria.

As I attempted to grapple with what had happened I remembered reading Elias Canetti's *Crowds and Power*. Remembered being in a crowd demonstrating outside St George's Cathedral in Cape Town in the 70s - of how the crowd suddenly seemed, simultaneously, to scatter and run - like a flock of birds, even though the police facing us had done nothing more than begin a quiet, though unmistakably menacing, advance on us. I distinctly remember feeling a panicked part of a greater whole.

So there you are - Brian Astbury's *Theory of Emotion*. I await, impatiently, the invention of a meter like a Geiger counter - which measures invisible radioactivity - that you can hold up in front of an actor, or, for that matter, any other human being experiencing real, true emotion, and measure on a dial the amount of emotion emanating from them.

Until such time I rely on my own internal Geiger counter.

The wonderful thing about such transmission of emotion is that good actors can recreate it. They can act like some strange two-legged wireless transmitter. The pain, the joy, the anger, the sorrow flows from them, no through them - from the character and into the audience – like wonderful, pure, clean water flows from the mains out through a tap.

Our job as teachers and directors is to enable the actor to make the connections which open this tap.

All the actor needs is supreme courage, an openness to experience, and a lack of vanity.

A Word about Vanity...

Why this last attribute? Well, sadly, I've seen more actors destroyed by vanity than have died spiritually by any other means. I tell my students to be careful of vanity. 'Every time someone applauds, or says: 'You were marvellous!', they are dripping acid onto you. This will rust you until you crumble to dust.'

As I said I have seen this process close-up and with some big international names. It is incredibly destructive. The person completely loses perspective and now only listens to praise. All critical faculties fly out of the window.

I had a very minor experience of my own in this area which might illustrate this.

Above I spoke of telling my students a 'bowdlerised' version of the incident with a father and son. Why 'bowdlerised'?

One day I was sitting facing a group of students on a LAMDA course, then called the Overseas Course drawing as it did on students from all over the world - mainly America and Canada. They were mostly experienced graduates coming to London for what amounted to a Brush-up-your-Shakespeare course. (It also covered Restoration and Chekhov/The Russians in a packed year).

I was doing a term with them on scenes from Shakespeare. They were divided into three groups of 12. I was meeting the first on a Monday afternoon. I introduced myself, asked each of them to tell us who they were and why they were here, and then initiated a general discussion on acting and theatre. The subject of emotion came up. I flew my theory of 'emotion-in-the-air'. I told the story of the father and son. Even at a five-year remove (at that stage) I found the emotion still overwhelming me. It was obvious that this had also communicated itself to the class. We moved on to Shakespeare and *Othello*.

The second group arrived on the Tuesday. The same process. The same discussion. Emotion once again raised its head. As I, once again, flew my theory a small, quiet voice inside me whispered: 'Don't tell that story.' However, I found myself on a natural path which led without strain to The Story. Once again I was moved. Once again there were tears among the listeners.

Sitting on the Tube going home, reviewing the class to myself, the voice said, really quite loudly now: 'Don't tell that story again.'

On the Friday I met the last group. Same process. Same discussion. Hello Emotion. In a slightly out-of-body experience I heard myself deliberately construct the discussion so that it led to The Story. The words came out of me. I felt nothing. The group looked back at me with 'So what?' expressions on their faces. The Story which illustrated the whole point I was trying to make had fallen flat on its face.

On the way home I promised The Story that I would never tell it again unless I absolutely knew that it was necessary. I apologised abjectly for my vanity. I had really enjoyed the effect I was having on the class.

I had not understood that it was not me that was having this effect - it was the original pain of that small, lonely boy. I was only its conduit. I was deeply ashamed of having betrayed him, using his pain for my own selfish ends.

I asked for a special dispensation for this book.

I have subsequently told the 'bowdlerised' version many times. Sometimes I am allowed to feel a small part of that original pain again. I battle with my overweening vanity, as it affects the listeners. In these moments I gain a small understanding of the problems facing actors as they try to recreate and communicate the emotions of their characters to their audience.

Actors, beware vanity. Characters will only share themselves with you if your intentions are pure, and your courage is great.

I have one final, cautionary tale.

It is related to the process I've just described; sometimes comes as the result of vanity, but more often through an unknowing, often subconscious application of a particularly dangerous technique of acting.

I call it the theory of *Holy Cannibalism*.

But first – another digression…..

As actors open themselves up to their characters all kinds of things happen. To communicate the character's feelings, as I've said, the actor must make a connection, or more often, a set of connections to those feelings. Frequently this is a big ask and, as I set out in the chapter 'Even my dog hasn't died', an ask fraught with problems.

Very few of us have murdered anyone. How many of you have inflicted what Hitler did on humanity? Yet somewhere some actor will find themselves wrestling with the problem of trying to understand why an abuser, a murderer, possibly even Hitler, carried out their crime.

I do not, cannot, will not believe that people are born evil. I believe that people are twisted out of shape by their upbringing and environment, and that, if we don't attempt to understand HOW this happens, then we are responsible for the fact that this cycle will keep repeating itself. More human beings will continue to be bent out of shape, and take their vengeance on the rest of us.

If we continue, for instance, to ignore the fact that child abuse is handed, for the most part, from generation to generation; continue to refuse proper training and support for our overloaded social workers; for the exhausted young parents, battling to survive and bring up small children in a hostile and uncaring world; support for the orphans dumped into care, where some are abused even further; if we continue to hide our head in the sand because, well, let's face it, it's much more important to spend that trillion pounds on a new nuclear defence system which, if ever used, would result in the end for us all!; if we continue to play the Three Monkeys with these issues - and please listen carefully to this - *then it is our responsibility* the next time some poor child known only by an initial - A, B, C - is discovered too late in the bottom drawer, dying of malnutrition, covered in cigarette burns and bruises, bones broken, brains jarred. *It is the responsibility of each and every one of us.*

I'm sorry if this makes you feel helpless. I sympathise. What can we possibly do?

Well, in the first instance, we live in a democracy. If there is no one to vote for - politicians generally being more interested in power than fighting for the dispossessed - then form your own party. You have a voice - let it be heard!

If this is too impractical for you, the second alternative is simpler - anyone can do it. *Attempt to understand.* Try not to get involved in a tabloid-style baying for vengeance. 'Hang the Swine!!' was the reasoned headline I once saw emblazoned on the front page of a 'newspaper' which would have had more dignity if it had been used to make toilet rolls.

This kind of blood-lust is difficult to resist. Hearing the tales of inhuman savagery, listening to the sobs of the aggrieved victims, it is difficult not to want an eye for an eye. Go on, go down that road. Hang the Swine. But when the next Swine does the unspeakable to the next victim, please remember that, by refusing to understand, identify in time, heal the perpetrator, you bear a part of the responsibility for what happened to that next victim.

We live as part of a society. The privileges of that society also carry responsibilities.

What can we do?

I left South Africa because I could see no way through the morass. Fortunately Nelson Mandela could. The process he used involved understanding and forgiveness.

Learn the lesson.

My apologies for the rant. Well, no, I'm not really apologising.

So, how do we learn the lessons?

We need to understand that we are being taught 'lessons' all the time – some good and valuable; others which can be deeply harmful and affect us in ways which are almost invisible to us – until we understand how they're delivered and how they function.

We receive these messages daily through newspapers, TV, advertising, the attitudes of family and friends, the examples of role models in reality and fiction.

I have heard the following cry many times throughout my life

So….. let's deal with it….

'Why does everything have to have a message?!'...

I choose to work through the medium of the arts. Through stories and metaphors. All the arts have the ability to pass on this understanding. Not to preach, not to lecture - to create metaphors of understanding. Sadly many artists abdicate this responsibility. They just create – ignoring the fact that everything you create has some message or other. 'Oh no,' people used to say to me, 'not the 'message' again! Why does everything have to have a message?!' I have news for people who think this way: EVERY story or play or film or soap has a message. Disagree? Ask most artists why they create art and a substantial majority, especially in the written arts, will respond: 'Because I want to communicate ...'

I leave you to ponder what is contained in a 'communication'. And on the responsibility of the communicator as to how the 'communication' is received, and what effect it has on the listener.

I grew up in the area immediately after the Second World War. In my late teens I had a fixed set of attitudes and beliefs. The early political ones I spoke of above. More ridiculously I 'knew' that I would finally meet this beautiful woman who would be 3-4 years younger than I was, and a virgin! Go ahead, laugh. Fortunately for me I met a divorcee with three children who was 16 years older than I was - exciting much gossip in the innocent early days of the 60s - before the Sexual Revolution. I was on the receiving end of a crash course in Changing Attitudes.

Where did I get these attitudes? Certainly not from my father and mother. As gentle and wise as they were they did not discuss such things with me. I learned from books, but mainly - film. Film after film washed this message over me until it became an accepted belief.

Everything has a message. If you don't want to end up blindly accepting tenets with which you probably wouldn't agree if you devoted a minute's thought to them, then you had better start getting used to the fact that propagandists really know how to use this system - and that they're targeting YOU.

I'm exaggerating? In the early 80s my wife and I had a lovely game. I was unable to work in London yet; she had the odd afternoon off from her labours at the National. We would watch matinee films on the telly. Many of these were the sort of Betty Davis/Barbara Stanwyck black-and-white melodramas made during and shortly after the Second World War and the Korean War that followed.

The game - such as it was - involved the moment in the film when the 'heroine' committed adultery. 'She's dead!' we would cry. (Afternoon film matinee-ing is a simple pleasure). And, sure enough, at the end of the film the adulteress would pay the price. Mostly death, but, for instance, in *Jezebel* Ms Davis loses everything that means anything in her life because she dared to wear a red dress to the ball, instead of the more generally accepted white number! Am I being simplistic when I say that the message of that film for me is: 'Don't step out of line. Conform!'?

Why the rash of 'The Adulteress Dies!' films? Well, during the Second World War millions of soldiers left wives behind to fight The Last Just War. Whether consciously or not the film-makers sent out the message to their forlorn wives - stay faithful, adultery is a dangerous business.

I'm not necessarily saying this was a wrong message. I am saying it was a definite Message.

Another possible way a 'message' has affected all of us. In the immediate post-war atmosphere many nations - appalled by the slaughter – move towards abolition of the death penalty. The way has been led by the United Nations, and every year the list of countries supporting this move grows. Prominent among those voting against UN resolutions for a moratorium on the death penalty are America, China, Iran.

In America there was initial post-war support for the move against the death penalty. And some states abolished it. Opposition reached an all-time low of 42% in 1966. However, despite a Supreme Court ruling in a case in 1977 that the death penalty was an unconstitutional punishment, and subsequent limits to the death penalty in the next decade, public support rose to an all-time high in favour of 80% in 1994. Recently this has begun to recede again, but many States retain the final penalty. In 2004 a poll revealed that, when not offered an alternative sentence, 71% supported the death penalty. As I do a final edit of this book the TV news tells me that in Arkansis yesterday a man was executed by a firing squad! This is the 21st Century.

Given the worldwide move against the death penalty after the Second World War, why is it that the people of one of our greatest democracies have become so much in favour of this barbaric sentence?

You may of course agree with them. I am more interested in how this came about. In understanding this process.

It's only my own personal theory, of course, but throughout the 60s and 70s right up to now, actually, a stream of films has come out of Hollywood all carrying the same 'communication': Some people are so horrible, so 'evil', that there is only one thing to be done with them - kill them.

If you can't think of any example of this genre, then you obviously haven't been going to the movies for the last 40 years or so. Given a jog to my memory, I could possibly come up with more than 100. And not obscure, B-movies either. They starred Clint Eastwood ('Are you feeling lucky?' - didn't we all feel a sense of happy satisfaction as he blew the ugly, unshaven, unkempt, obviously 'evil' villains away?), Mel Gibson - come on, you can all add to the canon.

One film that did attempt to go against this vigilante trend failed almost completely at the box office - despite starring the up-and-coming Michael Douglas. However, it is proving to have legs. I often see it in our own schedules now. *The Star Chamber* is worth a viewing. It has the guts to challenge our assumption that villains all look the same - and are very easy to spot. We all know what a villain looks like. The stereotypes are constantly thrust in front of us by film after film.

One evening in the 90s I came home, switched on the telly, and began to prepare my supper. On the screen a cheery, plump Uncle-figure was smilingly chatting. I smiled back at him. I would certainly have entrusted my granddaughters to his care. Then his words seeped into my brain.

With his broad and friendly smile he was saying: 'For the first few days I keep them chained to the bed. But then they lose the desire to run away ...' By then I was pinned to the screen as he told us how he had killed several young men after keeping them imprisoned for several days. I had an uncle who looked just like him. He was a favourite of mine.

Other men who did not fit the stereotype: John Wayne Gacy (33 murders – a respected member of his community – fundraiser for charity through the "Jolly Joker" Clown Club), Robert Berdella (6 murders), Jeffrey Dahmer murdered 17 young men, cutting them up and keeping some of the pieces in his fridge. Seen a picture of Ted Bundy? Dr Harold Shipman?

Films generally choose not to deal in such subtleties. It's pantomime. Hiss the villain. This really prepares you for the Dennis Nilsen that lives next door and looks ... just like us.

This kind of thinking ends up with people battering on a house where the owner has a sign proclaiming that he is a 'Paediatrician' as they bay down the streets looking for paedophiles. In case you don't know - this actually happened.

As these attitudes, these stereotypes, these communications wash over us - day by day - we unconsciously accept their tenets.

We have to understand this process. This will enable us to be able to deal rationally and logically, not blindly in some animalistic desire for vengeance. Understanding the problem and its causes enables us to find ways to heal and to halt the cycle.

Theatre can help. So can film. The artists who work in them need to take responsibility for their actions.

By way of this large digression, we arrive back at the poor actor who is opening up his/her psyche to the depredations of a character whose experience of pain is infinitely worse than the vast majority of us, thankfully, ever experience. But, as I've said, watching the actor communicating this emotion to us can help us, prepare us - just in case it does ever happen. And for those to whom it is already happened - grant them the comforting feeling that they are not alone.

So, in order to understand, the actors enter the world of the character. I actually always feel that the reverse happens - actors allow the characters to enter them, to explore all the riches of their subconscious (as discussed under Image Streaming) and use whatever they find in order to create themselves.

For some - who have not even lost a dog yet - this will mainly consist of those pure baby emotions (see Rebirthing) in any of many and various combinations (the colour theory of emotion has a validity here) that will create the imaginative response to the characters' needs.

In others, the character will find more concrete and accessible, understood images and feelings. The conscious experience of pain and loss, once out of the un-understanding world of the baby, is there - open to the needs of the character. There are many systems based on the use of such memories.

They are VERY dangerous.

If the character should ask for a memory of trauma or death - and you have experienced this - what should you do?

Do you know about cannibalism? That it generally isn't about snacking on somebody tasty-looking? It has a deeper significance. For some, a portion of the vanquished enemy is eaten to make sure that said enemy goes directly to the deepest dungeons of hell without passing Go.

For others, if a deeply-loved relative dies, it is your sacred duty to eat a portion of this person - to protect them in the next world.

Holy cannibalism. Unthinkable to us, but an act of the purest love and sacrifice for them.

So, should the character decide that he or she needs access to that memory of someone precious passing on, my answer is that, yes, the memory can be used. It would be almost impossible not to.

HOWEVER - forgive the caps - this whole paragraph should come in them - HOWEVER, you should NEVER, NEVER use such a memory to trigger an onstage emotion.

If such a connection has been made the actor should treat it with care and reverence, trusting that it will be there when needed. Do not go looking for it.

I can't stress this enough. If the actor uses such a trigger through vanity (as I did in my class), but even more dangerously, if an actor is forced to repeat this every night through a run in an inadequately prepared situation, the ghosts of that situation will come back to haunt you. And that haunting can have catastrophic results.

Let me tell you how.

In the late 80s my wife worked for one last time with Athol. The play was *The Road to Mecca*. A three-hander, it had been inspired by a South African artist, Helen Martins, who had lived and died, without recognition, in a small hamlet called Nieu Bethesda in the Karoo region of South Africa. Very late in her life she had - with no previous training or experience in art - suddenly begun to convert her house and garden. Internally the walls and ceilings were coated with coloured, crushed glass in huge designs. There were many mirrors and many candles.

Externally she filled her garden with statues of owls and camels and Wise Men and mermaids sculpted out of wire-frames covered in cement. More crushed glass formed eyes. Above all this, suspended on wires, hangs the word 'Oos' - Afrikaans for 'East'. In one corner was a large outdoor cote filled with white doves. Helen Martins had become fascinated with the idea of Mecca, the pilgrims who travelled to worship there, and its flock of white doves. Where the owls came from I have no idea.

The small village, while doing their best to care for her, thought, with some justification, she had gone insane. Possibly she had. Was Van Gogh mad? Is some form of madness a condition of great art? Or maybe the artists are the only sane people? This is not a subject for now.

Apparently only one person had responded to her art - a young woman, visiting from the big city.

Finally, at the age of 78, crippled with arthritis, almost blinded by the glass dust (a coffee-grinder was used to crush the bottles), her work finished, Helen Martins took her own life.

Athol took the situation and based his play around it. It is not a biographical play. The actual young woman was, I am told, horrified to find out what the character suggested by her part in Helen's life did. The third character is Marius - a Dutch Reformed minister. Every South African Afrikaner town has one. The original had made it his charitable business to look after Helen. Athol used his artist's licence to set up a situation in which the play can - rather wonderfully - explore themes universal to all artists. As a vision of the artist driven to create without thought of recognition and reward it is, I think, unequalled.

It was premiered at Yale University. Yvonne was not in that cast. Its professional world premiere was in Johannesburg where Yvonne was joined by Elize Cawood as Elsa and Louis van Niekerk as Marius. I did not see this production but by all accounts Elize - coincidentally the wife of Wilson Dunster, one of the original cast of *Orestes* - gave a very fine performance.

The play was taken up by the National Theatre in London with Bob Peck and Charlotte Cornwell taking over. Charlotte became an absolutely marvellous, feisty Elsa. I saw this production many times. When I first read the play both Yvonne and I had doubts about the speech in which Elsa tells Helen of a love affair with a married man which ended in an abortion (no doubt the reason for the actual woman's horror). It seemed clichéd and rather 'cheesy'.

However, Yvonne told me that in Elize's hands it had been very moving. In Charlotte's hands it was the same. I would watch (or listen over the tannoy) as, night after night, two fine actors hit the emotional moments square on. Watching Charlotte, without emotional overload, plumb the very real pain of every woman who has been in this situation each night - like the pure tone of a very painful bell ringing - was an experience for which I will always be grateful. I had always known that the Yvonne could do this. Seeing two actors of such calibre recreate, transmit, communicate repeatedly - without fail - was a lesson in Zen.

There was a considerable barney about the New York production. American Equity was unwilling to allow Yvonne to take the role in New York. This battle won, the play opened Off-Broadway in 1988. Athol was now playing the Minister, Marius, and the cast was joined by Amy Irving.

I flew over to photograph the production and provide a photo for the poster, arriving in time for the first dress rehearsal. I had been working at LAMDA until the day before leaving, had been awake for 36 hours straight (Can you sleep on an aeroplane?). I slumped into a seat. Designers and tech people apart, I was the only audience.

What followed was a triumphant proof of

> **Astbury's 4th Law of Theatre**
>
> ***Bad theatre puts you to sleep
> no matter how wide awake you are***
>
> ***Good theatre keeps you awake
> no matter how tired you are***

Bad theatre makes my bum start to hurt and my eyelids droop within 30 seconds.

As happens with all good theatre the play seemed to be over in half the time it had actually taken. This remains the most perfect production I have ever seen. I know I'm biased here, but I'm not alone - ask any of those who also saw it. One young actor told me later that she had decided to be an actor directly as a result of the National's production.

Yvonne's relationships to the other actors in her casts had always been good. She had bonded even more deeply than usual with the other two Elsa's. Now she and Amy had formed what was close to a mother/daughter relationship. Like Charlotte (and, surely, Elize) Amy took on the emotion and, especially in the 'abortion' speech, communicated quiet, deeply-felt pain. Not for the first time I found myself in tears.

Yvonne and Athol always had a 'special relationship' as actors. As a director he knew her better than anyone. Any thought of sleep vanished from my mind.

I photographed the final dress the following day; the play went into previews and opened. I finally lived through the weird experience of a New York opening and the party afterwards. The New York Times delivered its Delphic oracle - a generally favourable, but rather carping, hedge-betting review. There was some depression at this but, fortunately, the award season was upon them and Yvonne and Amy shared the Obie award (the major Off-Broadway award - the Tony being for plays in theatres classified as On-Broadway) for Best Actress. In South Africa she had won the Vita award; in London the Olivier Award (this, as in New York, should have been shared with Charlotte, but the London award doesn't operate that way).

Word-of-mouth was good and audiences flocked to see it. A fallow period in my teaching allowed me to return to New York before the end of the third month of what had been scheduled to be a six-month run. I found Yvonne in deep distress. Amy's agent had - unbeknown to Athol and Yvonne - only signed her up for three months. While she now was desperate to stay with a play which had become as precious to her as it was to Yvonne, she had also - earlier - committed to a film. She couldn't get out of this.

The final week of Amy's run was more than usually emotional. Their relationship had become even deeper, extending beyond the bounds of the theatre walls. An over-wrought final performance, topped by an emotional curtain speech by Athol, a shared meal - and Amy was gone.

The search for her replacement had commenced, obviously, as soon as Amy's situation became apparent. Various actors were suggested, and I was privileged to go with Yvonne to a matinee performance of Terrence McNally's *Frankie and Johnny in the Clair de Lune* to see one of the strongest candidates. At that stage only well-known in theatre, Kathy Bates was to rocket to Oscar-stardom in the film *Misery* shortly after *The Road to Mecca*.

Yvonne was immediately impressed. Kathy is a very fine actor indeed, and her onstage relationship with the other actor was sharing and very strong. Yvonne met her and liked her very much. A straightforward, down-to-earth, complex human being, she told me. No sign of vanity. Athol also approved.

Kathy began to rehearse, and here we are, after this long preamble, at the reason for this tale.

The process of replacement in a case like this is rather brutal. The actor rehearses with replacement actors - hired for the occasion - who read straight off the book, duplicating the moves written down. As the other actors are involved in the run of the play they are, obviously, unable to come to daily rehearsals. Kathy's situation was even worse. Her director was also acting in the play, so, for the majority of rehearsals, she was being supervised by the Company Manager. Company Managers (my daughter is one) are frequently called on to do this. But, as most of them will admit, they are not the director.

Monday was Yvonne's 'day off'. Kathy would come to our small apartment - I would go for a walk - and she and Yvonne would attempt to work their way through the play.

Yvonne was very worried. 'She's really struggling. We need a proper rehearsal process.' They weren't going to get it.

Amy left on a Saturday. There were rehearsals on the Monday and a dress rehearsal on Tuesday afternoon. That night Kathy opened. As good an actor as she is she was nowhere near ready. Everybody tried to keep her spirits up. The big emotional speech was, as yet, disconnected.

Yvonne was very angry that such a process had been foisted on a fellow-actor. Kathy kept trying. But you can't rehearse on stage in front of an audience.

At the end of her first week I left to return to London to my teaching.

Three weeks later I received a phone call at 4 AM. 'I've just been through the worst experience of my life.' Yvonne's voice was calm but tense. 'Just before interval I was in the middle of a scene when it felt as though someone had switched off the lights. I found myself sitting in this weird place. There was what looked like half a room surrounding me, a woman I didn't know sitting opposite me, and a whole group of people watching me. I didn't know where I was. The worst thing' - and she started to cry - 'was that I didn't know who I was.'

When she had calmed down she told me that she had apparently dried in the middle of the scene and just sat there. Kathy had tried to improvise, feeding her cues, but to no avail. The lights were dimmed (no curtains) and she was taken backstage. The audience was asked to take an early interval. She finally emerged from the state, was given a glass of water. At the end of an extended interval she had gone back on and managed to get to the end of the play. Both Kathy and Athol (whose character only came on in the second act) had helped her through one or two more 'moments'

'That is the most terrifying thing that has ever happened to me.' she repeated.

There was little I could say or do.

The run progressed. It had already been extended by three months.

There was talk of a further extension. Yvonne had won another award from Theatre World. The 'freezes' continued. They never actually had to stop the play - Kathy got very used to having to shepherd her through them. 'She's being fantastic - I can't imagine how awful it must be for her.'

This was New York. Yvonne was taken to psychiatrists - I think she was even given a brain scan. I'm a bit hazy on this as she became very unwilling to talk about what was happening. Nobody could find anything wrong with her. Our phone bill shot through the roof, but it was not - apart from the barest bones - about what she came to call 'The Terrors'.

They began to get worse and it was arranged that I would fly to New York to support her.

Yvonne was always a very private person. She rarely talked about her acting process because she felt that, if she did so, it might desert her.

I had a regimen. After spending the day with her - we occasionally ventured out to museums or art galleries - I would have to walk her the three blocks to the theatre, sit in the dressing-room with her until she went on stage. Then I had to leave - she did not want me there at the interval. At the end I had to be waiting in the dressing room to walk her back to the flat.

I was there for a month before I had to return to direct a play at LAMDA.

As the time approached for me to leave she became increasingly nervous. She was being pressured to agree to a further six months extension to the run. The play had become a very hot ticket. Unfortunately I could not stay.

The run was due to end in three weeks when I got another call. She had told them that, not only was she refusing to sign for the extension, but that she couldn't complete the run, and wanted to end a week early. 'The Terrors' were getting worse. The producers had little choice.

I fetched her at Heathrow. She was in a very bad way. Distressed because she had had to let Kathy, Athol and the rest of the team down. Absolutely certain that she would not have made it through that final week.

At home she took time off. She had started painting previously as a relaxation. Not pictures - it had all begun when she decided to paint the rather grotty surround of our bath. Daisies. She slowly developed technique. Furniture. Anything that didn't move for a period of time got painted. I had to be careful.

Now she launched into this with her customary fervour and concentration. I would arrive home to: 'There's a rather sweet table/hall stand/wash-stand outside No 34/46/22 - I've asked - they're throwing it out.' - and I would have to go and fetch the item. I became very good at getting rid of woodworm. Six months went by. Her agent was asking when she would go back to work.

One day a packet arrived containing scripts and a personal letter from Arnold Wesker - three one-person short plays. She liked Arnold, was a great admirer of his work, loved the plays. But: 'I can't. I don't know what to tell him. I'd love to - they're different from anything I've ever done - but I don't have the courage. I know it will happen again.'

She made an excuse, felt that he had thought she didn't like the plays. Couldn't tell him the real truth. Later her agent, Lou Coulson, found her work in telly. This was not a problem - she didn't have the worry of carrying a whole play.

She only went back to the stage once more in her life. Director/playwright Terry Johnson asked her to play in the production of *Death of a Salesman* that he was doing in York. Desperate to find out whether she would be able to brave a whole evening on stage again, but unwilling to do this in London, she accepted. The run went well. A happy cast and only one or two minor twinges for her.

The Road to Mecca was to have a run in Washington at the Kennedy Centre. She was asked to do it. Same cast. She refused. It apparently went very well.

Then plans were made to film the play in South Africa. Athol wanted Kathy to play Elsa. Yvonne - fearing also that this would trigger memories of the stage experience - preferred Amy. Athol would not budge.

In her personal life she was becoming ill. We found she had a liver condition called Sclerosing Cholangitis. The doctors could find no reason why. She was a non-smoker who only drank the odd glass of wine.

The Road to Mecca had been a culmination for her. The role she had lived her life for. She finally decided to do the film with Kathy. 'I like her. She's very good. I'm sure that, now she's had the benefit of a proper rehearsal period for the Washington run, she'll have connected to the character.'

She was losing weight fast. Leaving for South Africa she smiled at my worry. 'I'm okay. I want to do this. I'm not letting anyone else play Helen!' I laughed at her fierce possessiveness.

The calls from their rehearsals in Johannesburg were very positive. Kathy was not stupid or insensitive and obviously knew that Yvonne had fought for Amy. 'She's being so supportive, so understanding. It's lovely working with someone who has no malice. We've got a very good relationship going - and she really has taken on all of Elsa's pain. She's a completely different kettle of fish to Amy, but that's okay - it's bringing new things out of Helen.'

The filming was a very happy experience.

She arrived back. Her condition had deteriorated even further. The wonderful team of doctors at the Royal Free Hospital in Hampstead did everything they could, but the disease spread.

In December 1991, on Friday the 13th, her consultant phoned me. She had developed lung cancer - it was a secondary infection, spreading probably from her liver. How long? Three to six months. They were going to try chemotherapy. This might mean her losing her hair, of which she was very proud, and which I had loved for 30 years.

On Monday, January 13, 1992, surrounded by all three of her daughters, she slid from her coma and on to the next stage.

Once again, to the point of this story. While I was in with her in New York, after the attack, we would occasionally, gently, talk about it. I did not want to push this while she was still playing, but she was obviously desperate to find some reasons, some way out.

She would not describe what was happening - continuing to refer to it only has 'The Terrors'.

I must emphasise here that this was NOT stage fright. That is a completely different phenomenon. This was a paralysing, terrifying state.

One Sunday we were cooking our supper in the small kitchenette. She had done the Sunday afternoon matinee and was looking forward to her evening off, her Monday off - the next performance was on Tuesday evening. The performance that day had been a good one, free from the slightest twinges. Kathy was being a rock - she completely trusted her to be there if it struck again.

So we talked. She had no idea where this came from, or why. She had a history of stress diseases - a colon condition had plagued her for years before it was finally diagnosed, then cured by doctors at Cape Town's Groote Schuur in the early 80s. Then she developed a frozen shoulder - another stress condition. She had no idea where the stress came from. Generally attributed it to the normal stress that an actor undergoes nightly.

We explored various ideas and possibilities. Nothing. I said to her: 'You base a lot of this character on your mother, don't you?' She was standing with her back to me, grating cheese. She started to cry. Cursing myself, I tried to comfort her. We ate the meal, and she had another of her daily doses of repeats of *Cagney and Lacey* - which she loved.

It was obvious that we had hit a nerve. But it was one she was not yet ready to explore.

Back in London she began to feel free to talk about it. She knew Olivier had had a famous bout - asking the actors on the opening night of the run of *Merchant of Venice* not to look him in the eyes. His wife, Joan Plowright, is quoted as saying that he told her 'I've got to have some tranquillisers, because if I don't have something, I'm going to walk out of that stage door and get on the first bus that comes.'

Ian Holm took a break from stage performance for nearly 18 years. Derek Jacobi had a five-year absence. One day we saw the singer, Elaine Paige, on a lunch-hour programme, telling of her bout with something similar.

She started asking other actors. 'Everybody is too scared to talk about it.' she said. So she began to plan a book on the subject. She would interview anybody willing to talk; approach psychologists or psychiatrists in an attempt to find answers.

The final disease ended that ambition for her, but set me on a path that I am still following.

Any answers? Only a theory. *Holy Cannibalism.* The ghosts which are contacted by the character allow themselves freely to be used in order to communicate real feeling, real pain. As long as this loan is treated with reverence and love. In my small case vanity got in the way. In Yvonne's, a brutal, unthinking, inconsiderate process forced her, night after night, to allow the character to draw on her most precious memories in a production which had lost its way. One evening her ghosts said: Enough - and switched off the light. The fault was not Kathy's - she was trying her damnedest.

In hindsight Yvonne should have insisted on a break during which she and Kathy and Athol properly rehearsed and bonded. At the time, of course, she didn't even think that this was possible - as I'm sure it wasn't. Too many financial considerations.

I've written this down at some length as a warning to those who tamper with systems based on using personal memories to trigger nightly performance; to those who force actors into unnatural situations and expect them to pull the deep, painful connections required for real performance out of some magician's hat.

The consequences are appalling. I do not use that word lightly - I lived with someone suffering from them for nearly three years - the last ones of her life.

Mostly 'The Terrors' are unleashed because of untenable, forced situations. I have, once, had the painful task of advising an actor in a production of mine to pull back from her role - in which she had been doing wonderful, rooted, connected work - because one of her fellow actors had decided to play a very painful scene for laughs. It was too late in the run to do anything about it. I was scared that she would harm herself in the way that Yvonne had.

But vanity can also bring it on. Actors are in this extraordinary situation. Nobody goes up to a lawyer or an accountant and says: 'You were absolutely marvellous! What you did tonight changed my life!' Acid. 'How do we cope?' young actors ask. I can only pass on Yvonne's method of dealing with praise - which, thicko that I am, I only worked out after she had gone.

My final story to illustrate this. One night I picked her up from a performance at the National. We drove home, I made her supper (She wouldn't eat before a performance. Living with an actor for 30 years wrecked my eating and sleeping patterns), we watched some late-night telly, talked a bit ... Finally she was wound down. Actors, just in case you don't know, are subject to a nightly blast of adrenaline - without which they cannot perform. Adrenaline (it's actually a chemical called Epinephrine) puts the actor on a real high. Leading to

---

Astbury's 5th Law of Theatre

The Worst Possible Time to talk to an actor is immediately after a performance

---

At this time the only permissible thing to say is: 'You were marvellous, darling!' That adrenaline rush can quickly turn really nasty. The only person who can dare to trespass this rule is the director, and even s/he needs to tread with extreme care.

In my experience the come-down time is about two hours. We stood up to go to bed. 'Oh ...' she said, an afterthought dawning, 'Peter Brook was in tonight.' I looked at her in total amazement. It would have been the first thing I would have blurted out. 'What did he say?' 'Oh ... he was very nice ...' 'Yes - but what did he say?!' 'Oh, god, you know me - I can never remember. He was very nice.' I knew when I was licked. I had been this way before. She never could remember.

I made an arrangement with Pauline, her lovely dresser. She would kibitz when someone famous came backstage and pass it on to me. She proved a worthy spy.

I only realised much later what the process was. If someone complimented Yvonne she would accept it with her normal sweet, shy graciousness, and then promptly consign it to some limbo hidden deep inside. In this way it couldn't rust her.

'It's not an easy process -', I tell my students, 'but you have to learn to practice it.' In most of the eyes I can see that this good advice is not going to be heeded. Praise is too seductive.

In September, 1991, we were sitting quietly watching the telly. It was about 8.30. She was getting weaker each day. The phone rang. An excited voice from South Africa asked to speak to her. She came back from the phone. 'I've won the Vita Best Actress award for *Mecca*.' (The film). When she was nominated they had asked if she would go out for the award ceremony, but she was not well enough. We celebrated with a mug of hot chocolate.

Almost an hour later we were still sitting watching the telly. She had her feet in my lap. I was looking at her. 'What?' she asked. 'You've forgotten, haven't you?' 'What?' 'You won an award tonight.' 'Oh.' she said, and smiled at me. Went back to watching the telly.

I sat and thought about the incredible excitement of her first award - the Three Leafs Arts Award - in Cape Town in 1965, given to her for two performances in different plays. It was presented by Maurice Chevalier. About the equally incredible excitement of her Olivier Award in London for Mecca, when she made the best acceptance speech I've ever heard (and Imelda Staunton - as Best Supporting Actress - made the funniest), dedicating her award with typical humility to 'all the nobodies in the world'.

I have been a very lucky man.

The Final Stretch

I left Mountview and resumed my freelance career. I found myself back at LAMDA directing a final year production of Gorki's *Summerfolk* in the MacOwan Theatre. I was a bit trepidaceous about how these methods would be received by a cast who had no grounding at all in them. The previous year I had been in South Africa, where the 25th anniversary of the founding of The Space was being celebrated in Cape Town by a range of theatres. I was to direct a production of *The Guise* - now unbanned - with a cast of established, and in some cases, award-winning professionals. They had taken to the methods with open-minded alacrity (except for one - an old friend of mine - who could not cope with under-reading). So I was fairly confident.

The young LAMDA actors were a delight to work with, talented and willing. From this experience one more example of the efficacy of image streaming.

The actor playing Zamislov, a clerk/assistant to the main character - Basov - is having an affair with Julia, wife of Suslov. The same problem arose as we'd had in *Matchstalk Man*. There was no information at all about the character in the play. Phoning Gorki was not possible. One day we did a small exercise in communal image streaming which I won't bother with here. We had half-an-hour to fill at the end of a long day. The following morning the actor came over and handed me a handwritten page. 'This was my image stream.' It wasn't very long. He saw himself as a very young child. Asleep in his room he is awakened by sounds from his mother's bedroom. Scared, he tiptoes down the dark hallway to where a crack of light comes through the part-open door. He peeps through. His mother is in bed with a man he doesn't know. He realises she is a prostitute.

Short and simple, but it galvanised the scene he had with his mistress. The self-destructive qualities that the actor playing her had been detecting came into sharp focus. The scene became brutally sadomasochistic, as Zamislov took his revenge on all females. An actor, thrashing hopelessly lost, found his raison d'être.

The exercises we have developed I continue to use and pass on to others who wish to find the energy at the heart of all good characters. They help the actor to open up their imagination to the vast storehouse of their brain with all its resources; to find that flow that is at the heart of being 'in-the-moment'; to connect to the deep feelings in emotions; to release and integrate these so that they can communicate them to an audience.

There are still many more exercises to be discovered and developed. I have found, for instance, the value of Grotowskian techniques such as the Plastiques in helping the actor to contact the emotion trapped in their muscles and to abandon themselves to 'thoughtless' acting. I cannot teach these exercises - too old and decrepit - but all actors should learn them.

Others will find other methods. Not all methods work for all people. Each individual is different. It is an exciting field. The battle against the body/mind defences - those that cripple and repress - is never-ending.

At the heart of those battles stands the actor - alone on the stage in that terrible darkness - going where we dare not, but need to.

The Exercises

Before we start with the basic exercises as worked out at LAMDA, developed at Arts Threshold, and refined at Mountview I first need to introduce you to four techniques.

Under-reading

If I ruled the world all directors would be forced to use this system. However, I do understand the problems people have in accepting that it could work for them - I had them, too. I was introduced to the technique by a wonderful director, the late Tessa Schneideman, when I engaged her to direct a production of *Volpone* with 3rd Year acting students at Mountview. I remember sitting through a tortuous, three-and-a-half hour rehearsal about 10 days before it opened as the actor playing the title role struggled with the lines as they were fed to her. It was a confusing, cacaphonic experience. It did little to endear the process to me when the majority of the rest of the cast expressed their cautious approval. However, 10 days later Tessa produced, out of the hat, a wonderful production of the play with her all-women cast, skateboards and all.

Later, with the same year group (and some of the same actors) she did *The Love of the Nightingale* for us. This time all reservations on the part of the actors were thrown out of the window. One after the other they raved about the process. 'Never felt so free.' At the rehearsal 10 days in advance most of the cast already had their lines and it was not nearly as tortuous. Once again intense and magical performance resulted.

The one thing I am is a Doubting Thomas. I still didn't feel - despite Tessa's urgings - that the process could work for me. I mostly worked with 2nd Year students in truncated, 14-hour a week rehearsal periods. It would take too long I reasoned.

One extraordinary day in late November - I think it was in 1997 - I found myself on a plague-site. Flu had decimated the School. Nearly half the student population as well as several of the teachers were at home, coughing and wheezing. In my own rehearsal four of the cast of 15 were present. Only two of them were in a scene together - and that was the second last scene in the play. We had not touched it yet. I had no choice, and they had all worked in classes with Tessa, so I asked the other two to under-read. Revelations and Roads to Damascus! I watched in complete amazement as the two actors seemed to vault lightly over the first week of rehearsal. Freed from the constraints of 'script-in-hand' they could use their whole body, did not have to keep looking down at a script - thus breaking the flow - confident in the knowledge that the lines would be fed to them. I started to use the system rather tentatively. The actors loved it! All my reservations were decimated.

Can you concentrate with two voices delivering the same text, one after the other? Not a problem. After the first time through the other voice seems to fade into the background and you no longer notice it.

Surely the actor will pick up on the under-reader's rhythms and inflexions? Nope. The only time this happens is when there is a rather sneaky defence mechanism operating and the actor is, in fact, avoiding connecting with the text. Easy to spot, even easier to deal with (Make the actor wait for a count of 3 before delivering the line).

What happens if there are not enough people to under-read? I directed Olwen Wymark's *Brezhnev's Children*. 12 women are on the stage almost from beginning to end. There are monologues but mostly the dialogue bounces back and forth. There are two other character who pop in and out - two doctors (It's set in a Moscow maternity hospital). One of them is by far the smaller role. She became the under-reader for everyone - except obviously in her own scenes. The first two rehearsals were chaotic as she rushed around trying to make sure that everyone knew who was supposed to be talking. Then it settled quickly into a good rhythm as the actors became accustomed to it. It was hard work for her, but kept her very busy in what would otherwise have been a rather boring rehearsal process.

In a self-directed piece three actors chose a one-act play in which all three characters were onstage all the time. Under-reading was impossible. Somebody had sent me an Internet link to a description by an actor of working with Phelim McDermott, one of the most innovative directors in Britain. He described the process whereby they used a form of under-reading in which they recorded it onto a tape player and then played it back as they rehearsed. I told the three of this and they tried it out with great success. The only thing they had to do was re-record it as they had done the first one too slowly.

Another wonderful actor, Isabelle Gregson, devised her own show - *There's Something in the Fridge That's Trying to Kill Me* - with the writer Chips Hardy. In the first version - done at E15 Acting School - she had to direct herself, working alone. She recorded her text onto a mobile phone. Worked perfectly. The show went on to great success at the Edinburgh Festival.

I now use this system as a matter of course. I have found, over and over, that it speeds up the process enormously. Actors also say things like: 'It's like having a guardian angel on your shoulder.' It helps them learn their lines more quickly though IT IS NOT A SUBSTITUTE FOR LEARNING THE LINES. Pardon the caps but some actors can be very lazy.

So, how does it work?

The actor goes onstage without their text. This is carried by their under-reader.

(I've borrowed a scene from some unknown to illustrate)

Under-reader: (loud and clear) *'To be or not to be...'*

Actor: *'To be or not to be'*

Under-reader: *'That is the question...'*

Actor: *'That is the question'*

Under-reader: *'Whether 'tis nobler in the mind...'*

Actor: *'Whether 'tis nobler in the mind'*

Under-reader: *'to suffer the slings and arrows...'*

Actor: *'to suffer the slings and arrows'*

Under-reader: *'of outrageous fortune...,'*

Actor: *'of outrageous fortune,'*

You get the idea. The under-reader feeds the actor not more than 7 words at a time (see rules below). The actor speaks their line when ready, taking pauses where necessary. They should not get sucked into taking on the rhythm of the under-reader, or feeling that they have to say the line immediately.

The first time around the under-reader also reads in the stage directions that apply to movement, actions and time - *Shakes hand, Moves to door, Lights up, Fade*, etc. Not the ones about the character's emotional state - *Cries, Shouts*, etc. This is dropped in subsequent read-throughs.

In a multiple character scene the under-reader responsible for the reply must wait until the other character has begun to say their line before 'feeding' their own actor.

Thus (if our playwright had decided to make this a two-hander)

Under-reader 1: *'That is the question'*

Actor 1: *'That is the question.'*

Under-reader 2: *'If you're just going to stand around!'*

Actor 2: *'If you're just going to stand around!'*

As the process develops the under-readers must begin to feed the rest of the line as soon as the actor is speaking theirs.

So - in this scene:

Under-reader 2: *'If you're just going..'*

Actor 2: *'If you're just going..'*

Under-reader 2 (Starting as soon as the Actor has started to speak): *'..to stand around!'*

Actor 2: *'...to stand around!'*

This is to aid the flow and not keep the actor waiting. Just in case you think that the actor will not be able to hear the new line while speaking the old - step-forward once more The Amazing Right Brain. It only happens if the actor doesn't hear the line if outside noise from other under-readers drowns it out - see rule 3 below.

There are four rules associated with the process:

1. The under-reader should not attempt to be polite. Read the lines loud and clear! Follow the actor around, but stay just more than an arm's length away so that the actor can feel free to turn or make expansive gestures without bumping into you.

2. Obey the Left-Brain rule - no more than seven words. Try to chunk the text into meaningful phrases of three and four words. The same person should under-read for the actor every time if possible. In this way you learn where the actor is pausing appropriately. It takes a little work to be an under-reader. You should mark up the script, to make sense of what you're feeding the actor.

3. If the actor does not hear the line they should not stop and say: 'Line?' Instead they just repeat the line they have just said, thus staying in character. This tells the under-reader that they haven't heard.

4. Very importantly: There will come a time when the actors start to think that they know the lines and they will get very irritable with the under-readers and finally say that they no longer need them. You can, if you wish, listen to this and drop the under-reader. This will result in the Legions of Defence Mechanism No 1 rushing out of the camp in which they have been sulking, (see Defences) to do what they're good at: snatch the lines from the mouths of the foolish actors. Ignore the actors' pleas - persevere. What actually happens is that you get a quite extraordinary period in which you are listening to two voices speaking the same text, one - the actor - being about two words ahead of the other. What happens here is that if the actor loses the text for the briefest instant it is immediately there and the flow remains uninterrupted. When do they stop? Well in practice what actually happens is that they just gradually fade away ...

Being slow of mind it took me some time to work out why under-reading works so well. It is, of course, a Left-Brain Disabling Device. The poor left brain is so busy coping with trying to relay the seven bytes of info that it leaves the acting to the amazing Right/pre-conscious brain.

Mind-Mapping

This is an incredibly powerful technique. It's taught to most students in schools these days in the form of brain-storming, or spider diagrams. Sadly, once we leave school we seem to put these 'childish things' behind us. A pity. To learn more about Mind-Mapping read one of Tony Buzan's many books on the subject. They all teach the basics, which are all you really need, though the developments can be real fun and a real help. Dyslexics (the Actors' Condition - dyslexia - it's amazing how many actors are dyslexic) are now taught to mind-map as many of them operate better through imagery.

So, a quick basic introduction. Why don't you take 10 minutes and try it out for yourself?

Start off with an A4 sheet of paper in landscape mode. Obviously a pen or pencil. Draw a smallish circle in the centre - enough to write one or two words inside. Draw seven lines radiating out in all directions from the circle, to about one third of the way to the edge of the page. Put another small circle at the end of each line. OK. You're set. Now, I'm going to ask you to put a word or two in the central circle. Then, without conscious thought, and as quickly as possible, you are to write in each circle a word or two (don't get loquacious) that pops into your brain as you think of the central word. It is VERY IMPORTANT that you don't a) slow down, b) think consciously, c) judge or attempt to rationalise what you've written.

You will find that some of the new words will lead to further thoughts. Speedily draw another line from that particular word, pop a circle on the end, and enter the new word there. These circles might each grow 4, 5 or 6 extra bubbles. It's great fun. You don't have to fill all seven initial bubbles - or you might need more. It's your mind-map - construct it how you will.

UNDER NO CIRCUMSTANCES should you get seduced into writing sentences! One word, two maybe, three possibly. More - NO!

As it grows you might find that words in different bubbles on different extensions seem to connect. So connect them with a line. Put a symbol on that line which represents what the connection is about. (A little heart for love; a heart with a broken line through it for whatever that suggests to you; a lightning bolt for anger or an enemy or ....) Make them up for yourself. If you want to, use different colour pens.

Just go very, very fast. If you get stuck at any point, take the word on which you are stuck, turn over the page, put it in its own circle, and off you go again with a new mind map. It actually works best with A3 sheets of paper, but not everyone has access to these.

When you're finished you'll probably find that your bubbles have spread over the page in what looks like an unholy mess. Some bubbles sprouted many others, some didn't. There are connect lines running all over the place. Some words/thoughts are repeated.

Actually what you've drawn is not a bad symbolic representation of the brain, with all its nerves, dendrites and synapses. This is how it works - and that is why this is such a powerful technique.

So - have a bash. If you wish you can take the name of a character you've already played, or, even better, a character you are about to play, and place it in the central circle. If you want to try something else (nothing to stop you trying both - or more) there is a selection of possible words at the end of this section. Don't peek at them before you are ready to go. Then don't ponder on them. Select the first one that grabs you, and GO!

OK. I'll assume that most of you have tried it. It only takes 10 minutes or so, after all. For these (and you unadventurous few who did not try will now not know what I'm talking about): How was that for you? Looking at your mind map - does it cover your thoughts about that central word. Do any of the words surprise you?

Mind-maps can be used in various ways. Above is described the fast, subconscious, instinctive way. There's also a slower, left-brained, rational way. Remember what that student said about how Stanislavski would probably be using mind-maps instead of Actioning if he were still around?

As you read a play, build a conscious thought-out mind-map of the narrative. Spider diagrams are probably better here. A spider diagram starts with one line from which other lines sprout like branches or arteries. You'll end up with the whole play filleted and spread out in all its acts and scenes, the characters in those scenes, what happens, etc.

After this, build a quicker, less thought-out Character Mind-Map (bubble style). By this time you should have a strong idea of the characters and their relationships, so you'll be able to go faster. The heightened speed is used to put the mind back into instinctive, subconscious mode. It's surprising what you will already have learned from a basic reading of the play, and from that first Narrative Mind-Map.

A further use is if you hit a problem with the character somewhere in the rehearsal period. A quick mind-map around the problem can untie all sorts of knots.

An illustration of how mind-maps work. I introduced the technique to those students who were on the Road to Damascus with me. I had first done a rapid character mind-map the night before. Then I had taken this and turned it into something more structured and rational, using colours and symbols. I showed them both. Platonov's character had a riot of connections to all the women - hearts bleeding and broken and yearning (can't quite remember how I symbolised 'yearning'...). There was one oddity. In the first speed mind-map one bubble had been filled with the word 'hormonal'. 'I have no idea where that comes from,' I said, 'or how it connects to the play. But you can't censor or judge or rationalise – so there it is.' There were guesses. Most centred around the various female characters and their attraction to Platonov. 'We'll find out.' I said, and left it there.

In the final week of rehearsals we were working on a set of three small scenes (subsequently cut) in which Platonov is brought letters from his various paramours by servants. After the first - delivered by a young woman - Todd (the good-at-improvising American) said: 'He's even flirting with her!' We incorporated it into the scene. The next message was delivered by an old nurse. Halfway through the scene Todd stopped and said: 'He's flirting with her, too!' And Platonov was. After the rehearsal he and I sat and talked about it. 'He flirts with ALL women,' said Todd. 'It doesn't matter what their age or their look. He is constitutionally unable not to flirt! He loves all women!' Like a light bulb the word appeared above our heads: 'Hormonal'. 'He's incapable of NOT falling in love with a woman. Sonya walks into the room - he loves her. She leaves and Anna arrives - he loves her. He gets home to his wife, Sasha - he loves her. Marya enters, with her hands which smell of formaldehyde - and he loves her! The maid, the old nurse.... all of them. It's a disease.'

So - Platonov loves all women. This fact explained all the rest of his actions. By loving them all he, of necessity, hurts them all. He can't stand this - because he loves them. It slowly drives him mad with pain In his last scene with Marya, just before Sonya shoots him, he is hallucinating, not aware who he is talking to, telling her how he hurts everyone. Finally she says: 'Where does it hurt?' 'Being Platonov hurts.' he answers. (One of the best-known adaptations surprisingly leaves this crucial line out).

All of this from the word 'hormonal' on a mind-map.

Nowadays, when I'm working on a written play, I begin by asking each actor to do a rapid mind-map of their character. This is very early (many actors have only read their own, highlighted parts at this stage, the naughty buggers), but it is generally surprising for them to find out how much they already know. Then, having focussed them in this way, we move on to the first Image Stream.

Another area in which Mind-Mapping is very useful is in the dreary task of learning lines.. I'll spare you the stories of how I found this and just give you the technique.

Take the speech or scene you have to learn and split the sentences into the thought processes and meanings that lie beneath the words. Taking them in order, build a slow, considered mind-map (or spider drawing) assigning one or two words to each thought process. Do NOT use the words in the speech. When you are finished, put the text away. Now, I used to say: 'Try and do the speech using only the mind-map.' With some struggle the actor would be able to find most of the processes and meanings of the actual lines. Sometimes they wouldn't remember all processes, and, frequently, they might not even refer to the mind-map. But they always found the basic sense.

One day I was using this technique with a class of 1st years at E15 who had had to do a writing exercise (see my book *Knit Your Own Theatre*) in a devised adaptation of a novel. They had each been given a character about whom there was little information in the book. They had made interesting educated guesses at the possible backstory of their characters (The process we used was also good at tapping into the mystical areas which open up in Image-Streaming). However, I had to get through 15 such stories and some of them were struggling to keep the class's attention.

The third actor, a young man, had found a surprisingly angry heart under what had seemed the placid exterior of his character. I asked him to do the process again, this time as an anger-run. He set off willingly and was soon in such a fine old temper that he even tore up his mind-map and stamped on it.

At the end the person who had been following his written text said: 'About 80% of that was word for word what is written here.' It was the other 20% that was fascinating the rest of us.
Several more deeply buried unspokens had erupted to the surface. Had he planned these? No, he said, he just suddenly found himself saying them. It was as though his character - whose life in the actual pages of the novel was undescribed - had leapt at this opportunity to tell his story.

We began to do anger runs as an addition to each new character's story. After two more such extraordinary sub-textual stories, where details undreamt of by the actor/vehicle had emerged, we junked the first struggle-through with mind-map alone and went straight for the anger run.

It was an exhilarating afternoon.

The following day I asked them to do these speeches straight - I allowed them to hold the mind-map if they wished, but no-one actually referred to it. We dropped the anger run. You have to try this for yourself. All of them could reconstruct their full text - not necessarily with all the actual words, but definitely with all the thought processes underlying these - sometimes better expressed now - and all the new elements.

I now teach this process very quickly in one session. The actors are asked to select a speech, mind-map it but NOT attempt to learn it. They arrive in the class clutching their pieces of paper. Very few of them believe they will remember anything. It is very satisfying to watch as, one after the other, they find that the basics of the speech are lurking inside; to see their surprise as the anger run springs the speech from its trap. My favourite was a young man who had deliberately chosen a Shakespearean speech with all its difficult language. In his first anger run he found more than half of the actual words, and all of the processes and meanings.

As I write this my edition of *Mind* magazine brings me news of tests which proved that people remember best when they only have one word to describe the process. (*Scientific American Mind*, volume 20, number one February/March 2009: 'Avoiding the Big Choke')

The same article confirms another process: the more you bring your conscious mind into the process of carrying out an action (whether it be playing a sport or acting a part) the more likely you are to 'choke' - to freeze, to forget. Defence Mechanism No 1.

(Suggested words for a beginning mind-map: 'Happiness'; 'I am...'; 'You never...'; or make up your own)

The Basics of Image Streaming

Done alone:

You must have a tape or digital recorder capable of recording of at least an hour. Digitals are better for this. You wouldn't want to have to stop in the middle of a stream full of fish to turn the tape over.

Character Image Stream:

Close your eyes (not forgetting to switch the tape on) and think of the character. If you're just starting say: 'S/he looks like...' and describe, height, hair colour, clothes until the images start to arrive. Describe them in as much detail as possible. Sights, sounds, smells, textures, temperatures - let it be as sensory as possible. Follow the stream - don't attempt to influence its course. Don't judge, attempt to rationalise or understand the images. JUST. DESCRIBE. THEM. Nothing is unimportant. If you find yourself in the room with no doors or windows, look around - there may be a trapdoor or piece of paper on the floor. Go down through the trapdoor. Is there a message on the paper? If there's nothing, what's the temperature? Or is there a smell?

Try not to stop and think. Keep up the pace.

Done with a partner:

It's best to start off this way, though there is a rule for the partner. Resist the temptation to get involved and attempt to influence the stream. The partner's role is mostly limited to taking notes. If an actor gets stuck you are allowed to ask the following questions: 'What are you looking at?', though more useful is just the little, gently prompting word: '.. and...' For the rest, let the stream take its own course, no matter what your opinions of it may be.

The person doing the streaming just follows the method set out for doing it above.

It's important to understand that an image stream is as long as a piece of string. There is no such thing as a typical length. I've known really valuable ones which only lasted 5-6 minutes. The longest one I've been involved in was two hours 15 minutes. They end when they end. The 'streamer' should not become embarrassed or worried about the time they're taking.

There is one rare exception to this 'rule'. I once - and only once, thank heavens - had a serial attention-seeker in one of my classes. He absolutely loved image-streaming. During the first time after I introduced the class to it I saw his partner getting desperate. They had been going for nearly an hour-and-a-half. Listening in, I realised that all he was doing was indulging his already over-vivid imagination, careening off on ever wilder tangents to make sure it never had to end. He had the complete attention of another human being. Who was waiting for her turn. I finally stopped him in a brief pause for breath, as he had used up all the available class time, and made him promise to give his partner her time outside of hours.

But there has really only been this one. Not many actors are attention-seekers, are they?

At the end of both these methods the 'streamer' should review what they have said. It's longer when done alone. You have to listen to the whole tape and make notes. A partner will just take you through the 'highlights', mentioning things that interested them, pointing out themes, the recurrence of colours, etc.

Then, after both of you have gone for a pee, or a quick coffee, you change over.

One final Image-Streaming story to illustrate its efficacy.

I had directed an actor at the beginning of her third and final year - introduced all the techniques. Later in the year I received a phone call. She was playing Titania in *The Dream*. Her director was very good, but she was stuck.

'Have you Mind-Mapped?' 'No.' ' Image-Streamed?' 'No.' I put the phone down on her. What's the use of teaching techniques if they're not used? Did she want me to wave a magic wand? The phone rang again. 'Sorry.' she said, hurriedly, 'It's just that I can't get anyone to take notes for me.' 'Tape recorder?' 'Haven't got one.' 'Find someone.' I am a really horrid, unforgiving person (with a high rejection factor). A week later she phoned again. Desperate. Nobody would sit with her. She'd done the Mind-Mapping. It had clarified things but she was still in trouble. The opening was a week away. I have a rather regrettable, well-hidden soft centre. 'OK. Come in earlier tomorrow and I'll take notes for you.' I expect it's my excessive need for validation and approval, but there I was at 9.30 the following morning. I had a class at 11.

We set off. When her director had asked her for an image of Titania she had come up with a peacock. So we started with that. I'm not going to go into the detail that she did - the stream lasted one hour and 45 minutes, overrunning into my next class.
Just the highlights.

The peacock feather that came straight into her mind, immediately flattened into a road in front of her. Walking along the road she came to a large field. It was ploughed and the soil was dark and black. Standing in the centre was a very large three or four-storied object. 'It's got scales - like an armadillo.' she said. Then: 'Right at the top there is a sort of visor and I can see two eyes looking at me. It's Oberon!' She was quite indignant. Oberon stood aloof in his 'armour'. She looked down at the ploughed, black soil. A stalk of straw started growing rapidly out of the ground.

It must be obvious to you how much I love image-streaming. It liberates imagination and metaphor in ways which are, by turns, moving, puzzling and, in this case, hilarious. 'Streamers' get very physical, using their hands to draw shapes and to point at imaginary objects.

As the straw grew she followed its progress with her index finger. Up it came and up - until it was lodged in her nostril. 'Ooo!' she said, pushing her head up with pointed finger in nostril, 'it's lifting me off the ground... No!... It's pulling me down...', and her head started dipping to the floor. (Remember her eyes are closed through all of this...)

The nasal straw now pulled her into an underworld that I won't detail. She kept meeting up with Oberon - each time he was dressed in less armour. This culminated in a scene where she saw herself as a flat piece of green muslin, cut-out in the shape of a doll. Oberon appeared again - this time as another piece of cut-out green muslin. He came up behind and put his hand on her shoulder. A huge, melancholy sigh came from her: 'Ooooh...', she whispered, '... It's sooo long since I've been touched.', and a tear trickled down her cheek.

I'm not the brightest star in the sky. It had never occurred to me that Oberon and Titania are eternal beings. They can't die. So they live in this never-ending cycle of love-recrimination-hate-love.

The changeling they are fighting over came into this scene in a way that, for the first time, made sense to me. You'll see just how dim a star I am when I tell you that I can't remember how. In my defence it was pretty far into the time and I was beginning to worry about my next class, while frantically scribbling notes. I did ask her for a photocopy. She finally gave the original to me 10 years later. Actors - you just can't trust 'em...

I had determined before we started that I was going to tell her that she had to find someone to stream with her on *The Problem of Bottom*.

Now I don't want this book to be X-rated, but it's not my fault. That Will Shakespeare was a randy bastard. That's why there's a whole Dictionary of Sexual Allusion devoted to him. The apprentices in the pit must have had a high old time with Titania's drugged night spent with Bottom - the Ass. Why are children encouraged to study it?

Each Titania has to cope with the fact/hallucination of bestiality. I didn't particularly want to bring the subject up with this young Titania. I'm much too delicate.

However, the image-stream was ahead of me.

'I'm on a beach,' she said, 'It's lovely and warm and sunny... though there is a bit of a mist around... but it's nice... I feel great... it's like a happy drug... there are lots of really hunky men on the beach... it's like Baywatch....Oooo! there's this really gorgeous guy talking to me... he's really... Oh! he's lifted me up in his arms and he's carrying me... Now I'm sitting under a very tall pine tree... his head is in my lap... it's VERY big... I'm stroking his.... eyelash?.... he's so beautiful.... now I'm up in the crown of the tree - it's my bower.... I can just see him sitting there over the edge of the nest... my head is going up and....Oooo!!' She blushed scarlet. 'I'm not telling you what I'm doing....' Much as I wanted to know I let her stream in silence for a short while. Her blush was still fading when the scene changed and she was back and very angry with a laughing Oberon.

By this time we were 15 minutes into my next class. They'd already opened the door and I had waved them out. I could hear their chatter outside and was worried that other tutors in other rooms would start to get irritated.

She was now standing on the bank of a river. 'Please don't let her get in the river!' I begged the gods. This would probably mean the start of another journey! Cruel gods! A boat came floating by. 'Don't!' my agonised mind screamed. But she got into it anyway. 'It's very nice,' she said, 'Cushions all around, very comfy.' Just as I decided that 'long-as-a-piece-of-string' or no, I was going to have to pull her out, she said: 'It's so lovely and peaceful. I'm bobbing along in this boat. I'm smoking on a Hubble-Bubble...'

She gave a great sigh and opened her eyes, smiled.

I rushed her out and the class in.

The following week she was onstage giving the sexiest interpretation of Titania I have ever seen, to the great acclaim of all the eligible men in the school. Sadly this didn't include her Oberon, an actor carved out of solid oak. But she was happy.

Afterwards she told me that, back in rehearsals, everything had just fallen into place. 'I had a real basis, a real understanding of her.' Her director was thrilled.

The Joy of Image-Streaming.

The Anger Run

To a certain extent, this is a misnomer. It should really be called the Energy Run. It's the first, furious paddling of the surfer; the ignition key turning and telling the battery to send that short, sharp spark of electrical energy which puts the rest of the engine into action.

Pure energy. In our case anger is the energy pulse that works best.

The exercise is very simple. Just do the speech with as much anger as you can muster. There is no 'motivation'. The 'reason' is to release anger. It's not quite as easy as it sounds. It is rare to find an actor who can launch straight into a splendiferous rage without their defences jumping in quickly to shut them down.

Most opt out right at the start. Despite my prefacing the whole thing with statements like 'I want rage! Real, messy, loud rage!', and 'I warn you - I have very high standards of anger!' I will have to stop the actor quite quickly and remark: 'I don't remember asking for 'quite cross'.' It can take some time to get the actor revved up to the point where they begin to approach the lower slopes of 'really very cross'. Generally I push people by stopping them within 2-3 words of the start when it's obvious that anger will not be on the agenda. A few of these stops and most actors will start getting really pissed off with Me. This is fine. Whatever floats...

Permission Workshops - that early possible title. It's amazing how freeing this exercise is. For many it is the first time in their life they've been allowed to be angry.

The way in can be quite a struggle. I remember one such at Mountview. The actor had the most beautiful smile. It rarely left her face. 'I can't be angry,' she said, 'I'm just not an angry person.' I pushed and pushed. I had deliberately given her a very angry speech. In her 'anger.' run she kept bursting into embarrassed laughter. I put her through all the exercises, one after the other. It was rather brutal. At the end of a period of about 30 minutes, which culminated in her having to punch a big pillow over and over and over, she sat, panting, sweating, her hair all over the place.

Still smiling desperately. I let her sit for a while, then asked quietly: 'Why are you smiling?'

In one of the most moving moments I have ever had in a rehearsal room she turned her face to me. The smile slowly crumbled. Tears started to stream down her cheeks. Nothing loud, just the quiet dissolution of a mask that had been in place for far too many years. When she was able to speak she said: 'My mother died when I was 12. I had to look after my brothers - they were all younger than me. My father depended on me. I couldn't let him down. I had to be the stable one.'

So she smiled and smiled and ran the household - a mother at 12. Unable to show her feelings. Always taking second, third, fourth place. A carer. The smile became her mask.

The anger that began to pour out of her now was quite something to watch. I wish I could say that the mask vanished never to return, but it's not that easy.

So, finally you have got the actor to fully express their anger. Remember the rules:

- **no handling of any piece of furniture or prop**
- **no touching of another actor**
- **no kicking or punching floors or walls**

Once they're on the wave they're generally open to whatever happens. However, the Defences do not give up quite that easily. One day, early on, a young actor started off in a veritable tantrum which then started to slide slowly down the slope towards inaudibility. I was fascinated and let him go right to the end of the speech. Several members of the class were giggling. He finally ground to a halt in a whisper. 'What happened?' I asked. 'I dunno,' he said, 'It was like there was a volume,' and he indicated a spot on his shoulder, 'and someone was turning it down.' 'Someone?' I asked. 'Yeah. I expect that was me...'

Thus came into existence *The Volume Control Defence.* I will be publishing a book of 3000 Collected Defence Mechanisms (this is a joke...).

Defence Mechanism No 1 is always first (unless you use Under-Reading,) - the actor stopping and saying: 'I've forgotten my lines.' I am then delighted to be able to tell them that, in the light of all we now know about the brain, it is IMPOSSIBLE to forget your lines. They lurk for evermore somewhere in that Magnificent Brain of yours. So, therefore, there must be a reason why they are not readily available just at this moment. That reason, M'Lud's, is *Defence Mechanism No. 1*. Your defences have spotted a dangerous pattern on the horizon. Mostly they don't even know what it represents (the baby's 'un-understood' feelings - see Rebirthing). But they're there to protect you, so they press the red button and the Amygdala sends out the warning to shut everything down. Or fight. Or run like hell.

The actors' battle is to convince their defences that this old wall, with its 'un-understood' hieroglyphics is no longer necessary or useful.

In this battle the Anger Run is one of the most effective weapons.

Once the energy of anger is set in motion it is quite extraordinary how the released emotion morphs from one state to another. Standing balanced on these waves the actor is carried to wherever the character needs them to be. Making the connections necessary to play the role. All these exercises have that as their major aim.

Once actors get used to the exercises, to freeing their emotions, to allowing all those old walls to be broken down, it all becomes much easier.

Working with actors who have gone the whole route, I find that for most it requires very little more than the beginnings of an anger run before the wave is up and they can surf the scene.

For some it is even easier. I had worked with Lynsey at Mountview, where she was suspicious and resistant to what I was teaching. She now denies this, but I was there... In the last year of the course, with another director, everything fell into place for her. She stopped looking at me with deep mistrust. I used her in *Matchstalk Man*, which was only the second time I had actually directed her. In a subsequent play I cast her opposite a very experienced older actor. She had two short, but very intense scenes with him. On the first rehearsal of these scenes she zoomed into the core of the character, making quick, fierce connections - much to the amazement of her partner. 'Is she always this fast?' he asked me afterwards.

To tell the truth I was also a bit stunned. Also worried. I would normally have expected to get to that level of connection only after a week or so. What it did do, however, was enable us to work in more depth and get to the detail of the scene faster.

Really good actors find their own ways to make these connections. The more instinctive the actor is the more likely they are to break through for themselves. My wife managed fine, even before Athol arrived. Really good actors know where they have to go. The other kind learns to fake it. 'Oh look, shame, she's crying REAL tears.' Audiences are fairly easy to fool - that is, until they start coming up against the genuine article.

The Basic Exercises

We'll start with the basic exercises as worked out at LAMDA, developed at Arts Threshold, and refined at Mountview.

Please remember that each individual is different, these exercises do not all work for everybody. At the start these were formulated for actors to do at home, on their own. There are brave souls who have managed to do this alone, but most need others to be present and help. No matter how you choose to do them you should try each to its fullest extent, and then decide which of them work for you. It is rare for all the exercises to work for one person. A final LARGE warning. Please be realistic about the limitations and drawbacks of your own body, or that of someone you may be helping. People with weak backs or wrists or shoulders should be very careful of any of the exercises that put a strain on such areas. There is always an alternative exercise.

At first the basic exercises numbered four, so I'll start with these and add the newer ones that have come along since.

Exercise 1:

First do an anger run on the text.

Then, after checking that the actor does not have a weak or injured back, shoulders, or wrists, they are asked to push against a handy, strong nearby wall. They need to get quite far from the wall - far enough for their body to be at an angle of roughly 40 degrees to the floor. I'm not good at geometry or maths, but what this means is that they are not just leaning against the wall. Hands extended above their heads they attempt to push the wall over. You need to give them something to push against with their feet. I generally use another actor, against whose firmly-planted foot they can push.

As they push, using their whole body, hips, legs - they must not get stuck in one position - they recite the text.

When I started I used to make them do this as an anger run with some fairly spectacular results. This led to my 'boast' that 'I can destroy a strong man in 45 seconds.' I'll elaborate (though I don't recommend its use any more) as a) it's quite funny, and b) it contains an illustrative lesson on the power of the body's defences.

I had noticed that people tended to get exhausted and lose strength very quickly, sometimes literally dropping off the wall. One day a very strong, fit young man 'fell' after about 15 seconds, scrambled back up, 'fell' almost immediately again, scrambled up, etc. I must admit to thinking he was a bit of a wimp, but afterwards, when he had connected really well to the speech, we were talking. 'Don't know what happened there', he said, 'I played rugby for my first team at school. I was a lock forward in the scrum. We used to push against scrum machines. Nothing like that ever happened.' He thought for a short while. 'Let me try something.' He got up and started to push against the wall again. On and on he pushed, struggling, grunting, sweating - for several minutes. Finally he stood up. He was not even breathing hard. 'I could have gone on for a lot longer. But when I was doing that text all my strength just went.'

Drawing on my vast knowledge of medicine and the body I gave him what I hoped was the correct answer. 'When you're just pushing, that's natural and something you're used to doing. When you add the text and attempt to be very angry your defence mechanisms swing into action. They don't want you to get angry, to escape their control.. So they flood your muscles with lactic acid, which causes them to lose strength. It's like what would happen at the end of 80 minutes of a hectic game of rugby. You know how you feel?' 'Yes,' he said, 'Exhausted. This was worse though. I had no control at all.'

For a while we had great fun, culminating in a session with a rather muscle-bound actor who prided himself on his strength. To his intense chagrin and obvious humiliation he lasted for 18 seconds (we were timing) before dropping to the ground. I stopped using it because it was becoming a circus trick (the longest anyone ever lasted was 36 seconds) and distracting us from our task. I put the anger run first, before getting to the basic exercises, where it does its job very well.

So, just use the text normally - no anger run. Some will have no reaction at all as they push. Others make a major connection immediately and you should immediately move on to the next exercise when that happens.

Once an actor has made a proper connection it does not profit to keep going back to it.

While they are pushing against the wall - being VERY CAREFUL - there are two ways to help. One is to put some pressure on their back, shoulders, hips (ALWAYS ASK if they mind you touching them in this way. If they don't like being touched, don't insist!) This is because those wily defences will make sure that the pushers do not fully exert themselves while pushing. So, to quote Giles in *The Crucible*, you give them 'more weight!' Again BE CAREFUL! This is not a competition between them and you. You are ASSISTING them. This pressure has to be varied. Move from shoulder to shoulder, to middle-back (be especially careful here), to hips. Work with short, gently jolting motions, interspersed with long, firm pressure. What you're trying to do is catch them slightly off-guard, to fool their defences.

I say 'at least once' through the text, but you have to judge this for yourself. Remember that the Secret at the heart of most of these exercises is that you are attempting to exhaust the actor so that their defences will be so busy coping with complaints from the rest of the body that they ignore the text and its attempts to connect to their emotions.

If you are trying out this exercise on your own you can avoid the perils of *Defence Mechanism No 1* (*'Can't remember my lines'*) by putting a low stool or chair against the wall so that, as you lean into the wall, you can see the text. Another method is to record the text on a tape recorder. Several of my students use their mobile phones.

Exercise 2:

The second exercise involves the actor standing up, closing their eyes (and from this point on they keep their eyes closed throughout the rest of the set), turning away from the wall and then sitting against it as though there is a chair. So, propped against the wall, suspended. They should not get too low down as (due to that lactic acid) this can become excruciating. Their head should be against the wall - make sure they keep it there and don't extend their necks forward. In this position they ball their fists and start to drum with the back of their hands on their thighs. It's best if they do this with alternating fists but some people like both hands pounding at the same time.

Do this through once or twice. If they show signs of getting close to a connection don't be scared to repeat. Again it might show no signs of working at all - in which case, move on.

Exercise 3:

For the third exercise you ask them to slide down to the floor - eyes still closed. They then hug their knees to their chests VERY TIGHTLY. Pardon all the CAPS but it is important that the pressure is not only very tight but that it increases throughout the exercise. You will find that, as with pushing against the wall, their Wily Defences will encourage them to relax this grip. I usually appoint another actor to watch out for this and give them a little squeeze on the arm muscle to remind them.

If you have enough people then you can help in the following way. One person, who is generally the under-reader, moves in behind the actor. Standing braced against the wall this person puts their knees against the back of the sitting actor. The actor then pushes back against the knees (which give a slight resistance and forward push) and then pulls themself forward, using their stomach muscles, setting up in this way a rocking motion. The actor aids this motion by pushing back against the knees using their toes - not their heels. I'm not sure why this is important but it is. It works better if the actor pushes with their toes. The actor can put their head on their knees. It's a form of rocking, upright foetal position.

Again run the text - I often use this one six or seven times. It depends on the connection made. By this time, however, the actor should be becoming very tired.

At this stage I used to go on to exercise six, but then I discovered that exercises four and five worked really well, so, here goes.

Exercise 4:

This one seems to be almost innocuous but it can be very effective. The actors lie on their back, arms spread out sideways, and lift their legs straight up into the air. The toes are then pulled down towards the chest. They know when they're doing this properly because their hamstrings get very uptight and complain.

They should try to find a spot in this position where their legs start to tremble. This is usually found with the legs slightly bent at the knee, but for some it's with the legs kept very straight. It's a matter of experimentation for each actor. Finding this 'Tremble Point' is quite important, as it tells them their muscles are hovering on the edge of a release of the emotion trapped in them. Could this possibly be a genetic remnant left over from the animal response Peter Levine talks of in *Waking the Tiger*?

Run the text.

Exercise 5:

This one has a title - *Neelam's Exercise*. It is named after Neelam Parmar, who discovered it by mistake while setting up a speech she had written for herself in a self-devised project at East 15. The speech was set in a gym where the character was going through various aerobic exercises while complaining about the men in her life.

Doing endless sit-ups in rehearsal, Neelam found herself making multiple connections throughout the speech, day-after-day. I started incorporating it in the basic set, with Number 4, and it has proved very successful.

An interesting sidelight: Neelam's speech was used in an expanded devised work - *The Opening* - which was taken to the Edinburgh Festival in 2006. Because she was in another devised piece - *Terrorist! the Musical* (both pieces were products of the Contemporary Theatre Course at East 15, of which I was the first head, from 2002 to 2007.) - she developed her speech and handed it over to another actor - Jenna Wasling. The sit-ups worked well for Jenna, too. But halfway through the Edinburgh run she came to me. The speech was 'going dead' on her. The sit-ups weren't working.

I advised her to stop doing them - the speech didn't specifically require them. Instead she could curl up into a foetal position - whatever suited her. I also told her to stop expecting the speech to work, to stop trying to orchestrate the emotion. 'Let it surprise you.' It's the same old story: start to think consciously and everything vanishes. Being 'in-the-moment' means being in a semi-trance. Any conscious decision hauls you out of this state. While in that blessed state the pre-conscious brain just purrs ahead making its lightning-fast decisions before the spoil-sport conscious brain and its defences can sabotage them

Jenna, a wonderful and very courageous young actor, tried out all this. The speech came back. I met her several days later. 'How's it going?' 'Fine - except that I rather miss the sit-ups.' 'So go back to them - but don't make the decision until the moment before you have to start the speech.' This is good left-brain thinking. It gives the left brain a sop, so that it won't sulk, while, sneakily, the right-brain gets on with its subterranean work. She played happily on - varying the impulse each night.

So the exercise is very simple: on your back, legs pulled up, feet on the ground (a position known in Alexander Technique as semi-supine). The position of the arms is varied and depends on the strength of the actor. Very fit people, used to doing sit-ups, should clasp their hands behind their heads (Superfit people should have another helper giving them slight resistance by holding gently onto their arms as they sit up). This goes right down the scale to the Super-Unfit (this is where I fit in) who are allowed just to clench their tummies while lifting their head off the floor. While people tend to really know they have stomach muscles the following day, the aim is not to damage. Please be careful of this.

Exercise 6:

This involves the actor lying flat on their back, arms stretched out sideways (remember eyes still closed), and whispering the speech. They should do this using lots of air, panting and gasping where necessary to increase the supply. There should be no trace of 'voice' - no sound from the vocal cords. The body should be completely relaxed. The only muscles permitted to work are those of the stomach.

A variation of this - the Laughter Run - involves asking the actor to 'laugh' the line out. No laughing before or after the lines - just expelling the actual words on the laughter breath. Again, no use of the vocal cords.

As you get used to doing these basic exercises you will find that - if you are helping someone - you have to be as instinctively 'in-the-moment' as they are. It soon becomes obvious that an exercise is not working for the actor. Move on to the next, until you find the one that does. But, at first it is best to run through them in the above order.

THINGS TO WATCH OUT FOR... and why...

A Word about Tetany...

One of the most common phenomena arising from the exercises is a tingling feeling in the fingers, or a feeling of numbness in the lips and cheeks. It generally occurs after the actor has been doing quite a lot of deep breathing. This symptom is called Tetany.

Tetany is a condition which is brought on by forced over-breathing, resulting in a reduction of CO_2 in the blood. When I first started doing these exercises there was a great fear of Hyperventilation. I remember buying a book which gave dark warnings of its dangers. You were supposed to make the subject breathe into a brown paper bag to increase the levels of carbon dioxide in their blood. (This is now discouraged as it can lead to too much CO_2 in the blood). I discovered the magic remedy for hyperventilation brought on by over-breathing one day when I was summoned to a class where a young student was hyperventilating quite dramatically. Not knowing quite what to do, but knowing that I was expected to do something, I leaned close to her ear and whispered the magic words: 'Breathe. More. Slowly.' I then matched the rhythm of my breathing to hers and slowed it down. In less than a minute the hyperventilation had vanished.

Hyperventilation is mostly due to anxiety or panic. The magic words will cure this. There are other less common causes, but in all such, reassurance can help relax the breathing.

The symptoms manifest themselves quite quickly. It doesn't happen to everybody, but I've found that more than half of the people I've worked with experience it to a greater or lesser degree. Lesser I've described. A tingling feeling in the fingers, slight numbness in the facial areas. Greater can result in the fingers feeling really painful, the feeling spreading up their arms and, sometimes into the legs, starting with the feet and ankles. In the face this can build to the lips going so numb that the person speaks as though they have just come back from the dentist. At its worst the face feels as though it is constricted by a mask.

Most people experience only the painful/tingling fingers. The very worst case I ever saw was in a group exercise early on where one young man ended up spread out 'like a gingerbread man' - one of his mates observed. When we lifted him off the floor he came up in one piece, and I must admit to a moment of panic. It was very early on in my Mountview days and I'd just discovered the reason for the phenomenon. At that stage - in search of some sort of 'McDonald's Solution' to the problem of working with large groups - I was experimenting with group work. I gave this up later because it was difficult to devote adequate attention to cases like this.

However, after about 10 minutes of slow, controlled breathing (slowly in through the nose, slowly out through the mouth), he was back to his usual, ebullient, though slightly shaken, self. I researched the syndrome as thoroughly as I could. It puzzled me. Why did so many people display these symptoms with only the smallest increase in their regular breathing pattern? And why did it only happen to them once or twice and then not again? Before we examine this, however, some final words on hyperventilation.

I have worked with more than 800 actors now, pushing them all to the edge of hyperventilation. Mostly all you get is a case of tingling fingers or numb lips and cheeks - the first signs of tetany.

Two caveats to this. Be careful of pushing the breathing too hard, especially in a class. Some people slip into a rebirth memory state (More later) very quickly, and while this is not dangerous it is very time-consuming. I've had it happen once and it taught me to watch very carefully for the signs. If somebody quickly begins to show signs of Tetany, slow their breathing, making sure that it is quite shallow. Keeping them standing up is also a way to make sure that they don't enter the state.

Secondly, why do we need to know about tetany? Well, back at Mountview there was a singing concert one evening. There were about two or three a term at which each of the Music Theatre students would have to present a song. One young man sang his song, adopting the most peculiar stance. He had his hands buried in his pockets with his elbows kinked forward in the most uncomfortable way. He was also obviously extremely tense. Afterwards I questioned his singing teacher. She was equally mystified as to the reasons for his odd behaviour.

The following morning he appeared in my office. He was very worried.

'Last night as I was about to go on my hands suddenly did this...' He held up his arms with the hands pulled back almost at right angles, palms forward. 'I tried to straighten them out', he said, 'but I couldn't.' He illustrated this, trying with his hands in this state to pull the fingers forward into a normal position. 'I was really panicking. Then I heard my cue, so I just shoved my hands into my pockets and walked on. It was really embarrassing.'

I asked him whether he had been very nervous while waiting in the wings? 'Yes.' Had he been aware of breathing very hard? 'Yes - I was panting I was so scared.' Was there a tingling feeling in his fingers? 'Yes - they were really painful.' I explained tetany to him, and advised him to do a course in Primal Integrative Breathing. If I had not known what tetany was I would not have been able to help him. He went on to become a member of a rather famous band. As far as I know his fingers no longer trouble him.

So why do so many people display these symptoms with only the smallest increase in their regular breathing pattern? And why does it only happen to them once or twice and then not again?

The answer came in another group session which led me down a new and totally unexpected path. One that causes even more controversy; but one that seems to me to contain the explanation of many of the puzzles that have confronted me since that early question set off by Julie Hesmondhalgh's problem with having no 'affective memories'.

About 10 actors were stretched out flat on their backs, heads inward, in a large circle. They were all doing 'anger-runs' of the speeches they had selected. It was pure cacophony. I reiterate - I don't do this anymore. While the level of noise and emotion can stimulate and set off those who are shy of working on their own, it takes too many people to monitor it. But these were early days.

I became aware of someone on the other side of the circle making a very real connection. I was busy with somebody else doing exactly the same thing so I couldn't go around to her. When I finally did she had calmed down and was lying on her back with her legs drawn up to her chest. She was whispering the words of her speech, quietly - almost moaning them. Emma had just been teaching me the rudiments of hand pressure.

One that had worked a treat on me personally (back during my Bioenergetics therapy sessions) was a slight pressure on the chest at the base of the throat. You'll know the place. When somebody tells a particularly moving story many of the listeners will go 'Ohhh' with real empathy, and put their hands on their upper chests. It's a universal gesture. I've just seen it in a telly programme on a recently-discovered Amazonian tribe, used by a fearsome woman with bones stuck through her nose. But, as her modern visitor told her about the child she had left at home, the painted face softened and her hand went to her chest.

So, on this day, I gently put my hand on that spot. She moaned a bit more loudly, then started crying in a high-pitched voice. Her hands came up to try and take my hand away. Both were being held in the same strange shape. Four fingers clasped, fingertips together, opposite the thumb - like a mitten. They dabbed softly and with no power at my hand. I knew she was trying to get a grip on me. I took my hand off. Looking down on her I thought: 'This is a baby.'

Afterwards, when all had quietened down and we were sitting discussing the process - a regular part of those early workshops to find out what worked and what didn't, and to give them time to calm down - someone said: 'Who was that crying like a baby.' The actor herself didn't even remember it, but the people on either side of her identified her. I asked her about her experience. She couldn't remember much. 'But I did feel like a baby - really helpless, really lost, really weak.'

Rebirthing

The demonstration workshop had been held about a month earlier. In one of the discussions a member of the 'audience' had said to me: 'What you do is very much like rebirthing.' Now, I knew very little about rebirthing and what I did know wasn't good. A product of the New Age 60s, it had gained a large measure of notoriety somewhere in the 80s, I think, when a group who claimed to be practising it, placed a young girl in a sack and forced her to try and fight her way out. Rebirthing is supposedly a way of getting the body/mind to re-experience the circumstances of its birth, thus releasing many inbuilt tensions and traumas. The people with her became over-enthusiastic and ended up suffocating the poor child. This even featured much later as a case in the American drama series - *CSI*. I really did not want to have anything to do with such a process. What was it that I did I asked? It seemed that it was my way with breathing. I had actually drawn this from a process used in Bioenergetics. I asked Emma about it. She had actually undergone the process and was not wild about it. She did add that she felt that the fault may have lain with the practitioner she worked with. I began to ask around. I don't like putting my students through something I haven't done myself. It took me almost a year to find a practitioner that somebody would recommend. His name was Rick Zoltowski. A theatre director who ran his own company, he also practised as a rebirther. By this time the name had changed to Integrative Breathing as established and respectable practitioners realised that they couldn't fight the bad publicity which had resulted from the actions of those on the wilder shores of alternative therapy.

As I had waited to find someone there had been two programmes on the box investigating such alternative therapies. Both had included short and highly-coloured items on rebirthing, sending it and its practitioners up rigid. These practitioners seemed largely to consist of people with long hair, beards and beads, dressed in caftans, looking like throwbacks to the 60s, and generally 'practising' their 'arts' against a background of throbbing drums or gongs. As television it was very funny observing the work of people several cards short of a full deck. As intelligent contribution to debate and knowledge it wasn't.

I arrived at my first appointment with Rick, as full of trepids as any of my students would ever be.

He turned out to be an eminently sane, disappointingly ordinary-looking man. No caftan, no drums. Just a very ordinary flat on Highgate Hill. We talked about why I was there. My major Stanislavskian objective was obviously to find out what it was about the breathing techniques Integrative Breathing used that it seemed I was also using. A small secondary objective (Stan would have been proud of me) was the hope that the technique might be able to help me with the very high stress levels I was working under at Mountview. I had been reading up on Rebirthing (all the books still called it that) and it seemed that it could be of help here. Rick was fairly non-committal about the benefits. 'It's different for everyone' he said.

So I lay down on the pulled-out sofa bed in his lounge, he pulled up a chair, placed a large box of tissues next to me, and off we went. The first session was rather disappointing and also rather frustrating. All he was asking me to do was what is called Circular Breathing. You open your mouth and breathe slowly in and out. This has to be done in a smooth, uninterrupted flow. Breathe in deeply, fill the whole diaphragm and rib cage, right down to your tum. Then breathe out. Sounds simple. You are not allowed to catch or hold your breath at the end of the in or out breath. It's like smoothly turning a corner as you just let the relaxed out-breath flow out of you. I couldn't do it. My lungs started playing all kinds of tricks with me. Mostly I just could not go around that corner and let go. Just over an hour later the breathing part of the session ended with me in a state of terminal frustration.

I won't bore you with a long story about the 10 sessions I had with Rick. I will say that, if I ruled the world - which, sadly, I don't - all drama students (and, frankly, everybody else) would undergo this process.

By about session 7 my stress level had dropped from 110% to ± 5%.

Another 'benefit': I don't curse the world with my singing - I'm not that cruel. But in my car, with the windows closed, I love a good sing. Don't lie - I'm not alone here. I have a list of perennials, evergreens. One featured a note which I had never managed to hit. As my poor vocal cords struggled to reach up to it they would crack. Didn't matter in my car. But one day shortly after completing my course with the patient Rick I launched into it on the way to work one morning. The car groaned quietly in anticipation. But, dear Reader, I made it. For the first time. My car was flabbergasted - and grateful.

Even my vocal range had expanded. Another by-product: I found that I was no longer succumbing to the Road Rage which, up to then, had badly affected me.

What weird voodoo had Rick perpetrated? Well, none really. All he'd ever done was keep me on the straight and narrow as far as my breathing was concerned. I'd managed to conquer Circular Breathing in the second session, and then this started a wonderful process of release and integration. Nothing dramatic, no uncovering of deep, traumatic memories of my birth. Rather my conscious mind would go on holiday while my body - this is difficult to describe unless you've seen it - seemed to be re-enacting memories in order, subconsciously, to understand them.

This was before Goleman's *Emotional Intelligence* had introduced me to the brain. Before Candace Pert's *Molecules of Emotion* had proved that we do, indeed, trap emotions in our muscles.

With hindsight and much more experience my take on this is that during the actual process of birth, and in the 18 months or so that follow when the baby can't talk, many unexplained and seemingly life-threatening things happen. This huge, comforting integral part of yourself suddenly puts you down and walks away! Now, discovering that this huge, comforting thing is not a part of you, and knowing that it is the source of ALL - food, warmth, succour - you watch in horror as it leaves you and walks out of the room.

You have to put yourself in the booties of the baby. Time. The next 15 minutes of your life are going to be the merest blip to you. But, as Albert said: 'Time is relative.' At the moment, as I sit here, I can almost feel it streaking past me. I am filled with horror at how fast it has gone. But I can clearly remember thinking how unimaginably far in the future 1984 was. As for 2001... I'd better not blink or I'll miss the 2012 Olympics. Further back and I remember how, at the age of 10 or 12, the last week of term seemed to stretch interminably.

So, back to the baby. The first conscious second of life is a full eternity. Then the process starts. The 2nd second is half-an-eternity. The 3rd... do the maths yourself.

So when that big thing (not known as Mom yet) vanishes out of the door, unspeakable horror fills your soul. Without being able to articulate it with words and concepts yet you KNOW you are no longer going to exist. Your source of sustenance and nurture has gone. You wait, panic filling your tiny helpless body as the infinite seconds of eternity tick by. Non-existence seeps through your whole defenceless, feeble frame.

At the end of the blackest eternity through which you have ever suffered - impotent and filled with the knowledge that you are to cease to exist – at the end of this endless five minutes - 'it' comes back in. Feelings of relief and rage and pain flood your whole being. You let it know, loudly and in no uncertain terms, of the hell you have just lived through.

This is pure, 100%, undiluted feeling. No words, no concepts, just pure feeling. Un-understood. Horrible word but what other one describes it?

And for actors, the most wonderful resource.

Stored in the recesses of your brain, in the muscles of your body, all these 'un-understood' feelings.

In order to understand why these storehouses are such a wonderful resource, but also why - if they remain locked - they can be such a block to our ability to act and, even worse, to our ability to develop and grow as human beings; in order to understand why, we have finally come to the word that has been used a lot in this book - defences. We need to understand how these essential processes function - how they can, and do, save us; but how they can also chain us and stunt our lives.

This process - of understanding things from the baby's point of view - finally led me to another understanding. Remember that I had decided that there were Three Primary Emotions? I now believe that it is simpler (and more complex) than this. It's a journey. A journey which goes from perfect peace, through fear and anger, to pain. The baby lies, content, floating, in a temperature-controlled environment, fed on demand through the placenta and the umbilical cord, Mozart filtering sweetly in as s/he sucks at the comforting thumb and 'knows' (remember – no words or concepts yet...) that this is an absolutely fantastic way to live....Ummmm.

Suddenly! #?#!!! - terrible, strange things start to happen. The only lovely, warm home it has ever known in the endless eternity of its short existence - KICKS IT OUT! Contractions squeeze its poor, fragile frame, crush its head, and shove it into a frightening, terrifying, painful, inevitable journey. It does not matter that this is a destiny written into its genes. Peace is shattered, fear and pain are roughly introduced, forced upon the poor little thing. The journey can be anything from a quick 20 minutes to 2-3 days in our grown-up time. For the baby – still counting time in seconds that are each an eternity - this is the beginning process of their life. It will leave traces that the body will never forget (read *Molecules of Emotion* by Candace Pert), that will entrench rough patterns as the defences try desperately to cope with this avalanche of new information, emotion and threat - the patterns which will later form the basis of what I call The Un-Understood. And, following hard on the heels of the Pain and Fear that replace that perfect Peace, is Anger.

The Journey: Peace/Joy → Pain/Fear → Anger.

Another sidelight: Why does almost everyone suffer from Tetany? Think about it. Most of us share a similar experience. In our lives there was one person suffering from Tetany - our mother. Most birth processes encourage the mother to adopt a forced/panting breathing process?. Thus the cycle rolls on, mother-to-baby. I haven't done a proper survey on this, but I can tell you that several of the Caesarean birth students I have dealt with showed no trace of tetany. And don't get me started on the babies whose mothers decided very late in the process that they actually did want that epidural, and who, it seemed, were born asleep?

What I have found through the rebirthing process is that once this feeling, this tetany, has been experienced once or twice it goes away. It's almost as though the brain has said to itself: 'Oh, now I understand.' What was subconsciously un-understood becomes subconsciously understood. You don't suddenly get a thought in your head telling you what and why. But your subconscious knows that this terrible feeling is no longer a threat.

Defences

And so, very late but, I think, at the appropriate time, we arrive at an explanation of those processes that have played such a major part in everything talked of above - the defences. Actors need to understand what they are and how they function - the battle against their system of control will never end.

Remember back in the dark pages when we were talking of the brain and, especially, the amygdala? Well, it's back to there we must go now.

Generally, when I started introducing these exercises to a new class, after giving them a run-down on the brain, etc., we then move on to demonstrating the exercises. I call this part of the class - with due academic decorum - *'Say Hello to your Defences!'* This is because the vast majority of us have little idea of just how tightly we are controlled by these defences. I tell my classes: 'You may think you're in control of yourself - I'm going to show you just how out of control you are - how little actual control you exercise over your reactions.' It's really a very simple proof. Just one anger run is enough to drive most people into a state of fight, flight or freeze. Into involuntary action, over which they seem to have no control.

Then I can go further down the road of proving that, while they feel in a rather panicky way that they are going out of control, this is actually the first step on the road of going into control, of gaining real control of their emotions and reactions.

So let's look at what I understand to be happening within our defensive system.

Firstly, and very importantly, we NEED our defences.

A personal story which illustrates both the up and down sides of our defences.

When in 1992 my wife, my partner of 30 years, died, I knew it was coming, had had some time to prepare. Of course nothing can prepare you. If my defences had not rushed to my aid, shutting down all feeling, putting me - and the other members of my family - into a rather strange hyper-state - I don't think I'm being very fanciful in thinking that the pain would have killed me as well. Over the minutes, hours, days, weeks immediately after, I could assure everyone with total honesty, it seemed, that I was 'fine'. For weeks, even months, I 'coped' extraordinary well.

I even managed to feel a bit guilty about how well I was 'coping'.

My defences kept me alive.

Then time took me headlong into the downside. Not that I noticed.

I was running Arts Threshold in Paddington, while still earning my crusts at LAMDA..

I arrived one afternoon from a morning of classes. The Arts Threshold venue was in a church hall in the basement of a block of flats. As I descended into its depths I saw immediately that a) the front door was unlocked! (Meaning that anyone could walk in off the street and steal everything!), and b) the booking desk immediately inside the unlocked door was a MESS!, with flyers for other theatres strewn higgledy- piggledy around! Within seven seconds I was in a rage!! An envelope propped up amongst the MESS! caught my eye. 'Brian'. I ripped it open.

'Dear Brian,' it said, *'you are behaving most weirdly. We are very worried about you. Can we talk? Love, Julie.'* (Yes, the same one).

I locked the door and stalked around the dark innards, searching for culprits. Empty. Out the back were two arched coal holes dug in under the pavement. We had converted them into dressing-rooms. Clenched in anticipation in the women's side I found the letter-writer. The rest of the group, who had egged her on, had - cowards that they were - repaired to the local pub and left her to deal with me and the 'talk'. To say I was outraged is to understate shamelessly. You can understand - can't you?

I screamed at her. 'What the hell is this all about!!' She started to reply. I am not easily stopped in full flow. 'I come in here, the door's open, the place is a MESS!...' I'll cut the description of a quite ugly scene to the point where Julie - one of the bravest people on the planet – managed to get some words in. 'This is what we're talking about.' She was pointing at me. 'You come in here, and in seconds you're yelling at us...' 'Of course I am!! I've got every reason?.' 'No!' she said firmly. 'We've known you for nearly four years now and you NEVER lose your temper. Now you're losing it every day.'

The scene reached no resolution on that day. Swearing and cursing I stormed out and went home, leaving the ungrateful bastards to run the place on their own!

My home was a 20-minute drive away. I stormed up the three flights of stairs, switched on the kettle, and slumped into a chair. In the quiet I could hear myself panting. I became aware that my hands were shaking. I became aware that I was indeed behaving very 'weirdly'. I had once been described by a kind person in my Space days in South Africa as 'the calm centre of the hurricane.' I could count the times in my life when I had lost my temper on the fingers of one hand. Now it was a daily occurrence - and I hadn't even noticed.

Something was wrong.

I can't remember whether I apologised to Julie and the Cowards - I hope I did.

My defences had done a sterling job. Protected me from the emotion that would have seriously damaged me. Thank you. But then, like an unregulated police force, they became power-crazed. Kept me locked up - at least, kept all my emotions locked up. I've come to think of this in the following terms - if you consider your life as a waveform, then a healthy life has an evenly balanced set of ups and downs - you have to have both or life would be most boring. Some of us have rather higher peaks and troughs than others, but that's OK - we need to feel. However, our defences are set up to make sure that these 'feelings' don't get out of hand. So they build walls around each trough-moment to help you carry on your daily life. Their idea of an ideal waveform for you is fairly close to what, in a hospital, is called a 'flat line'. And you know what that means...

So these walls are spread like mountain ranges through your psyche, 'protecting' you. This would be fine - if your defences had the ability to break down the old, now useless, ones built-in. But they don't. Mine had built a giant stone castle around me, pulled up the drawbridge and sealed me from all feeling.

Emotions will not be denied. Will not be imprisoned. Will not lie down and die. They ferment, grow acidic, try to find escape routes.

This is only a theory of mine (and not an original one) but I think this incarceration causes illness, extreme stress, ulcers, cancer. Later I heard of the apparently quite well-documented fact that if one member of a couple who have shared a life dies, it is not unusual for the other one to follow 18 months to two years later. I have certainly seen this in my own experience. Had I not had my wake-up call it might have happened to me.

Instead I found a Bioenergetics therapist (it's a very physical, not talk-based, therapeutic method) to help me finally to express my grief. My later experience with Primal Integrative Breathing took me further down this road. So I survived. And learnt a lot about what it feels like to let go of emotion. About the fear of loss of 'control'.

You need defences. But you also need to know when to break down the old walls. If for no other reason than that you can be ready for all the new challenges that life throws at you, unencumbered by old and useless defences.

So, the actor stands in the rehearsal room with the dreaded script (though under-reading relieves them of this fear/crutch). Quite frequently, at a first reading, some small, true connections are made. However, as the process continues, the actor feels the emotion crawling up through their body attempting to find a way out along the legitimate route, i.e. up from the depths of the belly, via the diaphragm and lungs, up the throat, out through the mouth - and problems arise when this emotion is extreme. The character's very real feelings travel that path through the actor, trying to find sustenance and support on the way. Trying to feed off the emotions of the actor to give itself life.

What happens now - unless you are in the presence of an extraordinarily emotionally free and released actor - is that all the character's and the actor's emotions can do is join hands through the bars of the various prisons, guarded fiercely, but rather stupidly, by our aforementioned defences. They're stupid because they don't know any better. Especially if they're guarding a prison, patrolling a wall, built to protect a baby.Like the baby they had no words. No concepts to explain the 'trauma'. All they have is a very rough pattern which signals Danger! So, doing their job, they bolt the doors, lock the shutters. In vain the character's outstretched hand tries to join with and free the life-giving emotions of the actor.

Blocked.

What these exercises do is twofold. Firstly, they act as what I have called a Left-Brain-Disabling-Device. Remember that the poor little Left Brain can only hold seven bytes of information in its teeny palm at any one time? Well, fill it with several words and an action that has to be done, and it is soon clogged up, and relinquishes its responsibility for the acting process - surrendering it to the Magnificent Right (sub- or pre-conscious) Brain.

Your defences, however, are pretty tough and they love you much more than your mommy and daddy did - and that's saying some! They don't give up without a struggle. They don't want you to hurt, or to get too angry (wouldn't it be horrible if you lost control and tore the wallpaper down, or damaged someone?). They really don't want you to embarrass yourself (What if you burst into tears in front of everyone? Heaven forbid!)

Acting is impossible without these emotional connections; these displays of your 'vulnerability'.

Right up until her last play my wife - who was never very forthcoming about her rehearsal process, being very superstitious - would arrive home at a latish state of rehearsal and, in response to my query, would say: 'I had my weeps today.' I came to understand that this was the day in which she finally connected to the character.

Rather wonderfully there is such a moment captured on film. Another extraordinary actor, Judi Dench, is rehearsing *A Little Night Music* at the National Theatre. I think it was filmed for the South Bank Show. She is working on *Send in the Clowns*, and on a particular line you can feel the 'ping' of emotion radiating from her. A small tear trickles down her cheek. Afterwards, being very English, she apologises to her patently thrilled director for this 'naked' display of emotions. As the titles run at the end the cameras are recording the opening night (I think) from the wings. She is singing the song in that wonderfully cracked voice. As she delivers that line the same 'ping' of emotion, now safely connected and integrated with the character, radiates out.

This is what acting is all about. Actors allow the characters to show them just exactly what it felt like; characters demand that the actors descend into their underworld of pain and rage, despair, loneliness, shame, guilt - and emerge into the light to communicate this to their audience. Properly done, some members of the audience feel: 'Thank the gods I'm not alone'. For others it helps prepare them to cope should this terror ever be inflicted on them.

Acting, properly done, is a noble art. Much misunderstood because of that 98% of rampant vanities that hijack its truth.

To do it properly then a connection must be made.

And this is where the second purpose of the exercises comes into play.

Sorry about all these metaphors, but they help me to understand.

Surfing. A wonderful sport which sadly came too late for me. The surfer lies on the board on the swelling ocean. A wave approaches. The surfer begins to paddle furiously. The wave picks up the board. Its brave rider scrambles into a standing position, balancing precariously. The wave curls majestically and carries the exhilarated rider towards the shore. It's one of humanity's closest approaches to the ability to fly.

The metaphor should be obvious.

The actor surfs on an ocean of emotions. Catch the wave when it peaks and you can fly. Miss it and you stay in the same spot, bobbing quietly on a large ocean, little connection between you and its throbbing drive.

In the rehearsal room we are floating in a swimming pool. The actor and director have to create their own waves.

Enter the exercises!

All - from the basic pushing-against-a-wall ones, to the ubiquitous anger run - serve one major purpose: to create a wave of emotion. On this the character can surf with the actor. It doesn't matter if the character's emotion is not anger. Once the wave is set in motion it can take any form it wishes.

It's all about energy. Set energy in motion and things happen. The text, and what lives beneath its surface, will give that energy direction and focus.

All that is required now is that the actors learn to stand back and allow the characters to take what they need. When you get used to this process of 'allowing', it's a very quick and easy way to connect. It doesn't take long to find your 'weeps', for that single tear to mark its much deeper connection.

The process works best with people who are prepared to let go, to be vulnerable. At first it can take some time for those old walls to be broken down and cleared. But it's very healthy. In surprising ways. I came in on a conversation between three young woman attending a Sunday workshop at Mountview. 'Best thing about these classes is - my skin is lovely and clear for several days after...' The other two agreed.

Maybe I should have been a beautician. We worked out that it was the over-breathing that was probably causing the blood to get rid of impurities, taking in much oxygen and getting rid of all that carbon dioxide - it's a theory...

A Question of Control

A constant in the putting into practice of these exercises is the feeling that arises of 'I'm going out of control'. As I have said this is only a result of your over-zealous police force trying to 'protect' you from actually feeling any real feelings. So they blare out huge warnings in tabloid banner headlines. The closer you get to the actual connection the larger the headlines. Just as the tabloids over-use of large type has resulted in their inability to impart any real information - their readers having grown inured to 1000pt BOLD, black fonts - so your defences try to fool you.

You really have two defensive systems: the conscious, screaming-headlines, out-of-balance police force, and a much quieter health system that knows exactly how to keep you well. If you learn to listen to this one you will avoid most imbalances that arise psychosomatically. Let's face it - we all know it. It's constantly whispering quietly in your ear: 'You're eating too much', 'You really should exercise more', 'Smoking/drugs/cream cakes are BAD for you.'

Unlike the Bad Police Force defences that are whispering: 'You really are the worst actor on earth...', this health system can be trusted.

So, there you are, pushing like hell against a wall, and you suddenly feel a rather large wave of emotion surging up from your toes. 'MayDay! MayDay!!' yells the police force and tries to shut down all your systems. Generally it has no idea what it's protecting your against. It has just detected a rough pattern from your past that once spelt danger. Mostly these fears are based on baby memories. Remember? When that big thing, later to be known as Mom, left the room for unconscionable eternities, creating a scarred fear of abandonment which has no words to describe it - only leaving an inarticulate pattern. Now your police force is responding to this un-understood alarm call. It's only doing its job. Your job is to teach it that this particular pattern, this seemingly unbreachable wall, is, in fact, no longer valid.

I'm not going to kid you. This requires courage. An essential component of the actor's toolbox.

And there'll be a big problem confronting you when you begin. You've read this far. You've read about the fears of 'tipping over the edge'. Possibly my reassurances that - if you are in that small percentage that live this close to that edge - you will be protected by that deeper health system, which will either prevent you from doing it, or help you to 'act it out' - possibly these reassurances are not enough.

'What if...' What if I really do go out of control, slip over that edge, fall into chaos.

Well, let me keep up the reassurances.

Join the club. Every single actor I have ever worked with has had this fear. 'If I let go of all my anger I will rip up the carpet, break the windows, destroy the furniture. Hurt someone.' 'If I let go of all this pain - I will embarrass myself in front of all my mates; I will show that I'm weak and vulnerable. I will never be able to stop crying.'

To digress for a short moment on 'showing vulnerability': I don't know about you, but I don't go to the theatre to see some SuperPerson who can cope with anything life has to hurl. I go to be reassured that I'm not alone in my terrors, that somebody understands my pain. An actor's greatest gift to their audience is that vulnerability.

So how can I convince you that you will not topple into insanity?

Several more stories to illustrate the concept of 'Going Into Control'.

The first came in a LAMDA acting class when I was still experimenting - at that stage rather blindly. A young man whose name I have shamefully forgotten, and Connie Hyde, a tough, brave actor, were rehearsing a two-handed scene. The male character was very angry so I pushed the actor really hard. This was before I discovered the anger run. Suddenly his rage really exploded and he had Connie pinned up against the wall. The scene was electric.

He pulled away as soon as the last line was spoken. Still very angry. He was not happy about his actions. 'You shouldn't have pushed me that far!' he said. 'Why?' 'Because I could have hurt her.' 'But you didn't.' 'Yes, but I could have.' 'Did you feel that he was out of control? That he was going to hurt you?' I asked Connie. 'Not for a moment.' she said, 'Even when he slammed me against the wall, I knew he was completely in control.'

He was not mollified. Several other class members volunteered their opinion that, while the violence was very realistic, they had never felt that it was unsafe.

Story no. 2:

At Mountview several years later we were working on a scene. The young actor was holding his anger at arm's length, so we utilised the Pin-down technique. I don't like this exercise, and it would not still be in the repertory if it wasn't so effective. Also, if so many actors didn't specifically ask for it.

What happens is that the actor lies on the floor. Then, WITH GREAT CARE, the other actors take the following positions: One sits between the actor's legs with their back to the pin-ee. They hook their arms through the raised knees and hold on tight. This fairly effectively freezes the legs. No.2 squats over the stomach/hip area, knees on either side. THEY MUST NOT SIT ON THE PIN-EE! In effect they are like a jockey. Their job is to 'ride' the middle part of the body. They also put their hands on the collarbones but, again, THEY EXERT NO PRESSURE, only provide resistance.

Pardon all the caps, but they're necessary. This exercise has to be carried out with real care.

Two other actors place one hand on the pin-ee's shoulder and with the other hold on to the wrist. Now here caps are not enough, but they are all I have. YOU MUST UNDER NO CIRCUMSTANCES LEAN YOUR WEIGHT ON THE SHOULDER OR ARM! YOU CAN

DO REAL DAMAGE TO BONE AND MUSCLE! The object, once again, is only to provide resistance.

If you have one more person s/he guards of the head so that it can't bang on the floor. Otherwise just put a low pillow or folded-up jacket under the head.

The object of the exercise now is that the pin-ee - while doing the speech - attempts to get up, to throw off the pin-ners.

I will say it once more - THE PIN-NERS ARE ONLY THERE TO GIVE RESISTANCE. ON NO ACCOUNT SHOULD THEY EXERT PRESSURE!

The exercise is exhausting for the pin-ee, and quite tiring for the pin-ners. It took me some time to realise that the reason that people kept asking for it is that it makes them feel safe from all those 'what if's' above.
The first time I realised this was when a smallish group of women were attempting to hold down a large and very strong young man. I remember looking at him and thinking that he'd be able to throw all of them off with a flick of an arm.

When we spoke afterwards I brought this up. His reply raised another interesting issue. 'Probably,' he said, 'but I wasn't thinking about that really. It was interesting. Whenever the character felt strong in the speech I knew I could easily have got out of it. But where he felt weak I just didn't have the strength to do anything. I felt completely helpless - like him.'

Characters take over the actor.

So, there was our angry young man being pinned down by seven other actors (two on his feet to help with the legs). And he was getting truly angry. So angry that he started to spit at the one 'riding' him. Not, I hasten to add, wet spit - more like the action that gives rise to the expression 'spitting with rage'.

During the bonny struggle that followed the actor closest to me, who was giving resistance on his arm, lost control. He managed to wriggle his hand out of her grasp and reached up to grab at his 'ride'.

What I am now about to describe happened a 100,000 times faster than it takes to write down or even to read.

I reached my right hand out to help her regain. I saw his eyes flick to my hand. His hand shot out and grabbed my middle finger, bending it back on itself to within a millimetre of snapping. But he stopped. We regained control of the arm and the exercise kept going.

Afterwards, as we did an exhausted sum up/calm down talk, I said: 'You really wanted to break my finger, didn't you?' His eyes glinted. 'You're bloody lucky. I wanted to snap it right off!' 'But you didn't.' 'No. But you're still bloody lucky.'

I expect I am. Accidents can happen. The interesting part is that I could feel him stop. Sure, there was a nanosecond as that hand streaked towards mine when I felt 'Ohhh s**t ...', but in the nanosecond thereafter, as his fingers closed around mine, I had no further feeling of panic - just knew that nothing serious would happen. Hindsight? No, that's what I 'knew' in the moment.

The next story does not concern acting.

There was a knock on my door (always open) at Mountview. It was a Music Theatre student - Craig Giovanelli. He came in and closed the door - always a bad sign. It meant that the student had something serious and private to discuss. Craig was (and still is) a darkly good-looking young man of Italian extraction - of which he was very proud. He was also known as one of the strongest young men in the school. Nobody messed with Craig.

'I'm having problems with my group.' he said. We would remix the groups each term in the hopes (vain) that they would finish their course having worked with all the other members of their year. In this way they would learn how to cope with the vastly different characters and acting styles of their mates. It was fairly early in the term and he was still adjusting to his new group.

'They p**s me off! They're w*****s! I've been getting REALLY angry in class. I'm scared someone is going to push me too far and I'll hurt him.' One of his tutors had mentioned that Craig was being baited by two rather foolhardy mates.

I attempted to work my way through the issue with him, to calm him down, find a solution which would keep him in the group. He wanted to be moved. 'I'm going to lose it and hurt someone.'

We were heavily involved in this when there was a hammering knock on the door and, without waiting, it was opened.

Dan Poole's head appeared around it, fairly high up (Dan was approximately half-way from 6 to 7 foot tall). 'They're here!' he barked, 'The guys who mugged X.'

X was a sweet, small young student who had, the previous week, been held up with a knife (he thought - he never saw it) to the ribs in the main Wood Green thoroughfare and robbed of his wallet by two young men.

The school was in an ooze of sympathy for him.

What had happened today was that the two young robbers had recognised him in the street and followed him back to the School. Obviously not belonging to the Brain of Britain Club they had followed him into the building, up the stairs, and into the canteen - where he had taken refuge with some mates. Dan had seen this, knew that Craig was with me (my room was across the hall from the canteen), and here he was.

Craig jumped into action. My heart plunged into my trainers. Here was an already enraged young man rushing into an inflammatory situation.

He didn't, however, go into the canteen. X was safe - there were many other students there to protect him. Instead - followed by Dan, with me bringing up a reluctant rear - he sprinted down the stairs. There was only one way out of the building. We stood in the reception area, me behind Craig and Dan. The two young men came down the stairs, having realised their mistake. As the one saw Craig and Dan waiting he sat down on the lowest step, his hands on his knees, head bowed. 'I'm cool, man...' he said.

The other was not going to go easily. He began to dance around the area as threateningly as he could, trying to work his way past the two guardians. One hand was in his pocket in an attempt to make us believe that he had a knife or a gun. I, for one, was fooled.

Once again - in fractional fractions of the time it takes to tell - the following happened: Craig slid into the space, feinted one way, in the next instant had Stupid Mugger's other hand bent behind his back, and - in one smooth movement - pushed him to the ground and was sitting on his back.

The police were called, the muggers removed, the excitement began to die down, and I invited Craig back into my office.

'So, tell me what just happened?' I said. 'Errr...' he said, indicating that I'd been there and should know. 'OK.' I said. 'I'll tell you. You've just been in a situation where, if you had broken that guy's arm, stomped on his chest, punched his face to pulp, you would have been surrounded by a cheering, approving crowd, flushed with blood-lust and the desire for revenge for what he had done to one of our favourite, defenceless students. Instead - and I have to express my admiration here - you disarmed him cleanly and clinically. If it had been a Fight Test you would have got top marks. I think most of us are a bit disappointed that you didn't even seem to give him a teeny bruise. Yet, just before this all happened, you were telling me of how you might lose control and damage some of your mates. What do you think the chances are?'

'They are REALLY p*****g me off.' he muttered, but left to bask in the adoration of just about every female student in the place, and the deep green glow of envy from all the males. Except X - for whom he was The Greatest Superhero.

You don't go out of control - you go into control.

A Word about the Imagination

Something interesting happened one day in a rehearsal which not only solved a problem with what to do with people with weak or injured muscles, but also opened a further window onto the power of the imagination.

I was working with a rather large and powerful young actor. He wanted to use the pin-down exercise as it had once been very successful for him. Unfortunately on that day we only had three other actors - all women. We tried, but it was pretty obvious very soon that he was far too strong.

Mercury screeched to a halt, slight irritation on his face at seeing it was me again. This time the message was startlingly simple.

'Lie down on your back.' I told him. Obediently he stretched out. 'Put your arms out sideways in a sort-of crucifix formation.' He did. 'Now,' I said, relaying the message from the gods with great faithfulness and not a little doubt that it would work, 'you have iron shackles on your arms here and here' - and I indicated each wrist - 'here and here' - and I indicated each ankle. 'You also have a large hoop around your waist which is pinning you to the ground. All these are made of the strongest iron and are IMPOSSIBLE to get out of. Now do your speech and try.'

You really can trust the gods. As he struggled and sweated - now with the four of us sitting calm and unfussed, watching him - the most extraordinary thing happened. The battle was now with himself. Afterwards he said: 'It was amazing - I was really trying to get out. I thought: 'This is stupid - there are no shackles', but I couldn't lift my arms, couldn't move my legs. It was like there really were shackles holding me down. Then I forgot about the reality and the speech just took me over.'

The speech DID take him over. All the appropriate connections were made.

I have subsequently used this technique many times and rarely use the pin-down technique any more. Good actors don't need it.

A sidelight on this. I was working with two actors at E15 on a very confrontational scene. We were sitting outside on the grass on a lovely sunny day. In the scene the power switched hands three or four times, ending with the woman triumphant. I had two very strong-minded actors - neither of whom was much willing in their ordinary life to give way to anyone else.

I asked them to embrace each other (the two characters were lovers) while lying on the ground and then attempt to roll onto each other to establish control. This while doing an anger run. Interestingly as her character took the power the woman was able to roll the man onto his back - ending in triumph as the scene demanded. The actor said: 'As she took the power, my muscles lost power.' He was much bigger than her and could easily have kept her pinned down.

The imagination is directly connected to the muscles.

This also set me on the track of exercises for people for whom it would be difficult. There is always an alternative exercise involving the use of the imagination. It generally involves the creation of an imaginary tension through an imaginary exercise.

The final story illustrates the importance of this 'going into control' and the trust that is needed between actors.

At The Space we were doing Wolfgang Bauer's *Magic Afternoon*. This very violent play has an area in which the man slaps the woman, not once but several times. The actor in question was Vincent Ebrahim. The two experimented with various stage slaps, none of which looked convincing. The nearest member of the audience was two feet away. Finally they decided that he would just have to slap her for real. Again they experimented. If he cupped his hand it made a really loud, convincing sound while, at the same time, not hurting as much. However, he had to hit her on a very specific area of her cheek, along the jawbone. Too high and he would hit her in the eye, too low and he hit her on the jugular. It also had to be at the right angle as getting out of sync really hurt her.

The performance provoked more controversy than almost any other that we did. Audiences would gather outside afterwards to argue about its issues. The violence of the slapping was horrifying. I kept in touch with her through the run. 'It's OK,' she would say, 'My ears ring for a while, but he's never missed the spot yet.'

Actors have to be in complete control of their emotions, able to communicate intense rage while free of the fear of harming their partner.

Of course there will be accidents. Ted Whitehead's *Alpha Beta* is famous for its knock-down, drag-out fight between the couple whose relationship it is filleting. We did it at The Space with Yvonne and a wonderful actor, Percy Sieff. Once again the audience were within arm's length. Even worse they were on three sides. Any form of stage fight was out of the question. Neither Yvonne nor Percy would countenance it.

They carefully choreographed a fight which looked horrifically real. The stage fight maxim is: 'It's not the action - it's the reaction' (Stan was right). Over a six-week run they pummelled each other mercilessly. There were small accidents, mostly involving a set rather overloaded with furniture. Yvonne would sit mournfully in the bath counting her bruises. Percy and she had a little competition as to who could count up the most.

On the second-last night of a very successful run Yvonne tripped over a chair, went off-balance, and fell straight onto poor Percy's punch.

It was a measure of their trust that Percy was not withholding any power - he was expecting her to be in position to fold over the blow and give the reaction. Instead he fractured a rib.

Percy was in a state of shock despite Yvonne's reassurances that it had been her (and the chair's) fault. She played the last night tightly strapped up, with Percy being far too careful. The fight lost all of its power.

There is little room for faking in theatre.

Exercises for disabling the Left Brain

It's not rocket science. I started using left-brain-disabling-devices - without knowing I was - very early on. While working on *The Guise* I asked a poor actor, Tim Chipping, to tap dance while playing a scene. Another person who has never forgiven me - but it worked a treat. On another occasion I asked a young actor in an audition process to do her speech while rearranging the 12 or so chairs that were on the stage in different patterns. She did it so well that we took her.

The point is to get the actors to do something which will take their minds off the lines - disable the left brain. Meisner used it all the time. Perform a possibly unrelated action while playing the scene.

Some of mine:

- Two actors grasp each other's wrists and swirl quickly in a circle, pivoting on their toes. They are not allowed to run around the circle - this immediately identifies the Control Freaks, who hate to lose control of their legs. It is coincidentally a very good exercise for scenes of heady young love, or drunk scenes, as they get very dizzy.

- If you turn a table upside down you will often find that it has a narrow brace underneath. Make the actor balance on this (as though on a tightrope) while doing the speech. Another good one for control freaks.

- One which works for many different types of scenes is to seat the one actor on the floor next to the other, who is standing. The seated one puts their arm around the leg of the other and clings on for dear life while the other attempts to walk away. A variation is to have one actor putting their arms around the shoulders of the other from behind and hanging there, dragging their feet, while the other actor walks around. Both these work a treat when the scene is about one or other feeling trapped. I use it often. It has the double advantage of disabling the left brain and making the actors very tired and lowering their defences.

- Make them jog on the spot, but give them a journey along a road with traffic lights, pedestrians, dog poo which they have to imagine as they run. Works well for duos. End it in the park where they are getting very competitive and racing towards their latte.

- Get the actor to draw a picture of the other actor, or the scene.

- Make them lay a table...

- ... set out chairs and tables

- ... build a nest of chairs (watch out for damage)

- ... juggle

- ... skip

- ... cut a string of doll shapes out of a newspaper

You get the point. Frequently there will be something in the scene which will dictate what to do. As I said - it's not rocket science.

The Whispering exercise.

This may come as a surprise but I actually do use some Stanislavskian exercises. The best one is the Spoken Thoughts run. In this the actors don't speak the lines, they speak the sub-text.

After using this a few times with good, if rather stilted results, I started to tweak it. The actors had to be quite far down the line in their understanding of their text for it to work.

So we used under-reading instead. The under-readers read the lines - the actors, instead of repeating these, speak their sub-text. This worked slightly better, and could be used much earlier.

Then I added another element. While the actors (with under-reader) spoke the actual text I had at least one, sometimes two, other actors follow the character around, whispering their unspoken thoughts in their ears.

This is the most fiendish Left-Brain Disabling Device. You often find actors trying to run from their own thoughts, putting their hands over their ears to shut them out. 'I thought I was going mad' - several actors have said. Your own internal voices can do that to you.

This exercise obviously requires a certain amount of added person power, but is really worth it if you have that.

The Circle

An exercise which can help with the process of integration is what I call The Circle. You can do this on your own. It can also be done with two or three actors in a scene. The process is simple, but needs time - about 40 minutes to an hour.

You start off with a straight anger run of the speech or scene. Then, without pause, you go back in and repeat this, carrying over any emotional baggage from the first version. This process is then repeated over and over and over - hence The Circle. You never stop to discuss, or rest, or pee. You may take a quick swig of water. Each repetition is given its own new impulse. These can be anything. Decide as you restart. Laugh, try a different accent, skip, stamp, play it as a six-year old, as an audition for East Enders - use your imagination.

You need to do at least 15-20 repeats. If you run out of ideas, go back to an anger run.

Now, *very importantly*, there will come a time when you get really, really bored with this exercise. You will think: 'What am I wasting my time doing this stupid Circle for?' It is *very, very important* that you do not stop here. You need to go on for at least four or five more repetitions. You will know how many. I call it the Zen Barrier. Some time after you have passed through it you will suddenly experience a moment which I love to watch happening. It's as though a light bulb appears above the actor's head in which a thought is flashing like a neon sign. It says: *I can play this scene any way I want to.'*

Once you've reached this stage - and don't stop till you do - you really will be able to do that.

I've used this exercise to cure actors of the inability to learn lines. When they find that the thoughts are more important than the actual words - and that these are embedded in their brains - they lose the fear of 'losing lines' which has been crippling them.

A word about auditions

These exercises were originated to help actors with limited time and without access to directors. They can be used for this, if you have the courage to work alone.

A word of warning though. This kind of work takes its time to settle in. Image-Streaming, Mind-Mapping - these can be used overnight to help you find the hidden depths of the character. However, beware of the anger run. Releasing large amounts of emotion also releases much adrenaline, and this can have a numbing effect the following day. You should always allow at least 2-3 days to elapse while the released emotions are integrated.

And **never, never** use these exercises in an actual audition. The panel will think you have gone insane.

...and a final word...

....about using these exercises. I wish that I could say that one exposure to them would solve all your problems. Unfortunately it's not that easy. The defences I've spoken about NEVER give up. They can't. It's their job to protect you. But once you've cleared all the old rubble you'll still be dealing with all the new excrement that Life throws at you. Each day your defences will protect you from some new trauma - and build another wall. When it's served its purpose they will NOT tear it down. You will have to force them to relinquish their hold. This is where these exercises come in. A quick anger run is normally all that's needed to re-adjust the balance.

Acting is a wonderfully healing process. Every new character offers you the chance, while grappling with their scars, to deal with your own.

One thing you MUST remember: your defences are endlessly cunning in their protection, their desire to keep you from the experience of pain, or anger, or fear, or any one of the multitude of feelings that make us human beings. They know every button to push that will trigger a block in you. They know because they ARE you. Your job is to keep a beady eye on them. Separate the good walls from the no-longer-useful walls. In this quest being an actor is a Very Good Thing. But you must be an alert, inquisitive actor, armed with a magic sword - the words 'This is a defence. Why?' Not 'Is this a defence?' Because if you ask this the cunning defences will supply the answer: 'No it isn't!' - and they will lead you to the comfort of deadened, imprisoned feelings, and your ability to act, to live, will be shackled.

Don't let them do this. Be aware. Stay alive.

Epilogue

So, here we are, almost at the end of the journey. The old, true cliché says that it's not the arrival that is important - it's the journey itself. Mine has been rich and varied. I have had several journeys, paralleling each other, through life, relationships, career.

The one I set down here has been one of the three important journeys of my life.

To sum it up is almost impossible. The discoveries continue. As I write Jessica Beck, who pushed me into writing this down, is making new discoveries of her own. The field of Alba Emoting - set out by neuroscientist, Susana Bloch - is fascinating her. A workshop with the Song of the Goat Company from Poland opened up further exciting possibilities. Like all good directors she mixes and matches. As two of my ex-students, who have been kind enough to provide me with quotes at the beginning of this book, point out: There is no one method. Only new discoveries.

What I set out here has changed constantly. I hope the process of change has been clear. Even now, every time I work I find myself adapting the methods to the needs of the individual.

Take it, try it, bend, twist, reconstruct it. Don't let it calcify. These exercises are not the Holy Writ. Keep experimenting. Keep exploring. Keep your mind open.

I'd like to end by going back to the source. Theatre. Its ability to assist in the process of change.

As I sit here - in the final short phase of my life - I'm gripped by the urgency of time. I've talked about the baby's concept of endless time, and my old-age concept of 'racing' time. As I now streak down the final furlong this sense of urgency has me by the throat.

Our species is hugely arrogant. We have been around for the smallest molecule in the tiniest grain of sand on the huge Sahara of time. The dinosaurs will have outlasted us by several hundred thousand years. A New Zealand scientist gives humanity another 80 years as I write, before our cancerous growth has gorged on its own resources and we will follow many of the beautiful other creatures to extinction. Wonderful, complex, exquisitely crafted, intricate beings that we drove - through our greed, our selfishness and our lust for power - to oblivion.

We kid ourselves that we're this marvellous species - so much more intelligent, more sentient, more noble - than the ignoble beasts. We have, we boast, created Art in all its forms. We fill our museums, our concert halls, our theatres with it. We are superior.

Name me one painting that can compete with any ordinary everyday blue sky, filled with clouds; any sunset, any animal moving without vanity around our plains and forests. Which piece of music can compete with the natural sounds of the forest, the sea, a river, the song of a bird.

All we can do is imitate. We are not creators - we are plagiarists. Our short space on this jewel of the planet has resulted in huge ugly scabs. If Earth was a patient it would be covered in bandages, walking on crutches.

Am I exaggerating?

Look around you.

What can we do about it? Well, in the first instance, we have to take responsibility for our own actions. We are not all bad. As Phillip Zimbardo points out in his essential, seminal book - *The Lucifer Effect* - only about 2% of us are heroes - but that that 2% can have a disproportionately large effect. Bertolt Brecht - for all his flaws as a man - kept sending out one message right to the end of his journey: *'Take responsibility for your own actions.'*

Sadly, what comes out of the mouths of endless numbers of the 98% are the words: *'I was only doing what I was told'* - in many languages and many variations.

Many, not all, artists are such heroes. I am not an artist or a hero. I work in an art form which I've seen in my own experience can change things. I have tried to give others the skills with which to drive this change. They use theatre to give voice to the voiceless, to expose those who abuse their power, to explain the complexities of life, to provide succour, to heal.

But we are running out of time, and life has a nasty way of crippling us as we struggle to survive, to blind us to the realities that loom. I sometimes think of it as a giant Tsunami of Doom gathering its forces of final destruction and racing towards us, sweeping increasing numbers of the 98% into its tumbling grasp. In its way stands another small wave of energy, preparing to go into battle to fight the flood of ignorance and greed, brandishing their weapons of Reason and Understanding - and real, true emotion. Can they win? I won't be around in 80 years' time to know the answer. Your children will.

Why am I so pessimistic? After all I've seen South Africa and the USSR - two seemingly impregnable monoliths - fall. I've seen the beginnings of the awareness that race, gender, class, religious discrimination and other bigotries are wrong.

But our disease, like any good virus, is able to morph itself into new shapes, sometimes more powerful.

Colonialism - with its gunboats and soldiers wiping out the indigenous populations in search of gold and diamonds and food to feed the gargantuan appetites of the various Home Countries - has adapted itself so successfully that most don't notice that it still flourishes. Economic Colonialism it should now be called, as it spreads its paralysing tentacles, making poor, vulnerable countries dependent on us economic giants.

Slavery was abolished nearly 200 years ago, wasn't it? Tell that to the billions of people living below the most minimal standards of poverty, working at all ages, at all hours, to feed and clothe the greed of far-away countries, to fill our need for the trinkets that we can't do without - though they have to.

Maybe we should just all give way to Humanity's last burst of hedonism.

The only thing Pandora managed to prevent escaping from her disastrous box was Hope - a mixed blessing. I cling to mine.

As I compulsively watch my television screen I mourn the endless excremental programmes that capitalise on our greed and our false hopes - for fame, for applause, for the drug of Celebrity.

But, amidst the dross, are other programmes.

I came to the understanding that slavery was alive and flourishing because of a series of programmes which took incredibly spoiled young people from our bloated society, transported them to the heart of the 'slave' colonies, and made them attempt to survive as those slaves have to.

I have had my faith in our appalling species bolstered by programmes which take ordinary people and show them how they can be extraordinary; programs which show the heroes among us as they fight to expose corruption and abuse; as they fight to save our environment and all the wonderful creatures with which we share it. I have seen theatre and film which exposes, questions and debates, photographers who courageously record injustice.

Sadly many 'famous' artists abdicate their responsibility, deny the sometimes false and dangerous messages that their work communicates, seduced by fame and money. But there are those who celebrate beauty and the human spirit; who contribute, not subtract.

There is much that can be done in our field, our wide field. Not just theatre - also film and television and the growing Internet - which is opening up huge possibilities.

Can you change it all? No. Change rarely comes through the actions of a single person. It comes through the combined small, ordinary actions of ordinary, committed individuals.

Mandela, Gandhi, Martin Luther King would not have made one jot of difference if they had not been able to guide, to surf on the multiple energies of multiple ordinary individuals. They were leaders, yes, but leaders require prepared and active followers.

It works both ways. In Britain we are currently in a huge economic mess because we allowed first Margaret Thatcher and then Tony Blair to exploit our greed.

It was not their fault.

Brecht, again. In his under-rated version of *Antigone* he has his Kreon/Hitler round on his followers:

When I attacked Argos, who sent me?' The army, he says, went to bring *'metal from the mountains at your request.'* (For 'metal' you could now read 'oil'). The citizens tell him that they trusted him *'and we closed our ears, fearing fear. And again we shut our ears when you tightened the reins even further.... But now you're beginning to treat us as you treated the enemy. How awfully you lead your double war.'* Kreon snarls: *'Your war!'* and he goes on: *'You eat the meat, but don't like to see the blood on the cook's apron.'*

If enough of us allow something to happen, then it will happen. The leader we need to crystallise it will come along. Mandela, Hitler, Gandhi, Stalin, Martin Luther King, Thatcher, Pol Pot, Berlusconi.

But time is running out. As you read this another species will become extinct. As you read this another baby will die of starvation or abuse.

You don't have to go to Ethiopia or the depths of the Amazon rainforest. Draw a circle of half a mile radius around you. In that small enclosure a woman will be being battered, a child abused; someone will be suffering racial hatred; someone will be being bullied. All of them need help - someone to speak for them, take up their cause, confront those that abuse the power they have over the weak.

That somebody is you. You can make a difference.

But beware - there is a rule. The rule states that there is no fence on which you can sit. You either help - or hinder. There is no middle ground. Your decision not to help makes you responsible for its consequences.

So, don't sit in your bedsit fighting the easy battle (in our Western cultures) to 'survive'. The battle which leads to your doing nothing.

I can't tell you how many times I have been told that 'I haven't got the time.' My answer has always been: 'What are you doing between 2 and 4am?' Years ago a group of young American actors creating a very strange production of Troilus and Cressida with me at LAMDA were distressed to find that our plan to turn the prologue into a musical number would have to be scrapped because we didn't 'have the time'. I left them at 6.30pm as they headed off for one of the schools productions that they were required to see.

The following morning, as we gathered for our only dress-rehearsal before the 'opening', they said: 'Can we show you our number?' Miracle of miracles, they had cobbled it together - complete with tap-dancing trio. It evoked equal measures of hilarity (from the students) and horror (from the staff) and is still one of my favourite treasured memories.

How? The play had ended at 10 pm, they had a pizza, and then started working at 11.30 in the front room of one of their digs. At 3am they had licked it.

This is a frivolous story. Fun - but it didn't rescue the universe.

If people really push me ('I work all day in a call-centre, I'm tired, I have to have a life, etc, etc.') I trot out my South African story.

At The Space in Cape Town in the last three years our company grew increasingly multi-racial. Many of the new actors came from the townships of Langa and Gugulethu. Most had full-time jobs - jobs that make your average day in a call-centre look like a trip to Disneyland. I describe an average schedule.

'Wake up at 4.30 or 5am in the house they share, frequently with up to 10 other people - sometimes without running water or electricity. Catch at least one bus and a train to their place of work, to start at 7am. Work through - with a 30-minute lunch break (if they're lucky) - to 6pm. (That's an 11-hour shift - and this is a minimum, not an average.) Catch at least one bus and a train to The Space, arriving at about 7.30. Have a quick bite to eat in The Space Caf. Start rehearsals at about 8. End rehearsals at 11.30ish. TALK! About Theatre, The Revolution, Life ... No more trains running. If lucky, one of the Space people will have a car and can cart them back to the township by about 1.30am. To get up again at 4.30 or 5am.'

When do they learn their lines I hear you cry? *'What do you do between 2 and 4am?'*

We are incredibly spoilt. Pampered. Cosseted.

Worse yet - we don't appear to believe in anything. Those actors had a huge reality. A great injustice to fight.

What do we have?

Go into that half mile radius. A child is waiting for someone to speak of their pain and suffering. People are lost in the most terrible abyss of hidden oppression, unacknowledged abuse. They face corruption, watch helpless as politicians strip away the protective cover of their rights.

What use is theatre in all this?

My final story - the reason I remain living in hope.

In 1978 I'd finished more than seven years running The Space. In all those late-night talks I mentioned above, despair had insidiously crept in among the white members of the company. What use had our seven years of struggle been? What had we accomplished? Had we changed anything? Worst of all: was Theatre, after all, not just a middle-class wank?

I had already decided to leave - unable to take up arms, fearful of becoming ever-more justifying of my privileged lifestyle. My wife had been offered membership of the National Theatre in London. We had announced that The Space would close. Athol Fugard - many years later - described the late 70s as: 'The darkest days in South Africa.' That was politically - but personally for me, too, they appeared to be without light. Apartheid was a huge granite monolith. Impregnable.

One day Sue Johnson from the burgeoning Feminist movement came to see me. She asked me whether I'd seen the play being done by the women of Crossroads?

Crossroads was an illegal squatter camp that had been set up by the wives and families who had followed their husbands and fathers to the factories of the Big City. It was just after the Soweto uprising and world attention was focused on South Africa. The women - a formidable bunch of fighters - had made Crossroads an international cause célèbre with their stubborn resistance to authority.

I knew nothing of it. I asked around. A drama therapist who worked in the townships finally tracked down a performance. One Thursday afternoon on a cool Cape Town mid-winter day we found ourselves sitting outside the tin-shanty Community Centre with a rowdy, rambunctious audience of women and children.

Before us unfolded a wonderful, sprawling, epic narrative tale.

It told of a legendary woman. She and her three children had followed their man to Cape Town by walking the 500 miles from somewhere in the tribal lands of the Ciskei. Somehow they had found him in the urban sprawl and set up a home - made from sheets of zinc/corrugated iron/packing-case wood/cardboard.

One day the authorities bulldozed their home to the ground. Wife and children were placed on a train back to the Ciskei. At the other end they got off - and walked the 500 miles back to Cape Town again ...

Once more they set up home.

Once more their home was bulldozed to the ground.

Once more they were trained back to Ciskei.

The third 500-mile walk back defies belief. No wonder she was a legend among these legendary women.
As the play was being staged she was, we were told, back in the Ciskei, and most certainly on her fourth walk back.

It was an exhilarating piece of theatre at its roughest. Rambling and hilarious. The cast had a wicked way with impersonating the officials who were attempting to rule their lives - much appreciated by the audience who knew these buffoons intimately.

Afterwards I was awed. Would they, I asked with trepidation, come and perform their play at our theatre for a week? This had to be explained to some of them. Not one member of the cast had ever been in either a theatre or cinema.

They came - and we had a joyous week. First one of the two children's choirs (we had to be VERY careful in balancing the amount of performances each choir had - considerable competitive pride was at stake) entertained the audience in The Gym - our large rehearsal room/theatre upstairs. Then The Women played out their archetypal tale in the unaccustomed, artificially-lit darkness of the main theatre.

The newly-founded Market Theatre heard about it and invited the production to Egoli - the city of Gold - Johannesburg.

Back in Cape Town The Space closed. I prepared to leave. I was writing a column for a small monthly magazine. One thing about the play had fascinated me. Nobody seemed to know how it had come about. I decided to find out and write my column about this process.

I went straight to Mrs Alexandria Luke. Known as MamaLuke she had played the leading role. A fearsome lady. In a properly regulated society she would probably have been Prime Minister. I tape-recorded my interviews. In the background of this one - over 45 minutes long - you can hear, every 15 minutes or so, a strange sound as MamaLuke sweeps the ever-invading sands of the Cape Flats as they try to take over her domain. 'If you don't do this', she told me, 'you end up with so much sand each day' - indicating with her fingers about 3 inches of depth.

No, she said, she hadn't started the Sketch (their description for what they had done). She knew that they had been growing increasingly impatient of the fact that all the journalists, photographers, television crews, seemed to be accomplishing nothing. They had decided to tell their own story. But who had come up with the idea, she did not know. Maybe it was Mrs Yanta?

Off I went to Jane Yanta. Yes, she said, they had wanted to tell their own story. No, she couldn't remember whose idea it was. Probably Muriel Mbobosi.

Muriel's shack was a joy to behold. Fiercely intelligent, she was the only one of the women who had had a proper schooling. Her husband worked in a label-printing factory and the wallpaper in their home was a riot of colourful beer and cigarettes ads.

She couldn't remember either. She suggested another one of the 12 core members of the group.

I travelled from person to person, ending finally back at MamaLuke - the puzzle unsolved. She didn't share my puzzlement. Who cared who started it?! 'Come.' she said, 'I must fetch water.' So, with her three children, all of us carrying buckets, we walked the half a mile to the only tap servicing this large community, and stood in the long, sociable queue, most of whom had seen the 'Sketch'. MamaLuke was a 'star'. A much more important star than any glossy Hollywoodian figure.

At home I listened again to the tapes. At one wonderful, epiphanic point my slow brain put it all together.

I had had the unutterable privilege of being allowed to be as close to the very roots of drama as is granted to anyone. These women who fought injustice and the invasion of sand; who had to bring up children, provide food, walk for water in a never-ending time-consuming struggle for survival; these women who were not white and middle-class, who had no idea what 'Theatre' was, had CHOSEN to tell their own story through this wonderful, eternal medium.

Theatre began around the fireside, in a market, as people told their own stories and heard those of others. The epiphany came when I realised that, should we finally manage to accomplish the inevitable consequence of all those nuclear stockpiles on which we have wasted so much money, and blow ourselves to smithereens - if a small group of children are safe in some underground cavern they will begin to tell stories - they will DO theatre.

Theatre is not some dry, intellectual concept. It grows, with us, from the soil.

I left South Africa with my faith reaffirmed, my despair alleviated.

14 years later Nelson Mandela was released and South Africa began its frightening, exhilarating new journey.

When I go back now I find old members of The Space flourishing in all levels of theatre and society.

Theatre can be part of a process of change.

Don't just sit there.

Accept your responsibility.

Bear witness to the stories of others.

Tell your story.

Feedback from workshops conducted by Brian Astbury

The practical work was extreme, visceral and obviously (speedily) effective. Useful to see how emotion can be tapped into – and to see it experientially happen in front of you.

Ben Webb - Theatre director

The Brian Astbury workshop was one of the most practically useful workshops I have been on, as he made sure he gave us actual practical exercises that we can use with actors....Witnessing other directors undertake these exercises made it easy to see the results, which were very moving, sometimes uncomfortable, but in my opinion this was a good thing as the electric atmosphere was felt by all - exactly how theatre should be.

Mel Hillyard Artistic Director for WriteTime with Eyebrow Productions and Director in Residence for Attic Theatre Company

he was clear, funny, candid and fascinating, also very uplifting and inspiring in his dedication to his craft and students, demonstrating how his physical techniques gradually release the actors' spontaneity and make them leave their brains alone and be completely and freely in the moment.

Orla Salinger Actress

…the results at the end of the session showed that his methods do exactly what it says on the tin! It was wonderful to watch the freedom and the daring surface through reticence and defence.

Jackie Kane Writer/director/actor

Thanks for the excellent workshop. I feel I have become a different director already after that day. It's given me a completely different perspective about directing and more importantly, what journey an actor is going through. I have always been appreciative of actors and admire what they do, but I feel I respect them even more now.

Shan Ng Theatre and film director (May Wong, 2010)

His techniques are beautifully simple and yet very, very clever. Whilst he makes the actor sweat and swear, the work becomes deliciously effortless, freeing and a joy to endure; I felt utterly in my skin. I find it hard to articulate the experience of working with Brian and I put this down to being in my right brain for the majority of the experience.

Ann Marcuson Actress

After the sessions with Brian I didn't work with the monologue for a year until I needed it for an audition. I prepared it as normal and was worried about my connection to the text after such an extended hiatus. However, on the day of the audition all the emotion was immediately accessible without me having to create or force a connection and the emotional speech came to me organically. I would recommend this method to any actor.

Ed Young Actor

Brian's technique is focused, ferocious and fearless. Like anything that demands stepping out of your comfort zone, when you give in to it, the results are exhilarating and enlightening. The exercises immediately propel you into extremely heightened emotional states, stripping away the barrier of logic, leaving you connected to the words and the character in a way that feels as though the words, emotions and sensations are totally your own. You lay yourself bare, but with that you open yourself up totally to all possibilities and, in the chaos and confusion, there is true acceptance of the moment.

Silvana Maimone Actor

His techniques allow emotional exploration of the text without over analysis or conjuring of personal memories. I found them liberating in the sense that I could let go of 'getting it right' and pumping emotions, which allowed space for authentic connections to emerge.

The results were sincere, resonant and engaging performances – essential for good theatre.

Fiona Geddes Actress

In one workshop, Brian was able to help me access emotions on stage that I'd never seen come out of me before. He provides fantastic instruction for everybody from seasoned actors looking to hone their skills to beginners who are just taking their first steps into the acting world.

Reed Doucette Oxford University Acting Workshop

I felt deeply liberated. It was a very inspiring experience to see actors explore different levels of emotions and energy. Afterwards I really wanted to take it into practice and take it further. I wanted to be emotionally spontaneous and creative enough to enter this unknown territory. Brian Astbury's workshop was a very intuitive and inspirational experience!

Joana Duyster-Borreda Oxford University Acting Workshop

There's nothing safe about a piece of good theatre whilst you're watching it - thankfully. Brian Astbury knows this and so his actor training and theatre-making methods have an element of risk to them (or certainly can feel as if they do) - again, thankfully. If you care about performing honestly and openly - without a host of bullshit mannerisms - and crafting performances that are based around following your true instincts, you might want to get to know his book and methods intimately. He understands what theatre is innately and in the truest sense; again, my advice is to pay constant and close attention. He's also warm, funny and in love with actors, so you're in considerably good hands.

Jordan Seavey   co-founder CollaborationTown Theatre, New York

In our theatre-writing workshop Brian created a non-judgemental, comfortable environment in which we felt free to experiment with our writing. Through a series of guided exercises Brian helped me to tap in to the character's voice in my subconscious and I left the workshop feeling invigorated and full of ideas that without the workshop, would never have come to me.

Fortuna Burke aspiring screenwriter, studying an MST in Creative Writing, Oxford University Writing Workshop

Brian freed more of my potential in three hours than I had previously managed on my own in twenty-six years. From the theoretical discussion on narrative structure to the more practical writing exercises, I came away feeling for the first time like I had something worth saying and the ability to say it. More than anything Brian instilled a belief in myself which I now realise is more important for a writing career than anything else.

Andrew Johnson Oxford University Writing workshop

Brian's workshop 'Unlocking Emotions' was a fantastic experience. Being put on a stage with your text when you are a writer is a refreshing and illuminating experience. The text comes alive in your head and in your body. When he worked my extract with an actress, I was so thrilled with it, I was in tears by the end of the session. Very effective stuff.

Carolina Ortega Playwright

What a privilege it was to witness the wealth of experience Brian Astbury brings to bear in rehearsals with actors for a special workshop Unlocking Emotions. Having sent in short extracts from scripts, writers had the opportunity of seeing actors interpret their work utilising a variety of demanding physical exercises developed by Brian to engage and fully explore the emotional content of each writer's dialogue. It was revelatory to witness the dramatic changes and development of the actor's journey as realised through the scripts as they were challenged by the demands of Brian's techniques and insight. It was perhaps the most perfect illustration of the unique ability of collaborative theatre to transparently marry the disciplines of writer, actor and director in one of the most rewarding workshops the LPC has produced.

David Bottomley Writer's Group Director, The London Playwrights' Collective

I just wanted to thank you for the work we did during the Unlocking Emotions workshop at the BAC last month. I had been struggling to finish my play. I had been rewriting and rewriting the last 10 pages for about 6 weeks. I couldn't get it right.

After your workshop, I had the courage of my convictions and listened to the characters. I then wrote what was true to them. I finished those last 10 pages in three days! I'm now working up a couple of other ideas and I hope I can use the same principle – and listen to my characters without interference from me and all my worries about getting it right.

Nicola Albon   Playwright, The London Playwrights' Collective

The exercises were intense and powerful, forcing us to strip away all of our preconceptions and focus solely on our natural emotional reactions to the text. The exhilarating feeling of having been pushed far beyond ones preconceived emotional capacity remains long after the session. The techniques I learnt are ones which will be useful in any future projects. A thoroughly enthralling and enjoyable day.

Maisie Richardson-Sellers   Oxford University Acting Workshop

Bibliography

Books mentioned in the text plus others for additional reading

GENERAL

The Lucifer Effect: How Good People Turn Evil **Phillip Zimbardo** (Rider)

How to Mind Map: The Ultimate Thinking Tool That Will Change Your Life **Tony Buzan** (Thorsons)

The Tipping Point **Malcom Gladwell** (Abacus)

Blink: The Power of Thinking Without Thinking **Malcolm Gladwell** (Penguin)

The Einstein Factor **Win Wenger** (Three Valleys Press)

Bioenergetics **Alexander Lowen** (Arkana)

Autogenic Training **Kai Kermani** (Souvenir Press)

Magic in Practice: Introducing Medical NLP - The Art and Science of Language in Healing and Health **Garner Thomson and Khalid Khan** - This book addresses many of the same issues that arise in my book, while giving clear instructions on how to cope with emotional states in yourself and others. Essential reading for those who aim to direct or teach, thereby exposing themselves to the emotions of others on a regular basis.

ACTING

An Acrobat of the Heart: A Physical Approach to Acting Inspired by the Work of Jerzy Grotowski **Stephen Wangh** (Vintage Books)

Towards a Poor Theatre **Jerzy Grotowski** (Eyre Methuen Drama Books)

Improvisation for Theater **Viola Spolin** (Northwestern University Press

Stanislavski and the Actor: The Final Acting Lessons, 1935-38 **Jean Benedetti** (Performance Books)

The Complete Stanislavsky Toolkit   **Bella Merlin** (Nick Hern Books)

Beyond Stanislavsky   **Bella Merlin** (Nick Hern Books)

Systems of Rehearsal: Stanislavsky, Brecht, Grotowski and Peter Brook   **Shomit Mitter** (Routledge)

The Art of Acting   **Stella Adler** (Applause Acting Series)

Different Every Night: Rehearsal and Performance Techniques for Actors and Directors: Freeing the Actor   **Mike Alfreds** (Nick Hern Books)

To the Actor: On the Technique of Acting   **Michael Chekhov** (Routledge)

Respect for Acting   **Uta Hagen** (John Wiley & Sons)

Sanford Meisner on Acting (Vintage Books)

The Psychophysical Actor at Work   **Phillip B. Zarrilli** (Routledge)

The Moving Body (le Corps Poetique): Teaching Creative Theatre   **Jacques Lecoq** (Performance Books)

THE BRAIN

Emotional Intelligence   **Daniel Goleman** (Bloomsbury Publishing)

Molecules of Emotion   **Candace Pert** (Pocket Books)

Human: The Science Behind What Makes Your Brain Unique   **Michael S. Gazzaniga** (Harper Perennial)

The Feeling Of What Happens: Body, Emotion and the Making of Consciousness   **Antonio Damasio** (Vintage)

Descartes' Error: Emotion, Reason and the Human Brain   **Antonio Damasio** (Vintage)

Looking for Spinoza   **Antonio Damasio** (Vintage)

The Emotional Brain: The Mysterious Underpinnings of Emotional Life   **Joseph Ledoux** (Phoenix)

Affective Neuroscience: The Foundations of Human and Animal Emotions   **Jaak Panksepp** (OUP USA)

INDEX

Acting types 71, 72
Alexandra Luke..*See* Women of Crossroads
Alhambra Theatre 10, 11
Amato, Rob 17
Apartheid 9-11, 14, 15, 17, 28, 77, 192, 206
Arts Threshold....1, 38-41, 47, 48, 127, 129, 149, 165, 180

Bates, Kathy 118
Beck, Jessica 1, 186
Bergman, Ingmar 11
Berman, Bee 17
Bernhardt, Ian 14, 17
Boesman and Lena 15
Bond, Edward 20, 73
Brain, The.....5, 6, 23, 24, 28, 37, 63, 64, 67, 70, 79, 80-85, 100, 107, 114, 132, 133, 135, 136, 139, 147, 153, 154, 161, 163, 164, 168, 180, 182, 198
Brecht, Bertolt 77, 103, 187
Brown, Emma.......2, 49-54, 157, 159
Bryceland, Yvonne......2, 13-21, 24, 26, 28-30, 40, 43, 73-77, 86, 115-125, 178, 179, 206
Burnham, Victoria 95, 96

Camus, Albert 17
Canetti, Elias 104
Catharsis 9
Cawood, Elize 116
Chekhov 26
Chekhov, Anton.........25, 27, 32, 56-58, 62, 67, 70, 87, 91, 93, 95, 98, 136, 137
Chekhov, Michael 20

Connection..........16, 25, 26, 35, 39, 40, 42, 49, 66, 82, 92, 105, 107, 114, 124, 134, 147, 148, 150-153, 157, 167-170, 177, 197
Cornwell, Charlotte 116
Crossroads 192
Croucher, Roger 21, 24, 55

Defences.......6, 8, 20, 23, 24, 40, 59, 81, 128, 130, 133, 139, 145-147, 150, 151, 153, 162-181, 185, 196, 198, 202
Directing. 8, 13, 19, 35, 36, 42, 45, 46, 49, 55, 64, 70, 72, 76, 77, 87, 129, 131, 184, 186,
Donald, Val 15
Drum Magazine 13
Dunster , Wilson 15, 29, 116

E 15 Acting School...........1, 70, 87, 153
Ebrahim, Vincent 178
Edinburgh Festival......38, 40, 41, 94, 127, 131, 153, 180
Edward Bond 20, 73
Emotion 4, 20, 23, 34, 35, 39, 42, 43, 49, 50, 54, 60, 62, 66, 81, 86, 99, 100-102, 104-107, 113-117, 124, 128, 145, 147, 153, 157, 162, 163, 166-169, 171, 184, 188, 196-198
Emotional Access 50
Energy.........4, 6, 55, 60, 61, 67, 104, 128, 145, 147, 169, 188, 198
Etcetera Theatre.....................40
Eves, Caroline 56
Exercises....................51, 149, 152-155, 169, 180-182

204

Fine, Moyra 18
Flynn, Bill 19, 76
Freud, Sigmund 4, 99
Fugard, Athol 13-21, 24, 28, 29, 73, 86, 115-119, 121, 124, 148, 192, 206
Fugard, Sheila 13

Gladwell, Malcolm 85, 201
Grahamstown Festival 15
Guy Butler, Professor 15

Hagen, Uta 20, 202
Hardwick, Lynsey 147
Hawthorne, Nigel 12, 102
Hesmondhalgh, Julie 157
Hofmeyr Theatre 12
Hong Kong Fringe Festival 41
Howarth, Donald 18

Image Streaming 90-98, 114, 127, 140-144, 184, 206
Imprinting 34
'In the moment'..........6, 28, 30, 31, 60, 65, 67, 70, 71, 80, 84, 85, 88, 89, 128, 153, 154
Irving, Amy 116

Jane Yanta... See Women of Crossroads
Jordan, Dr 12
Julie Hesmondhalgh .... See Hesmondhalgh, Julie
Jung, Carl 4, 99

Kani, John 14, 17
Karamitru, Ion 41
King, Martin Luther....9, 189, 190
Kingsley, Ben 29, 73

LAMDA........1, 21-33, 38, 39, 42, 48, 55, 106, 116, 120, 127, 129, 149, 165, 172, 190, 206
Learning lines 182
Lewenstein, Oscar 18, 28
Lindsay, Katrina 39
Lister, Moira 11

Malan, Robin 74

Mandela, Nelson.. 9, 18, 75, 109, 195
Mind-mapping................88, 90, 134-137, 184, 201, 206
Mohandas K. Gandhi.......... 9, 76
Mokae, Zakes 14
Mountview Theatre School .. 1, 2, 45-48, 52, 55-62, 67, 70, 86-90, 94, 96, 127, 129, 136, 137, 145, 147, 149, 156, 160, 170, 172, 174, 175, 206
Mowat, David........ 38, 40, 41, 127, 180
Muriel Mbobosi ...See Women of Crossroads

National Theatre........20, 73, 77, 116, 168, 192, 206
Nkonyeni, Nomhle 17
Ntshona, Winston 14, 17

O'Neill, Eugene........................ 9
Oklahoma 10
Orestes 16
Orton, Joe 19

Parmar, Neelam 153
Peat, Candace 161, 163, 202
Pentameters 40
Phoenix Players................ 14, 17
Pinter, Harold.................. 12, 102
Prophet, Chris........................ 19

Rebirthing..................114, 147, 155-163, 167
Re-create.................. 65-71, 182
Royal Court Theatre....18, 21, 28
Rudkin, David 74, 76, 77

Schneideman, Tessa 129
Seftel, Molly 14
Serpent Players 17
Sieff, Percy 178
Simon, Barney 14
Singer, Jacqui 19
South Africa.................9, 10-22, 38, 45, 61, 71, 73-77, 86, 104, 109, 115, 116, 118, 121-123, 126, 127, 166, 188, 191, 192, 195, 206

Soweto 75
Space Club 18

Space, The....2, 17-21, 28, 38,
    75-77, 127, 178, 191, 192,
    194, 195, 206
Spolin, Viola.................... 20, 201
Stanislavski, Konstantin.......... 4
Stanislavski, Konstantin.......4-6,
    19, 20, 31, 36, 38, 85-88, 135,
    201

Taganka Theatre.............. 29, 30
Techniques.... 34, 66, 83, 88, 90,
    91, 93, 96, 98, 114, 127, 129,
    130, 133, 134, 136-138, 140,
    145, 147, 149, 150, 164, 169,
    172, 177, 182, 184, 185, 201

The Island..............................18
Trinder, Tommy......................10

Under-reading.........83,129-133,
    147, 167, 181

Van der Westhuizen, Mr....11, 24
Vanity 105, 106, 107, 115, 124
Vanrenen, Maralin..................19

Walder, Dennis.......................18
Wasling, Jenna.....................153
Weale, Andrew.............. 1, 25-28
Wesker, Arnold.....................121
Women of Crossroads... 192-195
Woods, Billy.............94, 127, 147

Zimbardo, Phillip...................187

About the Author

Brian Astbury founded and ran South Africa's first non-racial theatre/arts venue, The Space, in the 70's, where he commissioned internationally famous plays like *Sizwe Banzi is dead*, *The Island* and *Statements after an arrest under the Immorality Act* from playwrights like Athol Fugard, Pieter-Dirk Uys, Geraldine Aron and Fatima Dike, South Africa's first black woman playwright. Many of the 'graduates' of The Space have gone on to become mainstays of the post-Apartheid South African theatre, TV and film scene. At The Space he began his career as a director.

In the 80's he moved to London when his wife, South Africa's greatest actress, Yvonne Bryceland, joined the National Theatre Company. Here he began to teach - first at LAMDA, then, in the 90's at Mountview, where he was Head of Acting, Directing and Musical Theatre Courses.

In 2003 he moved to E15 where he set up the Contemporary Theatre Practice course to teach actors, directors and writers the arts of survival through production of their own material. Later he headed the MA in Professional Theatre for Writers and Directors, before retiring in 2008.

Over the years Astbury has formulated the techniques for training actors, writers and directors described in *Trusting the Actor* in collaboration with students and professional actors. Many of these techniques have their basis in the use of energy and emotion to free the practitioner's imagination, allowing actors to understand and be able to access the mysterious state known as 'being in the moment'. He has also developed methods of accessing and freeing the imagination of writers through the use of mind-mapping and image-streaming.

He has done workshops on these techniques at the Young Vic, the National Theatre Studio, the London Playwrights Collective among others.

Printed in Great Britain
by Amazon.co.uk, Ltd.,
Marston Gate.